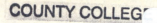

CLASSICAL THEORY AND MODERN STUDIES
INTRODUCTION TO SOCIOLOGICAL THEORY

Mark Abrahamson
University of Connecticut

Prentice Hall

Boston Columbus Indianapolis New York San Francisco Upper Saddle River
Amsterdam Cape Town Dubai London Madrid Milan Munich Paris Montreal Toronto
Delhi Mexico City Sao Paulo Sydney Hong Kong Seoul Singapore Taipei Tokyo

Editorial Director: Leah Jewell
Editor in Chief: Dickson Musslewhite
Executive Editor: Jeff Lasser
Editorial Assistant: Lauren Macey
Director of Marketing: Brandy Dawson
Executive Marketing Manager: Kelly May
Senior Marketing Assistant: Elaine Almquist
Production Manager: Kathy Sleys
Full-Service Project Management/Composition: Karpagam Jagadeesan, GGS Higher
  Education Resources, A Division of Premedia Global, Inc.
Cover Designer: Lisbeth Axell
Printer/Binder/Cover Printer: R. R. Donnelley & Sons, Inc.

Credits and acknowledgments borrowed from other sources and reproduced, with permission, in this textbook appear on appropriate page within text.

Many of the designations by manufacturers and sellers to distinguish their products are claimed as trademarks. Where those designations appear in this book, and the publisher was aware of a trademark claim, the designations have been printed in initial caps or all caps.

Library of Congress Cataloging-in-Publication Data

Abrahamson, Mark.
  Classical theory and modern studies: introduction to sociological theory/Mark Abrahamson. — 1st ed.
     p. cm.
  Includes bibliographical references and index.
  ISBN-13: 978-0-13-219291-0 (alk. paper)
  ISBN-10: 0-13-219291-8 (alk. paper)
  1. Sociology—Philosophy. I. Title.
  HM585.A26 2010
  301—dc22

                                                                    2009011341

Prentice Hall
is an imprint of

www.pearsonhighered.com

10 9 8 7 6 5 4 3 2
ISBN 10:   0-13-219291-8
ISBN 13: 978-0-13-219291-0

CONTENTS

PREFACE

This book grew out of several decades of teaching classical theory to students in sociology and related disciplines, although I was pleased to have occasional students in engineering, art, nursing, and other fields as well. My first objective in the course was to convey to students an understanding of the background of contemporary sociology. Toward that end, the reader will find discussions of the work of the major figures in the classical period of sociological theory. I have tried to stay close to the primary, albeit sometimes translated, works of the major figures themselves. I brought in the ideas of contemporary writers only when they seemed necessary to clarify or explain a particularly difficult concept in the original writing.

My second objective in both teaching and writing this book has been to present classical theory in a way that would lead students to appreciate its continuing relevance. The best way I have found to convey that contemporary relevance is by showing how modern studies are still being influenced by the insights of the major classical theorists. How the studies are being done makes no difference, so in bringing together studies for this book I have not cared whether they were based on surveys, natural experiments, participant observation, or secondary data analysis. Further, the methods of data collection and analysis have been described as briefly and non-technically as possible. The sole objective is to make clear the strong link between the ideas of the classical theorists and the issues being examined in the research of modern scholars.

I would like to thank the following instructors for reviewing the initial proposal or the various stages of this book. Their comments were insightful and helped to guide the book's development.

T. John Alexander, Houston Baptist University

Daniel Jasper, Moravian College

Ande Kidanemariam, Northeastern State University

Cheng-Hsien Lin, Texas A&M University, Kingsville

Stephen Lippmann, Miami University (Ohio)

Paul Paolucci, Eastern Kentucky University

John G. Richardson, Western Washington University

Given the way this book evolved, it could only be dedicated to the hundreds of students whose ideas and questions contributed to my own thinking in a way that made this book possible.

CHAPTER

1

Introduction

From even a casual glance at the sociological literature it is apparent that contemporary sociologists theorize about an incredibly diverse array of topics, and the ways in which they theorize are equally varied. It could almost appear as though there was no core and no boundaries to what was included, or how it was examined. In fact, some prominent theorists, including Jonathan Turner, contend that contemporary sociology has evolved into specialized, unintegrated subareas that share almost nothing with each other. He concludes that sociologists are not aware of any common intellectual community and that the result is chaos.[1] Turner makes an interesting point, and there is some merit to his observation, but I think he fails to recognize that just under the surface there is a discernable core, though this core is not large relative to sociology's many specialty areas. What, more than anything else, provides a modicum of coherence across sociological endeavors is theory, and sociology's classical theory in particular. It embodies a tradition that continues to guide many sociologists in the issues they study and the concepts they employ to clarify the issues. It is because of its place in contemporary sociology that classical theory continues to be vital reading material for people interested in better understanding the field.

Given the diversity among sociologists and the degree to which they tend to disagree with each other on all manner of things, there is a surprisingly high degree of consensus among them concerning which of the classical theorists have historically been most important to the discipline. Virtually every sociologist would nominate Emile Durkheim, Karl Marx and Max Weber as the classical theorists whose writings have been most important in shaping the field. Correspondingly, almost every book on classical theory allocates more pages to these three theorists than to anyone else. Following this tradition, we will devote two chapters to the work of each of these three men. Just behind these three in importance, according to most sociologists, is Georg Simmel, and a single chapter will be given to his work.

One additional figure warrants an entire chapter: Harriet Martineau. She may still lack the stature of the four men just noted because, as a result of gender discrimination, her contributions were overlooked for many years. Until very recently theory books ignored her entirely, but since around the turn of this century interest in her work has greatly increased among sociologists. New editions of many of the papers and manuscripts she authored nearly 200 years ago have also appeared in recent years. In the future reckonings of sociologists she will almost surely occupy a very important place among the major classical theorists.

All five of the theorists whose writings are the subject of separate chapters wrote during some part of what is now termed, "the classical period" of sociological theory. It stretched roughly from 1840 to 1920, and it was during this era that a number of (mostly European) scholars fashioned theories about society and social interaction that continue to influence contemporary work in sociology. The very first theories that might be considered sociological undoubtedly appeared well prior to this classical period. Some analysts might place them in the writings of the Enlightenment, 100 years earlier; others might contend that the first work in sociological theory actually occurred a couple of centuries before when Aristotle wrote essays about social organization in Greece. However, no earlier era contains writings that compare with those that appeared in the decades between 1840 and 1920 in terms of the directness of their link to contemporary sociological theory.

OUR APPROACH

Many of the classical theorists were very colorful figures. They fought in revolutionary wars, earned degrees in law and medicine, made and lost fortunes, overcame debilitating illnesses and, of course, wrote books. The families into which they were born and social conditions under which they lived undoubtedly affected what they thought about and what they wrote. One approach to understanding the classical theorists stresses the connection between the theorists' experiences and their theories. Familiarity with the conditions under which any person lived will certainly clarify the assumptions and meanings that lie behind the person's writings.

In this volume we will discuss the lives and circumstances of the theorists in the beginning of the chapter that introduces them, but this historical material will be limited to a couple of pages. We will deal briefly with biographies in order to devote more time to theorists' ideas and how they continue to influence what sociologists study and how they study it. If too much emphasis is placed upon a theorist's personal background, it can imply that a theorist's insights are confined to that particular time and place, and therefore, only of historical significance.

Our approach will assume that while some aspects of theorists' works may in fact only be of historical significance, there is also a timelessness to their theories, and it is this enduring quality that makes them of continued importance to sociologists. In order to illustrate the theorists' present relevance, each of the chapters that follows this introduction will discuss a number of contemporary studies inspired by and/or directed to their theories. A few studies of special relevance will be discussed in detail. They will be separated from the rest of the text, placed in research boxes which include non-technical discussions of how the data were gathered and more detailed examinations of what the study's findings mean in relation to the theory in question. Relating the classical theories to current studies clarifies how the theories still help to explain conditions in modern societies and it thereby highlights the enduring features of the theories. The reader should realize that these research boxes are to be read as integral parts of the text.

MODERNIZATION

Perhaps the strongest argument against the continued relevance of classical theories pertains to the transition from modern to post-modern. The most important social organizational changes that were occurring during the classical period can be summed up by the term, "modernization." Across much of Western Europe and the United States, modernization entailed a number of inter-related changes which slowly, but cumulatively, transformed societies. The most significant of these social changes entailed:

Industrialization. Technological developments changed the way people produced all sorts of things. Most importantly, machines increasingly replaced human labor, pushing people off of farms where their labor was no longer needed, and enabling the large-scale manufacturing of products at levels never previously experienced.

The changing organization of work in large-scale modern industry captured the attention of many of the classical theorists, and they described it, each in their own way. They also saw a new class of factory workers emerging, and they focused extensively upon the implications of this new class for social stratification and mobility and social upheaval. Many of the classical theorists also speculated upon how the availability of more mass-produced products would impact people's aspirations and relationships.

Capitalism. Associated with the growth of large-scale industry during the nineteenth century, particularly in Western Europe and the U.S., was the hegemony of capitalist economic systems. Their key features entailed: private ownership of productive enterprises, freedom for workers to offer their labor to the highest bidder, and markets for both goods and services that were relatively unrestricted by government regulations.

The classical theorists were divided in their views of capitalism. Those who viewed society from a Darwin-inspired evolutionary approach (a dominant theory at the time) regarded unfettered capitalism as benefitting society by assuring a survival of the fittest. However, the more humanistic and/or socialistic theorists saw the masses as oppressed, and viewed their suffering (as described in Charles Dickens' novels, for example) as demanding alleviation.

Urbanization.   Cities grew at a very rapid pace during this period. Large-scale manufacturing required the labor force associated with large and dense urban populations. People who were pushed off of farms migrated to cities because that was where they believed they would find more opportunities. And when people immigrated, they typically moved from rural areas in one nation to urban areas in another nation. By the end of the classical period, the suburban population surrounding cities was also beginning to grow.

As cities grew, the classical theorists believed they could discern attitudes and patterns of social relationships that were distinctive to concentrated urban communities. Most of the then contemporary theorists wrote about how differences in industrialization and urbanization were combining to create a modern type of social organization that was different from that traditionally found in rural or farming areas.

Secularization.   Modernization meant a diminished role for the religious institution as church and state were separated. In these more secular modern societies, the authority of the clergy and the ability of religion to influence other institutions as well as people's everyday lives were markedly reduced.

Almost all of the classical theorists noted the diminution of the religious institution and speculated about religion's likely place in societies of the future. Would it serve as a source of social integration, strengthening bonds among people and providing moral authority—or would modern societies expose religion as a sham for providing people with false ideas and beliefs?

Family and Gender.   Like religion, the family was becoming less central in terms of its interface with other institutions. With increasing migration and immigration, the predominant form of the family was changing from extended to nuclear. Virtually all of the classical theorists believed these trends would continue, and perhaps accelerate.

The role of women in modern societies, by contrast, was subject to very different predictions. Some theorists thought that women would (and should) continue to find fulfillment as wives and mothers, and remain subordinated to men in every institutional realm; but other analysts expected that women's aspirations and roles would move much closer to those of men's.

Political Order. While most of the social institutions were being rapidly transformed by modernization, political institutions initially tended to lag behind. Many features of governments continued to reflect the feudal period in which they emerged. They seemed obsolete, but it was not clear what would take their place, or when. In the meanwhile, people's attachments to governing institutions grew weak. Revolutions either occurred or seemed imminent in many of the nations experiencing rapid modernization.

The political turmoil led most of the classical theorists to ask questions about the fundamental nature of government and its future role: Would it play an important and autonomous part in modern societies, or just serve the economic interests of a capitalist class? And perhaps the most pressing question entailed whether gradual and peaceful modification of the political institution was possible, or whether change would eventually require revolution.

POST-MODERN RELEVANCE

Since sometime in the latter part of the twentieth century, most of the societies that began to modernize during the nineteenth century have been described as entering a post-modern era. There is not total consensus regarding precisely what the term "post-modern" implies, so the degree to which there has been a transformation of modern into post-modern societies is correspondingly open to debate.[2] Nevertheless, there is little doubt that some changes have occurred, and that has led to the question of whether classical theories, which developed in response to issues connected to modernization, remain relevant to explain phenomena in (at least partly) post-modern societies. There are a number of dimensions to this question, beginning with what post-modern entails.

Some analysts view nations as falling along a modern to post-modern continuum based primarily upon how industrial they are, and regard employment in manufacturing as the primary indicator. Thus, when a large percentage of a nation's labor force—perhaps over 25%—is employed directly in manufacturing jobs, the nation would be considered industrial, and therefore classified as modern. Following that criterion, most of the previously very industrial nations have de-industrialized (because their manufacturing employment has markedly declined) and they could thereby be considered at least somewhat post-modern. However, they have not completely de-industrialized. In the United States, for example, in 2005 there were still over 10 million people employed as production workers in manufacturing, and they constituted about 10% of the labor force.[3]

If a broader definition of modern and post-modern is employed, and other indicators in addition to industrial employment are examined, then the picture becomes even murkier. To be specific: changes in family and gender roles have continued largely without reversal; urbanization, especially involving the growth of suburban areas, has continued; secularization is more complex, though, and the degree to which religion has continued to lose salience varies both by nation and according to whether religious attachments are measured by people's behavior or their attitudes and values.[4] In sum, there is no doubt that the nations that modernized in the nineteenth century have moved, over the past several decades, toward becoming post-modern; but the movement has not been uniform, and elements typifying modern societies remain, and may persist for the foreseeable future. So, if modern and post-modern societies are viewed as falling along a continuum in which they differ from each other in matters of degree, then the issues the classical theorists were analyzing have become less relevant, but not irrelevant.

Other analysts stress the discontinuity between the modern and post-modern. To them, the differences are not matters of degree, but of kind. Post-modern societies are an inversion, or upside down reflection, of their modern counterparts. For example, while modern societies typically stressed design and completion, post-modern societies tend to emphasize chance and process. These overarching tendencies influence literature, art, archeology, etc. and correspond with transformations of sociological assumptions.[5]

However, even when a social issue or theoretical emphasis seems unique to post-modern societies, analyses of modern societies often provide an indispensable vantage point. To illustrate, one of the cultural features often attributed to post-modern cultures is de-differentiation: the tendency for categories and concepts that once had clear boundaries to "implode" and spill into each other.[6] For example, meal time in modern societies was associated with distinct times and places. Families convened at a set time around the dinner table. Now, people eat anytime, anywhere. Similarly, the real and the "fake" were clearly distinguished from each other in modern societies, and the fake was regarded pejoratively. Now, jewelers advertise "genuine zirconias," an oxymoron in modern societies because zirconias are fake diamonds. How could a fake be genuine? Similarly, movies formerly contained either drawn characters (i.e. cartoons) or human actors. Many animated features today, however, are neither, or both.

In modern societies the extensive differentiation of concepts and categories was apparently linked to differentiation in the division of labor. The icon of the manufacturing-dominated modern society—the assembly line—involved clearly distinguished jobs, and it functioned only by rigidly assigning every worker to one particular place. De-differentiation, then, may be a result of the dominance of non-manufacturing jobs in post-industrial societies because they involve less rigidly demarcated work organizations. In fact, home computers have even led to a blurring of the distinction between home and work.

Many of the classical theorists examined modern divisions of labor and the extensive kinds of differentiation attendant to them. They did not anticipate de-differentiation. However, the insights of the classical theorists, in focusing upon the importance of a society's division of labor, for example, continue to be useful in explaining changes the classical theorists did not anticipate. Thus, even when post-modern societies seem very different from modern ones, the classical theories of modernization often continue to provide a crucial vantage point for analyzing the post-modern societies that are emerging. In the future, the classical theorists will very likely continue uniquely to provide otherwise diverse sociologists with a common frame of reference to use in deciding both what issues to examine and how to examine them.[7]

THE SUPPORTING CAST

While we have identified a core group of classical theorists, including the five most important, it would be a mistake for the reader to conclude that there were no other major contributors to sociological theory during the classical period. In fact, there were an additional dozen or so men and women whose writings warrant notice. Some of them informed the thinking of the five core theorists; others helped to tie the work of core theorists to other major theorists; still others began theoretical traditions that remain vital today. Space precludes more than a brief discussion of these others, but no classical theory book would be complete if they were entirely ignored. They are presented next, according to their date of birth: earliest first. (This group excludes some historical figures that others might have included, but such lists always have arbitrary cut-offs.[8])

All of the following supporting cast theorists wrote during the classical period from 1840 to 1920, with one exception: Henri de Saint-Simon. He died before the beginning of the classical era, but warrants a brief note because he exerted a strong and direct influence upon many of the classical period's major theorists, Auguste Comte in particular. It is actually difficult to infer how much of the published work under the name of either St. Simon or Comte was done in collaboration with the other.

Claude Henri de Saint-Simon (1760–1825)

Saint-Simon was a very colorful figure. He was born into the French aristocracy, and made and lost several fortunes during his life. An idealist and an adventurer, he fought with the Americans in the Revolutionary War, serving as an aide to George Washington. For many years he struggled with psychological problems, however, attempting several suicides, and in his later years was committed to a mental hospital.

In his philosophical writings he envisioned societies becoming more equalitarian in a way that led many followers to consider him the "father" of modern socialism. For a decade after his death, "Saint Simonism"—entailing a unique combination of religion and science designed to improve conditions of the working class—was a very popular political perspective in Europe; and it also had a strong influence upon music, art and architecture of the time.[9]

Saint-Simon contended that the form of human societies and the nature of human thought changed along parallel tracks. Why not, he claimed, they are both parts of the natural world. The history of societies and of thought could be divided, he wrote, into a series of periods, beginning with domination by religion and superstition and culminating in what he termed, "Positive." In the latter period, which he thought was yet to emerge, a great emphasis would be placed upon impartial observation and measurement, and so scientists (and social scientists in particular) would be in powerful positions. Their knowledge would be used to benefit the working class, so the threat of their revolution would dissipate, making it possible for societies to disband armies and police forces. Not only would the working classes not have to be controlled, but because they would be content with their society, they could also be counted on to defend it in the event of an external attack.[10]

Auguste Comte (1798–1857)

Auguste Comte was small and sickly as a young man, but a brilliant student. He was also rebellious and as part of a student protest, left college, in Paris, at the age of 19. He returned home (to Montpellier, France), but was soon too bored to stay. He returned to Paris where he met the then 60-year-old Saint-Simon. The latter hired him to serve as a combination of assistant, secretary and collaborator. After five years together they separated in anger, the immediate impetus being conflict over who deserved the most credit for an essay they apparently wrote together. Comte felt exploited and believed Saint-Simon was trying to keep him in a subordinate position in order to continue stealing his ideas.[11] After leaving Saint-Simon, Comte suffered from chronic depression, attempted suicide several times, and never made more than a marginal living as a writer and lecturer. Few of his ideas were taken seriously at the time, and some were ridiculed, but later sociologists recognized his important contributions to defining and shaping sociology. Along with Saint-Simon he was also credited with making significant contributions to the development of modern socialism.

Comte was better organized as a writer than his older mentor, and presented more detailed and elaborate descriptions and analyses, though Saint-Simon's influence over the content of his ideas was apparent. Many of the theories presented in Comte's publications were re-formulations of materials Saint-Simon had written before Comte's birth, so the direction of influence seemed incontrovertible. For example, both men divided human evolution into three very similarly described stages, though the names they gave to the stages were different. Both also emphasized a positivistic science of society, though it was unambiguously Comte that first called this new science, "sociology." His agenda for sociology was to discover the natural laws of social phenomena, through observation and historical and comparative analyses. With this knowledge, he believed the new science would be able to help society overcome problems of disorder and conflict.

In *The Positive Philosophy*, a multi-volume work that he outlined before leaving Saint-Simon, Comte analyzed the social processes that produced stability and instability. (Harriet Martineau, whose own work is the topic of Chapter 2, translated and edited this work.) Using concepts that would be common sociological staples in future decades, Comte described society as a social system, comprised of interdependent parts. For sociologists, he wrote, the task is to understand both social order, as a static condition, and social development, as a dynamic condition. The most serious societal problems arose, in his view, when change disrupted the "harmony" among the parts.[12] What most keeps societies unified despite instabilities, Comte continued, are religion, whose common beliefs bind people together, and the division of labor, which promotes individual feelings of dependence upon others. As will be apparent in later chapters, Comte's views of social change and solidarity were important precursors to Durkheim's writing (see Chapters 7 and 8); and both Marx and Engels (see Chapters 3 and 4) praised his insights.

Herbert Spencer (1820–1903)

Herbert Spencer was too ill as a child to attend school so he was tutored at home by his father and uncle. His autobiography—a detailed recollection of over 1,000 pages—credited his father with having taught him to think freely and also shaping his personality in his father's image: eccentric, egotistical and solitary. He was a prolific and very influential scholar, but lived alone and suffered from a sketchily defined nervous disorder, opium addiction, chronic insomnia, depression, etc. August Comte and other acquaintances urged him to marry, claiming that a sympathetic wife would cure his afflictions, but he rejected their advice, explaining that it was too hard to find a woman who was both smart and attractive; plus, he recognized that he was too difficult to please.[13]

Spencer had read Harriet Martineau's (see Chapter 2) edited version of Comte's philosophy, and he strongly agreed with parts of it, and disagreed with other parts. He endorsed Comte's positivism and similarly assumed it was possible to discern social laws. Each also saw society as an integrated entity, resembling a biological organism. On the other hand, Spencer had a much stronger commitment to scientific objectivity, though he recognized it could be difficult to overcome one's emotional prejudices, and biases that were due to class, education, religion, etc.[14] Also unlike Comte, Spencer regarded social laws as so immutable that he thought individuals' efforts to engineer social change were unlikely ever to be successful.

The fundamental laws of sociology, according to Spencer, derived from the same evolutionary principles as in biology, psychology, geology, and every other science. Evolutionary forces move all phenomena from the homogeneous (which is simple and incoherent) to the heterogeneous (which is complex and coherent). To illustrate, consider how an infant responds to pain: body shaking, screaming, arms and legs kicking. However, as the child develops, responses become more specialized; for example, involving a verbalization without any body movement. Similarly, Spencer described societies as evolving from simple, undifferentiated systems, dominated by religion, to complex, differentiated systems, dominated by science and industry. He concluded that societies were in balance at both extremes, but went through a period of disequilibrium during the transition.[15]

During the latter decades of the nineteenth century, Spencer was the dominant theorist in sociology. He greatly influenced many early social theorists including Durkheim (see Chapters 7 and 8), though Durkheim went to great lengths to try to minimize Spencer's influence in order to emphasize his own originality.

Lester F. Ward (1841–1913)

Lester Ward was the youngest of 10 children born to an impoverished family that lived on a farm in Illinois. As a young man he was an avid reader, and interested in everything academic, but lacked the resources to acquire much of a formal education. He left home during the Civil War, volunteering to fight in the Union army. He was wounded in battle in 1864 and honorably discharged. Then he went to Washington, D.C. and obtained a civil service position and began taking night school classes. He eventually earned degrees in medicine, law, botany and geology! For a time he was most interested in applying his knowledge of geology, and went to work for the U.S. Geological Survey. Over the following years he published a large number of papers in geology and paleontology. However, Ward slowly grew more interested in the emerging field of sociology, and its issues dominated the last decades of his life.[16]

Ward read Spencer and Darwin and was impressed with their use of evolutionary laws to explain social conditions, but he believed they had exaggerated the degree to which people and society were shaped by evolutionary forces. People are unique among all life forms, he wrote, in that both individually and collectively they can exert force equal to, or surpassing, natural force. Thus, human design can control or redirect evolution.[17] Correspondingly, Ward thought it important to distinguish between pure and applied sociology, and he devoted a book to each. The former entailed the discovery of fundamental laws of social organization and change, many of which were evolutionary. The latter, applied sociology, was devoted to the betterment of society, and he believed it was possible because he did not regard social laws as completely deterministic. Ward's distinction between pure and applied sociology remained influential until the middle of the following century.

After writing about sociology for a number of years, Ward was finally offered a position as a sociologist—when he was 65 years of age. He became a professor of sociology at Brown University. He subsequently helped to organize what became the American Sociological Association, and was selected as its first president.[18]

Gustave Le Bon (1841–1931)

Le Bon lived to be 90 years old, and he was an active scholar throughout his life, publishing in a variety of fields. The young Frenchman completed studies in medicine, but did not practice as a physician because he had broad interests, ranging from archeology to physics before he turned to sociology. He wrote and lectured on diverse topics, and for a while made a living by designing scientific apparatus. His publication that has had the most enduring impact was, *The Crowd: A Study of the Popular Mind*. Published in 1896, though written years earlier, it earned him substantial royalties as well as access to some of the leading social circles in Paris where he regularly hosted lunches for a literary elite. In later years the book's analysis continued to have a very significant influence upon many of the most prominent early American sociologists as well as upon such diverse figures as Freud and Hitler.[19] On the other hand, some biographers have described Le Bon as having been in a marginal role in French intellectual circles where his work was not seen as creative and he was personally regarded as pretentious. For example, he apparently told Einstein that it was he—Le Bon—who was actually the first to propose the theory of relativity.[20]

The sociological question that preoccupied his attention concerned the way crowds acted in response to the series of political crises and upheavals that he lived through in nineteenth-century France. Mobs kept forming, and their members' actions seemed both out-of-control and unpredictable. In order to understand such mobs, he contended that when individuals form a crowd, they are transformed. They act, think and feel differently than when they are alone. Specifically, a crowd has a leveling effect, removing the variability normally found among individuals. The uniformities among individuals in a crowd cannot, as a result, be explained as due to the personal qualities of their individual members. The crowd emerges as a distinct form, Le Bon wrote, and it is neither the sum of, nor a reflection of, the people that comprise it. He was anticipating what later sociologists would call an "emergent property:" more inclusive levels (such as groups) have qualities not found in less inclusive levels (such as individuals). Similarly, a society would possess attributes (such as institutions) not found in small groups. (Emergent properties are further discussed in Chapter 7.)

Crowds also have a "dumbing down" effect as the members of a crowd tend to become less rational and more emotional than before they joined. People caught up in crowds act like they were hypnotized; as if their brains were paralyzed, he wrote.[21] They exaggerate an idea until it is completely distorted from reality because people in a crowd cannot tolerate ambiguity. How else, Le Bon asked, can we explain how mobs of people called for innocent people to be guillotined during the French Revolution? Finally, because people are disposed to subordinate their wills when they are in a crowd, they can more readily be influenced by leaders (or agitators) to act impulsively.

Vilfredo Pareto (1848–1923)

Pareto was born to an aristocratic Italian family that divided its time between Paris and Italy during his younger years. His college training, in engineering, was in Italy and he initially worked in technical positions in Rome and Florence. After his parents died, in 1889, he moved to a villa and spent his time writing articles that were radically pro-democracy, for the time, and very critical of the non-democratic Italian government. In response, the government blocked his efforts to obtain a university position. With time to study, he turned to economics and in a relatively brief period he authored several articles and books that were (at the time) regarded as major contributions to economic theory. Around 1900 he concluded that the leaders of the democratic movements he had been supporting simply wanted to replace one elite with another. All leaders, in his opinion, only wanted power and privilege, but he wondered why. Pareto wanted to understand the dynamics behind human behavior, and the "rational man" assumptions of economists did not seem very useful to him. In yet another career shift, his interests moved from economics to sociology.[22]

Pareto's major objective in sociology was to explain the non-rational sentiments that he believed shaped human behavior. People may claim that their actions are rationally motivated—following certain principles, for example—but they are really only trying to justify behaviors whose true motivation is affective. According to Pareto, logical, reasoned explanations are nothing more than after-the-fact rationalizations. Of particular importance to his analysis were the basic, perhaps instinctual, sentiments that he termed, "residues." They are the enduring human drives that are expressed in culturally variable ways. For example, the nature of sexual preferences and inhibitions vary from society to society, but they are always expressions of the same sexual residue. And within any society, people are dominated by different mixes of residues that describe their temperament. Pareto then combined types of non-rational sentiments with differences in cognitive abilities to describe various categories of people. He was especially interested in the people who comprised the elite segment. These people could be the most able—or—the people who were perceived as most able. Ideally, the two would be identical; but he thought that unearned advantages of birth could always lead to a discrepancy between the elites' actual abilities and the abilities attributed to them. Over time he expected that there would be cycles in which the governing elite consisted of people whose capabilities and temperaments varied greatly.[23]

While focusing upon elite groups in government, in economic and religious institutions, Pareto saw reciprocal influences among all the component units of a society. He described societies as social systems, and his analysis of the conditions under which the interplay among the interdependent parts of a social system would lead to equilibrium had a very major influence upon later sociological theory. For example, Talcott Parsons, the dominant theorist in sociology during the mid twentieth century, wrote that he was very highly indebted to Pareto's conception of social systems.[24]

Thorstein Bunde Veblen (1857–1929)

Veblen grew up on his family's comfortable farm in the Midwest. He was a middle child in a large family that valued education. (One of his older brothers earned a Ph.D. in physics.) He studied philosophy at Yale, also earning a Ph.D. in 1884. He was unable to find a teaching position, however, and falling ill, he returned to the family farm where he spent most of the next six years. While recuperating at his parents' home, he married a woman from a nearby farm. Then he returned to graduate school, studying economics at Cornell until he obtained a teaching position at the University of Chicago. He taught there from 1892 until 1906 when he was fired by the university's president for, "flagrant marital infidelities" after his wife told the university president he had multiple extramarital affairs.[25] Rumors of extramarital affairs continued to follow him from Chicago, and probably accounted at least partially for Veblen subsequently maintaining only brief positions at Stanford and the University of Missouri. After World War One he moved to New York and was among the founding faculty of the New School for Social Research.

Although nominally an economist, Veblen's most enduring contribution was in sociology. Most of his writings examined the incompetent way that owners managed their companies, and the adverse consequences that resulted for the entire economy. His analysis was much like Marx's in that he viewed the institution of private property as leading to excessive class differences and to inefficiency and waste. Once the possession of property became the basis for stratification in a society, it led people to ever increasing desires to accumulate wealth and possessions so that they could make invidious comparisons between themselves and others. However, he wrote, it is not possessions, per se, that lead to status, but the way people spend their time and the kind of objects they acquire.

The term that Veblen is best remembered for is, "conspicuous consumption:" the purchase and public display of expensive, but non-utilitarian commodities, such as high-priced cigars, rare artwork, fine jewelry, etc. He introduced this term in an analysis of what he termed the leisure class: the wealthy people who stand at the apex of the stratification system and who are above "vulgar" productive occupations. Their lives focus about a quest for status, but it does not make them industrious or frugal. Rather, their time is devoted to "conspicuous leisure:" clubs, sports, charitable organizations, and the like. Veblen concluded that the upper social class in a society with private property ultimately leads to "conspicuous waste."[26]

Charlotte Perkins Gilman (1860–1935)

Gilman's extended family included many prominent people, including Harriett Beecher Stowe, author of *Uncle Tom's Cabin*. Her own family, however, was poor and often dependent upon the handouts of relatives. Resolving to be self-sufficient, as a young woman she sent articles and poems to magazines and did not marry until age 23—older than the average for a woman in the 1880s.

When she did assume the roles of wife and then mother, Gilman was overcome by depression. She attributed it to the idleness enforced among women who were then playing conventional family roles. The fact that she also came slowly to realize that her "true passion" was reserved for women rather than men probably contributed as well to the strain she felt in her married role. Her self-prescribed cure for depression was to be as "productive" as possible, which for her meant writing articles, poems, novels and sociological analyses.[27]

The discrepancy between Gilman's high extended family status and her own poverty, and the disconnect between her innermost gay preferences and her overt heterosexuality were all played out in one of her early books, *Women and Economics*.[28] It was probably her most important work in sociological theory. In this book, much of which showed the influence of Karl Marx's emphasis upon class conflicts, she argued that it was neither housework nor "motherwork" that made women economically dependent upon, and subordinate to, men. Rather, Gilman argued, it was human society's excessive emphasis upon sexual differences that laid the basis for the continuation of women's subordination.

In both her fiction—she wrote novels, short stories and poetry—and non-fiction, gender was Gilman's focus. More specifically, she examined the institutional oppression of women from a variety of perspectives. In a sociological analysis of women's clothing, for example, she contended that their dress was symbolic of their subordinated role in society. First published in 1915, it was one of the first extensive sociological analyses of clothing and fashion.[29] She claimed that male dominance (i.e. patriarchy) had been a cause of social problems in every major institution: law, education, religion, etc. However, she was hopeful for the future, contending that men and women could work together to change these institutional patterns and create more egalitarian societies.

Charles Horton Cooley (1864–1929)

Charles Cooley spent almost his entire life near the Ann Arbor campus of the University of Michigan. He grew up there because his father was a professor (and later dean) in the university's school of law. He attended the university, graduating with a degree in engineering, and he briefly left Ann Arbor to work as a statistician in Washington, D.C. However, he soon returned to study economics and sociology as a graduate student. When he completed his Ph.D. he took a position on the Michigan faculty, and spent the rest of his career there. Although he had worked as a statistician, he felt that numbers were of little value in understanding what was most important sociologically: how people imagine each other. Toward this end, for over 40 years he kept a personal journal in which he wrote about events and his feelings in order to work out his sociological ideas.[30]

Cooley's writings made an enormous contribution to symbolic interaction: the study of how people's selves are a product of language and social interaction.

It is an approach which emphasizes how people's behavior is a product of the way they interpret situations rather than the social structure. To this day, the Society for the Study of Symbolic Interaction, a professional association of sociologists and other social scientists, honors the article or book judged to have made the most outstanding contribution to symbolic interaction during the previous year by presenting the author with The Cooley Award.

Two of Cooley's most enduring contributions to the sociological literature warrant special notice. First is the idea of the, "looking glass self."

> "Each to each a looking glass
> Reflects the other that doth pass."[31]

Cooley was trying to convey the idea that, in interaction, people routinely reflect symbolic pictures of each other to each other. We imagine ourselves from the other's standpoint, he wrote, and feel proud or ashamed. Cooley's second very enduring conception was of primary groups. He defined them as intimate, face-to-face associations, and believed that they were the universal bases of human nature and the core pillars of human societies. It was also in primary groups that he believed people's most enduring self-conceptions were formed.

William Edward Burghardt Du Bois (1868–1963)

W.E.B. Du Bois was raised by his mother in a small Massachusetts town where they were one of few black residents. A gifted student from a young age, at 17 he left home to attend Fisk College in Nashville, a predominantly black school. It was Du Bois' introduction to race relations in the nineteenth century South, and the discrimination he encountered had a long-term impact upon his thinking and writing.[32] After completing graduate study at Harvard—where he was the first black person in the U.S. to receive a Ph.D.—and the first of what would be many visits to Europe, he received a research fellowship to study an impoverished inner-city black neighborhood in Philadelphia.

He interviewed thousands of blacks in the local Philadelphia neighborhood and proceeded to do an exhaustive analysis of the data. The study was a methodological landmark, and its conclusion that the multiple problems faced by inner-city blacks were due to environmental rather than genetic variables was similarly well ahead of its time.[33] He also organized photo exhibits of African Americans in their churches, businesses and homes, all designed to reflect the pride and culture of his black subjects. His objective was to pressure white audiences into reexamining their conceptions of blacks.[34] Perhaps his work of most enduring influence, *The Souls of Black Folk*, provided a partially autobiographical chronicle of African Americans. In this book he stressed "two-ness:" a simultaneously double consciousness as an American and as a black that they (and he) had to struggle to try to reconcile.[35]

Throughout the first half of his career, Du Bois strongly advocated for the rights of African Americans: to serve as officers in the military, for example.

By the late 1920s, however, he became pessimistic about the prospects for racial equality in America, and the political positions he took and the viewpoints he expressed were viewed as displaying a Russian influence. Because of cold-war paranoia, he was considered a dangerous radical by the U.S. government. The government harassed Du Bois continuously over the last decades of his life until he died, in exile, in Ghana, at age 95.

Endnotes

1. Jonathan H. Turner, "American Sociology in Chaos." *American Sociologist*, 37, 2006.
2. See the discussion in Krishan Kumar, *From Post-Industrial to Post-Modern Society*. Blackwell, 2004.
3. U.S. Department of Labor, Bureau of Labor Statistics. Washington, D.C., GPO, 2006.
4. Surveys conducted in a number of European nations, over an extended period of time, are analyzed in, Pippa Norris and Ronald Inglehart, *Sacred and Secular*. Cambridge: Cambridge University Press, 2004.
5. See the analysis of modern and post-modern in, Ihab Hassan, *The Postmodern Turn*. Columbus: Ohio State University Press, 1987.
6. See the discussion in, Jean Baudrillard, *The System of Objects*. London: Verso, 1996.
7. With respect to the place of Simmel, for example, in providing such coherence, see Birgitta Nedelmann, "The Continuing Relevance of Georg Simmel." In Georg Ritzer and Barry Smart (Eds.), *Handbook of Social Theory*. London: Sage, 2001.
8. We have left out of this supporting-cast grouping some theorists that others might have included in their compilations. Here is a brief rationale for omissions some readers might question:

   William Graham Sumner (1840–1910) and Albion Small (1854–1926): The contribution of each to the development of sociology in the U.S. was considerable, but it was primarily organizational rather than intellectual. Few ideas from either have retained much influence, but each played a prominent role in building an historically important sociology department: Sumner at Yale, Small at Chicago.

   Sigmund Freud (1858–1939): There is little doubt about the enormous influence Freud exerted on the thinking of many sociologists, particularly concerning the tension between individuals and society; but it is difficult to view Freud's writings as having made a direct contribution to sociological theory.

   George Herbert Mead (1863–1931): Mead's influence, particularly upon symbolic interaction, has been extraordinary. However, Mead's effect upon sociological theory was primarily due to his posthumously assembled book, and the teaching of his students, and both occurred well after the classical period.
9. See Arthur J. Booth, *Saint-Simon and Saint-Simonism*. New York: Humanities Press, 1970.
10. See "On Social Organization," in F.M.H. Markham (Ed.), *Henri Comte De Saint Simon 1760–1825*. New York: Hyperion, 1991.
11. Mary Pickering, *August Comte*. Cambridge: Cambridge University Press, 2006.

12. August Comte, *The Positive Philosophy of August Comte, Vol I and II.* London: George Bell and Sons, 1896. Comte actually began writing the first volume in the 1820's, shortly after leaving Saint-Simon.

13. *Herbert Spencer: An Autobiography.* Part One. Whitefish, MT: Kessinger Publishing, 2005.

14. Herbert Spencer, *The Study of Sociology.* Ann Arbor: University of Michigan, 2005.

15. Herbert Spencer, *First Principles.* Palo Alto: University Press of the Pacific. 2002.

16. For a complete biography, see Edward C. Rafferty, *Apostle of Human Progress: Lester Frank Ward.* New York: Rowman & Littlefield, 2003.

17. Lester Frank Ward, *Outlines of Sociology.* Whitefish, MT: Kessinger Publishing, 2004.

18. For further discussion, see Arthur J. Vidich and Stanford M. Lyman, *American Sociology.* New Haven: Yale University Press, 1985.

19. Alice Widener, *Gustave Le Bon, the Man and His Works.* Indianapolis: Liberty Press, 1979.

20. Robert A. Nye, *The Origins of Crowd Psychology.* London: Sage, 1975.

21. Gustave Le Bon, *The Crowd.* New York: Dover, 2002.

22. Charles Powers, *Vilfredo Pareto.* New York: Sage, 1987.

23. Vilfredo Pareto, *The Rise and Fall of Elites.* Transaction Publishers, 1991.

24. See the preface to, Talcott Parsons, *The Social System.* New York: Free Press, 1951.

25. Elizabeth and Henry Jorgensen, *Thorstein Veblen.* Armonk, NY: M.E. Sharpe, 1999.

26. Thorstein Veblen, *The Theory of the Leisure Class.* New York: Modern Library, 2001.

27. Gilman's biography and a discussion of her work is presented in, Ann J. Lane, *To Herland and Beyond.* Charlottesville, VA: University of Virginia Press, 1997.

28. Dover Publications, 1997.

29. Charlotte Perkins Gilman, *The Dress of Women.* New York: Greenwood, 2001.

30. For a biography of Cooley and a discussion of his ideas, see Glenn Jacobs, *Charles Horton Cooley.* Amherst, MA: University of Massachusetts Press, 2006.

31. Charles Horton Cooley, *Human Nature and the Social Order.* Transaction Publishers, 1983.

32. For biographies of Du Bois, see David L. Lewis, *W.E.B. Du Bois,* Owl Books, 1994 (covering his early years) and Owl Books, 2001 (covering his later years).

33. For a summary and analysis of Du Bois' classic study, see Michael B. Katz and Thomas J. Sugrue (Eds.), *W.E.B. Du Bois, Race and the City.* Philadelphia: University of Pennsylvania, 1998.

34. David L. Lewis and Deborah Willis, *A Small Nation of People.* New York: Amistad, 2005.

35. W.E.B. Du Bois, *The Souls of Black Folk.* Walking Lion Press, 2006.

CHAPTER

2

Harriet Martineau

BIOGRAPHY

Born in 1802, in Norwich, on England's East Coast, Harriet Martineau was the sixth of eight children. Her father had a manufacturing business that initially supported the family in a middle-class life style, but gradually became insolvent during her late teen years. It was also during her teen years that she slowly lost all hearing, though in her autobiography, Martineau recounted periods of severe pain in her ears from the time she was five years old.[1] Looking back in her autobiography, she described her parents as having been strict and uncaring. There were few overt displays of affection or tenderness that she could ever recall receiving as a child. From descriptions of other, then contemporary Victorian families, however, the Martineau household may not have been highly unusual.[2]

A nervous and ill child who was mostly home schooled, Martineau was intellectually precocious. By the time she was 14 years old she had read the works of most of the leading economic and political scholars of the day: Malthus, Adam Smith, etc. She decided early in life that she wanted to write, but it was difficult to make a living as a writer, especially for a woman. And with her father's declining business she realized she would have to be completely self-sufficient unless she married well. The closest she ever came to marrying was when she was in her 20s and fell in love with John Worthington. He came from a poor family, and her parents discouraged the relationship. Their prospects improved when he became a Unitarian pastor, but he suddenly became ill and died. Though she was grief-stricken at the time, she later considered her ill health and nervous temperament poorly suited to marriage, and believed it would have worked out poorly had they been able to marry.[3]

Martineau's early efforts to support herself as a writer had very limited success, but she persevered and moved in with relatives in London in order to be closer to a variety of publishing outlets. Her "breakthrough" work was:

Illustrations of Political Economy, initially published in 1832. Current edition: Broadview Press, 2004.

This book contained a series of chapters that presented the ideas of the political and economic scholars she had been reading since childhood. The book was well-received, sold a large number of copies, and immediately gave her a prominent place in literary circles, even though colleagues could communicate with her only by shouting into her ear-trumpet.[4]

Martineau then decided to travel to America. She had read a lot about the young nation, and it piqued her curiosity; plus she felt that her deafness would be less of a problem in an English speaking country because she could at least read people's lips. She spent two years traversing the U.S. where she was treated like a visiting dignitary, and granted interviews with the most prominent people in the country. She also made a point of talking with ordinary people, men and women, adults and children, in cities and on farms. Because of the success of her previous book and the enhanced name recognition that resulted from her magazine articles, she could choose the publisher for the books that resulted from her American travels. There were two, a little over one year apart. The first presented a detailed picture of America, the second was the result of her reflections upon her methods in studying the nation, and her methodological advice to others. Specifically:

Society in America. Initially published in 1837. Current edition: Transaction publishers, 1981.

How to Observe Morals and Manners. Initially published in 1838. Current edition: Transaction publishers, 1989.

In these books Martineau displayed a sociological sophistication—in both theory and method—that was rare for the time. It was an important part of the body of work that led twentieth-century sociologists to identify Martineau as, "the first female sociologist."[5] However, until relatively recently, there was a wide-spread tendency to ignore and marginalize women's contributions to the development of classical sociological theory. It is only in the last generation that sociologists have recognized and appreciated what Martineau and other female sociologists gave to the discipline.[6] (It is interesting to note in this context that an edited anthology of Martineau's work, 150 years after it first appeared, received the distinguished scholarly book award from the History of Sociology Section of the American Sociological Association).[7]

Shortly after completing these two books she began what was to be a European tour, but after leaving Scotland she became ill. The degree to which her illness was psychosomatic was not clear, but it did physically incapacitate her for about five years. During this period she remained in her home, an invalid, able to do little beside write, though she did manage to complete several books, including a detailed account of her life as an invalid.

> *Life in the Sick Room*. Initially published in 1844. Current edition:
> Broadview Literary, 2003.

The basis of her eventual cure was as uncertain as the cause of her illness. She attributed it to a dubious therapy called mesmerism. In any case, she did recover, and for the next decade resumed a busy schedule of traveling, lecturing and writing. Much of her writing—in both books and columns in the London *Daily News*—was directed at improving the situation of women, and she was a leading feminist voice during a time of much public debate concerning women's roles. During this period Martineau also made another highly notable contribution to the new discipline of sociology. Specifically, she edited and translated the multi-volume work of August Comte, a Frenchman frequently identified as the founder of sociology. (See Chapter 1 for further discussion of Comte).

> *The Positive Philosophy of August Comte*, Translated and Edited by
> Harriet Martineau. Initially published in 1853.

According to Elbert Hubbard, a prominent nineteenth-century writer and publisher, her translation, condensation and editing of Comte's work would turn out to be her most enduring contribution. As she did with the ideas of the scholars in her first book, she captured the essence of what Comte had in mind, and presented it in a much more comprehensible manner than he did. In fact, she did it so well that her version of his work was translated back into French, and became "accepted as the text-book" of Comte's work while the original was "merely collected by museums . . ."[8] (However, as Comte's importance in sociology declined, Martineau's editing and translating of his work became less significant, and she is best remembered today for her own writings.)

After completing her translating and editing of Comte's volumes, Martineau again became seriously ill, and began her autobiography, believing she would soon die. She wound up living another 20 years, though, and wrote several other books before finally finishing her autobiography shortly before her death in 1876.

AMERICAN SOCIETY

In 1834, Martineau wanted to travel, and selected America as her destination. Like many people in England, she was fascinated by the new nation; and she felt her impaired hearing would present too much of an obstacle in a non-English speaking country. She landed in New York in September to begin two years traveling from North to South, to the Midwest, then to New England. She was eager to learn as much as she could about America, but was also concerned with what would today be considered questions of epistemology—*how* do people know what they think they know? Correspondingly, she paid close attention to her methods of inquiry, and kept detailed notes of where she visited, who she met and talked with, etc. She wanted to be sure she took in a broad slice of American life, and so she went to hospitals and universities, plantations and farms, weddings and festivals. She met with members of Congress, the President, Supreme Court Justices, and hundreds of "ordinary" people in cities and towns.

Her concern with methods led her over the next year to prepare a book on how to observe. In that book, she was very critical of people who go to another society and impose their own values upon what they see; however, as we will note, her book, *Society in America*,[9] contained many of the evaluative judgments she later cautioned against. Nevertheless, her book and deToqueville's *Democracy in America* were the two most significant sociological analyses of the U.S. conducted during the first half of the nineteenth century. Perhaps because of her gender, or due to the fact that her analysis of American society was much more critical than deToqueville's, his book soon became a classic while hers went relatively un-noticed. Her book sold poorly, and very soon went out-of-print until it was "re-discovered" 150 years later.

Unheralded at the time, she organized much of her description of American society according to the nation's social institutions: politics, economics, religion, family. Although such an organization would be considered rather commonplace today, it was highly innovative at the time she wrote it.

Politics and Government

Politics and government were the main subjects of the first part of *Society in America* (*SA*). As she found out more about politics in the U.S., she was struck by the discrepancy between ideals and reality. While professing a commitment to participatory Democracy, she found Americans actually to be politically naive, apathetic and misinformed. She singled out newspapers as both a cause and reflection of the underlying problem. Her critique of the political role of newspapers (the primary media in 1834) can be interestingly compared to contemporary critiques of (the more diverse) media.

She believed there were far too many newspapers, and that they gave the citizenry the appearance of being informed, but much of their content was distorted by political influences. Even though many of the distortions would eventually be corrected, she observed that, "lies may work their intended effect, before the truth can overtake them."[10] Finally, in another critique that closely mirrors contemporary criticism of the media's political role, she wrote,

> "The systematic abuse with which the newspapers of one side assail every candidate coming forward on the other, is the cause of many honourable men . . . being deterred from entering public life; and of the people being thus deprived of some better servants than any they have."[11]

The legal situations of women and people of color appalled Martineau, and she presented them to her readers as particularly vivid examples of the discrepancies between American ideals and reality. How could a government based, in principle, upon the consent of the governed not permit women to vote, she asked? Turning to blacks, she claimed that their systematic exclusion from schools, professions and churches was "disgusting." She was disappointed in how few people, black or white, railed against institutional racism in 1834. They accepted it as natural. Most people do not consider the possibility of arrangements other than the ones they are familiar with, she generalized, because they do not see "beyond the actual and immediate."[12]

Economy

The middle section of SA was devoted to the American economy. Even though the state of Missouri was then the western edge of the country, she was struck by the nation's size, and by its great material wealth in the form of: forests, quarries, salt, gold, coal, etc. She was certain America would prosper because of its geological assets and also its ethnic diversity. She argued that the population's heterogeneous backgrounds would ultimately elevate the intellect, character and wealth of the nation, even though many Americans were not aware of this benefit. In yet another statement that sounds like it could have been taken from today's news stories, she wrote, "America will find herself largely blessed" by the blending and absorption of diverse people, "however much she may now complain of the immigration of strangers."[13]

Martineau was also very sensitive to regional differences in work ethic and economic outlooks. She described people in the North as generally industrious and ambitious. By contrast, she regarded people in the South as typically trying to avoid hard work. Gender differences reflected these regional patterns. Northern women, she wrote, had fewer outside-the-home opportunities than Northern men, but hard work—whether in the home or outside of it—was the norm. Southern whites, upper class Southern white women in particular, typically looked down on hard work. These upper class women, she wrote, aspire only to being cultured (e.g. play the harp) and marrying young and well. "A more hopeless state of degradation can hardly be conceived of," was her judgment of these Southern Belles.[14]

As previously noted in the description of American government, Martineau was upset by the treatment of blacks, especially those who were slaves in Southern households. She condemned their forced menial labor, but she found the personal suppression of household slaves to be the, "grossest vice." The white male slave owners treated their female slaves as a harem for their own sexual pleasures, and then regarded them as though they were no more than inanimate pieces of property. Slave owners did not hesitate to sell both the women and their children (which had often been fathered by slave owners) even if it meant separating them. Meanwhile they flogged the black men without fear of any external restrictions. Abuses must always be wide-spread, she concluded, "when human beings are wholly subjected to the will of other human beings."[15]

Social Class

In the final section of *SA*, Martineau offered sociological observations on a variety of topics, ranging from gender roles and marriage and child rearing practices to religion and social class. (Her writings on women will be treated later in a separate section in this chapter.) Particularly notable here were her observations on class and caste. Despite its inconsistency with America's democratic ideals, she noted a tendency toward the creation of an exclusive aristocratic class based upon inherited wealth, but an observer had to "dig" below the surface to see it. Adults, she found, tried to disguise their pride in being among their cities' "first families," and to deny snobbish feelings toward people who recently earned their money (e.g. successful grocers). However, when she talked to their children, Martineau found them to be much more forthcoming concerning how class considerations permeated their lives, as illustrated by the following:

> "A school-girl told me what a delightful 'set' she belonged to at school . . . till several grocers' daughters began to come in as their fathers grew rich; and it became necessary for the higher girls to . . . visit exclusively among themselves."[16]

After spending two years traveling across America, she returned to London and published reports on her travels and descriptions of American society. She also wrote a chapter on how to observe, but it was not initially published. Upon reflection, she later decided that some of her descriptions of American customs had been too abstract, and perhaps reached too uncritically. Martineau then devoted herself to elaborating upon methods of observation and inference.[17]

HOW TO OBSERVE

In 1838 Martineau published what may have been the very first book to systematically discuss how sociologists ought to observe behavior in societies with which they are unfamiliar: *How to Observe Morals and Manners* (*HOMM*).[18] Most of her recommendations were applicable to studying any society, including one's own, though her emphasis was upon observing people whose customs were different from those that predominated in the investigator's home society.

Martineau began *HOMM* by insisting that it was easy to look at something, think that you are seeing it correctly, yet miss the point. Observers need to be trained, she wrote, in order to "see the truth" in what appears to lie before their eyes.

"The powers of observation must be trained, and habits of method . . . must be acquired before the student possesses the requisite for understanding what he contemplates."[19]

In this respect she felt that the people of her day under-appreciated the importance of following a systematic method when it came to understanding human behavior. People who lacked formal training in the subject would never presume to claim expertise in geology, astronomy or architecture; but, she complained, they do not hesitate to make a brief visit to a new country and immediately declare themselves experts in the country's morals and manners.

Ordinary travelers do not appreciate how limited their samples are, she continued. They see only a portion of the whole array of people, and worse yet, they impose their presuppositions over what they do see. To reach valid inferences from one's observations, Martineau offered the following principles:

1. Do not rush to conclusions. Hasty decisions force one's observations to fit predetermined opinions.
2. Do not generalize from limited observations. (Martineau illustrated this principle with the example of a British traveler in China whose host was intoxicated, so the English visitor concluded that all Chinese men were drunks.)
3. Recognize that observations are, at best, approximations to the truth; but take heart because when combined with the observations of others, they contribute to eventual understandings.

For a traveler's observations to have any validity they must be stripped of *ethnocentrism*: judging other societies by the standards of one's own culture. Do not be "perplexed or disgusted," she wrote, if you come upon people,

"Swallowing blubber, or scooping out water-melons, instead of regaling themselves with beef and beer . . . [or] eat with their fingers, instead of silver forks . . ."[20]

If travelers permit themselves to respond emotionally and in a judgmental way, they may miss the meanings of their observations. To illustrate, Martineau described what might happen if an outsider, who did not understand American political processes, observed town hall meetings.

"He will be tempted to laugh,—to call the world about him mad,—like one who, without hearing the music, sees a roomfull of people begin to dance."[21]

In sum, Martineau advocated that observers focus upon concrete events, take their time to interpret the meaning of what they see, and be cautious about generalizing. It was especially good advice for outsiders, such as travelers, but also useful for anyone who was concerned with the validity of her/his observations in any society.

In order to illustrate her principles of observation and inference, Research Box 2-1 presents a contemporary analysis of cell phone use among the impoverished residents of the island of Jamaica. By way of background, when this study was conducted (in 2004), there were an average of three cell phones per household in Jamaica, despite an average per capita income of less than $3,000 (U.S.). Almost everyone visiting the poorer cities and towns on the island was struck by how many of the apparently impoverished Jamaicans were regularly in conversations on their cell phones. How can their behavior be explained? Have cell phones become a medium of conspicuous consumption by which Jamaicans strive for popularity or prestige, even though they can ill afford it? Are outsiders correct when they denigrate the poor islanders for sacrificing "necessities" in order to purchase and use cell phones?

RESEARCH BOX 2-1

The Meaning of Cell Phone Use Among Poor Jamaicans

The Publication

Heather Horst and Daniel Miller, "From Kinship to Link-Up." *Current Anthropology*, 46, 2005.

The Research Question

Cell phone use among low-income Jamaicans has been very extensive, even when compared to its use among much wealthier people. Its prevalence can be observed on any street in any poor Jamaican town or city. How is this feature of Jamaican life to be explained? Is it an extravagance that the impoverished islanders can not afford, an effort to raise their social standing at the expense of essentials, such as food and shelter?

The Data

The investigators spent one year in two poor areas on the island, living with local families, participating in and observing everyday life in the selected communities. They also obtained socio-economic and demographic information about the residents of 100 carefully selected households who agreed to provide the investigators with detailed reports on their cell phone use. Among the information they provided was: the number of people's names and numbers they had stored in their phones, their relationship to these people, how often they called them, what they talked about, etc.

(Continued)

The Findings

Any interpretation of the place of cell phones in the lives of these people must begin with a recognition of their impoverished situation, and the relative lack of opportunities for upward mobility offered by the Jamaican economy. Fewer than one-half of the respondents in their sample had stable employment, i.e. working full-time, most of the year. Given the nature of the Jamaican economy, a majority of the poor islanders could work only intermittently and part-time: in construction or retail stores, picking crops, etc.

The respondents who provided detailed information had an average of nearly 100 names stored on their phones, and they often kept an additional handwritten list with hundreds more names in case their phones were lost or stolen. The people on their lists were: kin, "fictive" kin (e.g. a neighbor's aunt they also referred to as their aunt), former teachers and co-workers, people with whom they had once been romantically involved, friends, neighbors, etc. People standing in *any* of these relationships to each other could be expected, given Jamaican's norms, to help one pay bills, buy clothes, and so on—when/if they were able. Given the wide-spread poverty, people might have to try lots of names on their list before they found one able to help at the time. The respondents also stated that any type of job was *always* obtained solely through these connections, that is, social networking. Thus, routinely staying in touch with as wide a network as possible was the core "coping strategy" of these impoverished Jamaicans. When the cell phones first became available, even the poorest people on the island immediately purchased cell phones because they provided an extremely effective way of maintaining social networks. "It hardly seems surprising," the investigators conclude, "that the purchase of a cell phone is regarded as a priority by those who might otherwise be considered least able to afford them" (p 762).

The overall research strategy Martineau advocated was extraordinarily sophisticated for her time. It would today be described as, "multi-method" because of its reliance upon several approaches. Specifically, she advocated that a researcher utilize:

1. *Direct observation:* Carefully note what people do, with whom they do it, and how, she wrote. There may be important discrepancies between what people say and what they do (as illustrated by the previous example of nineteenth-century American adults denying they were snobbish), and a good observer will note these discrepancies. "From observations," she wrote, one "may learn more of the private life of a community than from the conversations of any number of individuals who compose it."[22]

2. *In-depth interviews:* While Martineau was concerned with the candor of people's comments, she nevertheless believed that in-depth interviews, as long as respondents were carefully selected to be representative of their communities, could add immeasurably to a study's value. However, to be useful, she repeatedly stressed that the interviewer must

sympathize with the respondent, and avoid both implicit and explicit condemnation.

3. ***Statistical records of births, marriages, occupations, suicides, etc.:*** These figures, she wrote, may, "afford more information . . . in a day than converse with individuals in a year."[23] However, she was sensitive to the fact that any society's official records could reflect the interests or biases of those who compiled them, and that if viewed apart from information obtained from observations and interviews, statistical records could impart distorted understandings. Contemporary examinations of the way governments "manipulate" data on poverty, unemployment, health, etc. provide a clear example of why Martineau had reservations about official statistics.[24] Nevertheless, she urged outsiders to seek such data, and settle for the best available data without insisting that they be perfect. To illustrate her persistent approach with respect to obtaining statistics on illness or death, she urged the analyst to,

> "Inquire for any public registers which may exist in all districts. . . . In case of there being none such, it is possible that the physicians of the district may be able to afford information from private documents. . . . If not, there remain the cemeteries."[25]

IN THE SICK ROOM

Shortly after completing her work on how to observe, Martineau became ill and for a number of years (1839–1843) was largely confined to her home. During this extended period, she spent most of her time writing, authoring numerous articles for popular periodicals and several books, including an account of the years her home was, in effect, an infirmary. Throughout this period of about five years she was frequently in great pain and sometimes felt too feeble even to hold a pen. She regarded herself as an invalid, and when *Life in the Sick Room* (*LISR*) was initially published she identified the author only with the pseudonym, "An Invalid."

The exact nature of her illness was never clear. In her autobiography she considered one of the likely causes to be anxiety and exhaustion from maintaining a busy work schedule while caring for a terminally ill mother when she, herself, was not well. However, she also believed that she was suffering from a serious and chronic physical malady, and this view was reinforced by some of the medical professionals she consulted. Physicians variously diagnosed her chronic genital pain as resulting from a tumor on her uterus or an ovarian cyst; but still others pointed to exhaustion, an unconscious desire to avoid caring for her mother, or some combination of the above.[26] (Persistent genital pain in women often continues to be a very difficult-to-diagnose ailment. For example, female college students who experience so much pain that they cannot sit through a mid-term examination typically have to consult half a dozen physicians "before finding one who acknowledges she has a real medical problem."[27])

Most people, Martineau observed, suffer debilitating pain for only brief periods. They consider their situations to be temporary, and so may be comforted when friends or family assure them they will soon be well again. When the suffering is not temporary, however, well-meaning attempts to console seem dishonest and are irritating to the sufferer. The chronically ill person, who does not expect a miraculous recovery, regards encouraging words as cowardly efforts by sympathizers to actually comfort themselves. She felt much better, she wrote, when someone told her there was no reason to try to paint a rosy picture of her condition.

> "One said to me, 'Why should we . . . make up a bright prospect
> for you? . . . the time seems past for expecting you ever to be well.'
> How my spirits rose . . . at this recognition of the truth."[28]

Furthermore, Martineau claimed, she never knew anyone else who, like herself, had suffered incapacitating pain for a long period of time who did not share her dislike of others' efforts at consolation. She generalized that everyone suffering a long-term illness or disability was happiest, in fact, when no friends or relatives even came to visit. Then no one had to feign optimism. Painters who are healthy, she mused, always draw pictures of a sick room full of sympathetic supporters. Their pictures distort the truth from the ill person's vantage point because, being healthy, they do not understand how comforting it is for really sick people to be alone so they do not have to pretend to be cheerful or optimistic.

Martineau's insights into the interaction between ill and well people anticipated some of the later theoretical analysis of Erving Goffman, and his writings provide a framework from which Martineau's insights can be further examined. People who are invalids, Goffman wrote, may have a "stigma" which he defined as any undesirable attribute that discredits a person's social identity. Some other examples of a stigma could include being blind or extremely obese, having a prison record or a deviant occupation (e.g. prostitute). In each case, people who do not share the stigma (i.e. "normal" people) tend to focus exclusively upon that one quality of a person, and it may be the only attribute of the person to which they respond. They may not, therefore, seem to recognize that the blind person also has a good sense of humor, for example, that the ex-con is also handsome, or the like.

However, "normal" people would usually deny that they only respond to the other's stigma even though their actions indicate that the stigma is so salient to them that they overlook the person's other qualities. The contradictory expectation this produces creates a quandary for people with a stigma when they interact with those who do not share the stigma.[29] Harriet Martineau must have wondered whether well people implicitly expected her to act like an invalid. Did they anticipate that she would get up to greet them? Pour her own tea? How could she know what they expected when they did not know, themselves. The inconsistent expectations of others—based upon their not fully accepting stigmatized people as being like them while simultaneously prompting them to act as though they were not different—makes relaxed interaction with most others very difficult for people with a stigma. Maybe that is what underlies Martineau's observation that invalids prefer not to be with healthy people.

It is interesting to speculate about whether the stigma associated with Martineau's illness would have varied according to whether its origin was considered psychological rather than due to a biological or hereditary condition. There would have been ample reason for her friends and family to have assumed her illness was psychological, beginning with the belief of many of the physicians she consulted that they were looking at a nervous condition. Further, it was certainly the case that Victorian women were, in Martineau's day, widely assumed to be fragile and susceptible to hysteria. However, some contemporary research on the negativity of stigmas suggests that beliefs about the origins of such illnesses may have made little difference. Seriously ill people are stigmatized in either case, according to a set of experiments, and while others sympathize, they also label ill people as different and often try to avoid interacting with them regardless of whether they infer the origin of the illness to be psychological or genetic.[30]

As her period of confinement increased, Martineau found that she especially wanted to be alone on days that had formerly marked important events in her life: birthdays, holidays such as Christmas, etc. When others were around, she explained, she felt pressured to act as though everything was fine in order to share the event. However, celebrating a birthday, holiday or the like brings home to the invalid, in a dramatic way, the difference between how one once observed the occasion and the present. When no one else is around to share the event, by contrast, she felt "unchained;" free to quietly remember the past without expressing platitudes about the future. Life was better without pretense.

The one exception to her preference for solitude involved a servant. The helpfulness of such a person, she explained, is "mechanical" and does not create obligations on the sick person's behalf. Ill people do not have to take the feelings of a servant into account and act as though they feel better than they do. The relationship between the invalid and her servant "is sustained with the least expenditure of painful feeling on both sides . . ."[31]

Here again Martineau's insightful reflections anticipated theoretical distinctions in Goffman's writings. He specifically analyzed servants as an example of a category he termed, "non-persons:" people in roles that require no consideration from others. They are treated as though they were objects; part of a room's furnishings.[32] (Other examples of non-persons can, in some social settings, include court stenographers, slaves, bodyguards, etc.) Thus, Martineau could receive the assistance she needed from a servant (i.e. non-person) without experiencing the discomforts that otherwise came from interacting with people who were well. Furthermore, in relating to non-persons, such as servants, Martineau would not have to hide the irritability she frequently felt. She was free to act however she wished.

ON WOMEN

Throughout her life Martineau focused upon the role of women in society, both as an interested observer and as an involved feminist who was committed to promoting change. In her native London, she closely followed women's issues in the work place and the household, often presenting her views in speeches, in newspapers and magazines. She was a very influential spokesperson for feminist positions in London. When her health permitted she traveled to other parts of England and Ireland, to France and America; and the observations she made during these trips contributed to her broad understanding of women's issues. Many of her analyses provided a comparative perspective on marriage, divorce, work, domestic responsibilities, etc.

Education and Work

The core problem faced by women in mid-nineteenth-century England (and elsewhere), according to Martineau, was a lack of educational opportunity. Because of this deficiency, women were not prepared for most occupations outside of the home. They had few chances, therefore, to demonstrate that they were as able as men to perform most jobs. Being largely confined to homemaking or to menial jobs outside of the home, females remained financially dependent upon males throughout their lives; first their fathers, later their husbands.

Martineau expressed some of her most deeply held views on education in response to a report of one of London's annual Queens College (for ladies) meetings. She found the Dean's comments in the report to be patronizing of women, but she gave him the benefit of the doubt, assuming it reflected a "happy complacency" he did not recognize in himself. He had advocated more education for women (and she of course agreed); but, the Dean continued, more education for women was important because it would make them better mothers to their children and better companions for their husbands. Martineau was sure he felt satisfied with the liberalness of his position, never questioning why the major purpose of a good education for women should be to increase their value to someone beside themselves. As long as that is how the education of women is to be justified, she wrote, most girls will not make much effort to excel in school.[33]

Viewing educational decision-making generally in mid-nineteenth-century London, Martineau regarded it as highly patriarchal. The senior officials in educational institutions were men, and decisions about children's schooling were made by fathers who, she wrote, were happy to make sacrifices to educate their sons, but expected their wives to figure out how to educate their daughters as cheaply as possible. Even in well-to-do homes of professional men, the typical father assigned little value to his daughters' education, claiming that, "it ought not to cost much to teach his girls as much as it is good for them to know;" and the working class father similarly believed that girls should be educated for, "managing the house and doing the needlework, and that all study beyond this is mischievous."[34] So, it was not just that girls in the mid-nineteenth-century did not need much education, in their fathers' view, but that "too much" education would actually be harmful to them.

Martineau's efforts to improve women's education took two directions. On the one hand, she directly attacked the philosophical foundations of arguments that held women to lower educational standards. On the other hand, utilizing Census figures she argued (very much like a contemporary social scientist) that the public conception of the work force was not accurate. Women were, in fact, much more involved in the labor force than was generally recognized, making inferior educational standards for women obsolete. Specifically, in Great Britain in 1851, outside of Ireland, she noted that there were six million women over age 20. The Census figures indicated that more than half of them were employed outside of their homes, she reported; and then asked,

> "Does this surprise our readers? If it never occurred to them before, they will be still further impressed by the fact that two millions of women, out of the six millions, are . . . self-supporting, like men."[35]

She proceeded to describe the number of women in varied occupations, from dairy maids to teachers, with the largest group employed in the manufacturing of clothing. Regardless of their jobs, Martineau noted that women were invariably paid less than their male counterparts. She attributed the discrepancy in part to men's prejudice and jealousy. The other cause, which she emphasized, was women's inferior training and education. To illustrate, she reported that thousands of women worked in retail trade, but they rarely ran or owned the shop because they lacked special training in bookkeeping and other relevant skills. The first step, she concluded, was to recognize "the facts" of women's employment according to England's latest Census. The next step was to provide the education that women (and men) required to fill their actual—not their imagined—positions.

Martineau envisioned a future in which both girls and boys would be similarly educated; discrimination against women in the labor force would diminish; and there would be more equality in women's and men's pay. Many recent studies make clear that in modern nations, such as the contemporary U.S., there has been substantial progress in all the directions previously discussed. However, wage equality remains elusive because, as the study summarized in Research Box 2-2 illustrates, the educational decisions women and men make have multiple dimensions and complex effects. An interesting question to ask in reflecting upon this study is: Do the educational decisions by which women disadvantage themselves in the labor market reflect a continuing patriarchal influence?

RESEARCH BOX 2-2

Education and the Gender Gap in Income

The Publication

Donna Bobbitt-Zeher, "The Gender Income Gap and the Role of Education." *Sociology of Education*, 80, 2007.

The Research Question

Since the 1990's, women have been more likely than men to graduate from a four-year college. Women's recent educational attainments might have been expected to reverse, or at least eliminate, the historic discrepancy between men's and women's incomes among young adults. However, even among young college graduates, the average yearly earnings of men exceed those of women by nearly $7,000; and these initial earnings differentials are strongly associated with earnings differentials later in people's careers. The central question is: What accounts for the persistence of this income disparity among young college graduates?

The Data

The study included a representative sample of nearly 25,000 people who provided data several times over a 12 year period. The respondents were first contacted (in 1988) when they were completing eighth grade. Most were 14 years old at this time. They were followed until 2000, when most of them were 26 years old, finished with college and in the labor force. The study included a wide range of data about the respondents, including: grades, test scores, college majors, economic aspirations, marital status, etc.

The Findings

The variable found to have the largest effect upon subsequent earnings was college major. Men were more likely than women to have majored in math, science and engineering, fields that were associated with high incomes after graduation. Women were more attracted than men to majors in the humanities, social sciences and education, which led to jobs with lower incomes. The investigator calculated the percentage of females in each major, and found that this variable independently accounted for about one-third of the entire gender income gap—far more than any of the other variables included, though several others were found to have relatively small effects: women were disadvantaged by starting a family before age 26; working part-time rather than full-time, and placing less value on having a lot of money. However, college major (i.e. percentage of females) eclipsed all of these other variables in producing a gender gap.

The investigator noted that in recent years there had obviously been some increase in the overlap among majors selected by men and women; for example, the number of women majoring in fields like engineering had increased as had the number of men majoring in fields like nursing. However, differences between men and women in their choices of major persist, and substantial variations in incomes continue to be associated with these different majors. Therefore, the investigator concluded, there is little reason to be optimistic that further increases in women's educational attainments will, in and of themselves, produce much in the way of declines in gender income inequality.

MARRIAGE AND DIVORCE

From her travels in the United States, Martineau knew quite a bit about marriages in America. She was also very familiar with what was occurring in her native England. In a more limited way, she knew something about marriage customs in several other European nations, and she had read a good deal of the history of domestic relations. She was able, as a result, to present a comparative analysis of marriage that was quite sophisticated for the time. She focused, in particular, upon the opportunities a man and a woman had, both as companions and as sexual partners, for obtaining enjoyment and satisfaction from marriage. In terms of the opportunities they afforded, she regarded marriage in virtually all societies—then contemporary or historical—as far from ideal.

Her focus was clearly sociological, seeking to explain marital quality as a function of social conditions and cultural values rather than individuals' psychological attributes. She wrote, "the corruption of society" is deep and widespread with respect to marital satisfaction; and as is usually the case, "the wrong will be found to lie . . . in the prevalent sentiments of society . . ."[36] This sociological perspective was quite exceptional for Martineau's period.

From her comparative analysis she inferred three variables that correlated with the ideal conditions for marital satisfaction in a society: the degree to which men's and women's roles were socially differentiated from each other; how much freedom young people had in choosing their mates; and the degree of restraint a society attempted to impose upon sexual activity. Martineau believed there was a tendency for societies to be similar on all three conditions, but for ease of presentation each will be discussed separately.

Gender Differentiation

One historically major type of gender differentiation and, therefore, unhappiness in marriage, Martineau wrote, occurred when societies emphasized the importance of courage to a man's honor. Men only had to be brave to be considered honorable. "The shallowness of the sentiment of honour is [a] great evil," she wrote.[37] In such societies, chastity for women was typically stressed, and women were put in a highly disadvantaged position. Men were obligated to act in an honorable manner only with equals (i.e. other men), and so they were free to use treachery in dealing with females. They could promise marriage in order to seduce a woman, then walk away; they could vow to love and honor, but not remain faithful to their wives; and in every case their honor was unstained when they failed to keep their word. The woman's virtue was not intact, though, and its loss was extraordinarily consequential for the woman. If a man loved her and left her, the woman's alternatives might be limited to begging or prostitution. This great difference in the power of men and women, Martineau wrote, was not conducive to husbands and wives bonding in a way that produced satisfying marital relations.

Another form of extreme gender differentiation described by Martineau occurred when men were supposed to be concerned with worldly matters and women were expected to be vain: preoccupied with makeup and fashion and other "trifling" matters. Given these expectations, there is neither an opportunity nor a reason for women to cultivate their minds. How, in such societies, she asked, can a wife provide meaningful companionship to a husband? What topics will she be able to discuss? Husbands will treat such wives as "playthings or servants" and seek social and sexual stimulation outside of the home.[38]

Finally, she returned to the issue of occupational sex segregation, this time examining it in relation to marriage. When women have few work alternatives, Martineau wrote, there will be an oversupply of potential labor for the available jobs, and as a result they will pay poorly. Women who want more in the way of luxuries may then be corrupted and choose vice over virtue. In addition, because limited work opportunities reduce women's alternatives, they correspondingly disadvantage women in relation to their husbands. In societies in which "the objects of life" are equally available to men and women, one may be certain of finding "the greatest amount of domestic purity" because, "if women were not helpless, men would find it far less easy to be vicious."[39]

Marital Choice

Martineau analyzed a wide range of societies in terms of how much freedom they gave to people in selecting their mates, and concluded that marital satisfaction was typically lower in societies that offered less in terms of freedom of choice. She saw 1830's America at the high end of freedom of choice, Italy and other nations (where women were committed to marriage before they could give enlightened consent) at the low end and England somewhere in the middle.

The quality of a marriage had to suffer, she wrote, if a father selected a bride or groom for his offspring as a means of obtaining wealth or status. Under these conditions, she asked, why would a husband and wife care about each other? Why would they expect their marital relations to be particularly satisfying? Martineau also felt that arranged marriages were particularly apt to lead to immoral, non-marital sexual liaisons (which she condemned). Despite being pledged to someone, young people might fall in love with another, and following their hearts may lead them to violate standards of marital and sexual conduct.

She made a point here of warning observers not to be misled by respondents' claims that their own society's customs were superior when it came to mate selection. People everywhere assert that their arrangements are the most pure, best from a religious standpoint, or the like. Do not take any of their boasts too seriously, she admonished. You find out how people really feel by carefully observing what is occurring with respect to non-marital births, extra-marital affairs, and so on. Only such observations will enable the analyst to infer the true "prevailing character . . . of domestic life . . ."[40]

Sexual Repression

Martineau also presented an interesting theory of how societies attempt to control sexual expression, and how such control impacts marital relations. Her basic proposition was that a society's emphasis upon "asceticism" (i.e. self-denial) and the actual amount of "licentiousness" (sensual indulgence) were directly related: the more of one, the more of the other. Underlying this assertion was her belief that human passions could only be restrained, not extinguished, so that attempts to suppress them in one place led to outbursts in others.

> "It may safely be assumed wherever artificial restraints are imposed on the passions . . . there must be a licentiousness, precisely proportioned to the severity of the restraint."[41]

One specific illustration of Martineau's proposition involved celibacy and multiple sexual or marriage partners. Whenever any class of people is expected to be celibate (e.g. clergy in Catholic nations), another class of people will have multiple partners, a kind of polygamy in fact, if not in name. Therefore, she expected that men and women would be most satisfied with monogamous marriages in societies that did not attempt to impose excessive and artificial restraints upon sexual expression.

Divorce

In mid-nineteenth-century England, divorces were very difficult to obtain. They were available to a husband by special petition, but even this limited avenue was not available to wives. In 1853 a commission was appointed to review divorce proceedings and to make recommendations to the government concerning the possibility of expanding the grounds for divorce and permitting women as well as men to institute proceedings. The latter possibility created a public furor, and Martineau weighed in on the issue in several articles for the London *Daily News*.

She began by challenging the dual standards that were being employed to keep women excluded as petitioners. For example, it was held that women would generally be more content if they knew they had to remain wed; this would presumably make them more inclined simply to accept their lot. However, the ability to terminate a marriage was regarded as good for men's happiness. Martineau pointed out the absurdity of the dual standard. She also turned to the assumption that infidelity was worse if a woman was guilty of it, hence husbands and not wives should have recourse to divorce on the grounds of infidelity. It is assumed, she wrote, that "any father would . . . rather see his son fall into vice than his daughter;" but, she noted, they overlook the fact that, "for the son's sins somebody's daughter must fall."[42]

Of particular concern to Martineau were cases in which a wife was stuck supporting herself, her children, and a lazy, unfaithful husband. Here she relied upon the previously discussed figures from the British Census concerning the "surprising" number of married women and mothers who were working because their husbands could not or would not support them. She used these facts again to buttress her argument to increase women's education. It was unworldly, she concluded, to assume that wives will be taken care of by their husbands. Furthermore, to deny women access to Divorce Courts, she wrote, makes even a mistress better off than a wife because, "a mistress can free herself from her tyrant at any moment, while the wife has no escape."[43]

In contemporary societies, where women's education is more comparable to men's, occupational sex segregation is markedly lower, and both men and women have greater access to divorce, the actual rate of divorce has markedly increased. Several studies have reported a direct correlation between women's labor force opportunities and the rate of divorce.[44] Explanations for this relationship have typically followed Martineau's expectation that when women can better support themselves, they are less constrained to remain in unsatisfactory marriages.

According to several recent studies, however, there is perhaps a surprising aspect to the correlation. These studies have compared the sex distributions of occupations and industries to the rate of divorce among people in these jobs. Among men, there is not much of a relationship; but among women there is a marked tendency for marital dissolution to increase with the sex mix of their occupations. For example, women working as elementary school teachers or nurses are in industries with relatively few males, especially when compared to women who are working as automobile mechanics or painters. The higher the percentage of male workers in their occupation, the higher the women's rate of divorce. Thus, it appears that sexually integrated workplaces not only result in women's greater financial independence, but also provide more of a "market" in which the busy working woman can conduct an extramarital search.[45] Perhaps working at similar jobs is conducive to the kind of companionate marriages that Martineau believed to be ideal.

Endnotes

1. Harriett Martineau, *Harriet Martineau's Autobiography.* London: Smith, Elder, 1877.

2. Gillian Thomas, *Harriet Martineau.* Boston: Twayne Publishers, 1985. See also Shelagh Hunter, *Harriet*

Martineau. Aldershot, England: Scholar Press, 1995.

3. See her *Autobiography*.
4. Roger Ellis, "Harriet Martineau." In *Who's Who in Victorian Britain*. London: Shepheard-Walwyn, 1997.
5. See Alice Rossi, "The First Woman Sociologist." In Alice Rossi, *The Feminist Papers*. New York: Columbia University Press, 1973; and Susan Hoecker-Drysdale, *Harriet Martineau: First Woman Sociologist*. Providence: Berg Publishers, 1992.
6. Patricia Madoo Lengermann and Jill Niebrugge-Brantley, "Classical Feminist Social Theory." In George Ritzer and Barry Smart (Eds.), *Handbook of Social Theory*. New York: Sage, 2001.
7. The book: Michael R. Hill and Susan Hoecker-Drysdale (Eds.), *Harriet Martineau*. New York: Routledge, 2001. See also the discussion in the review essay: Rebecca A. Allahyari, "An Ethnographic Primer." *Sociological Forum*, 19, 2004.
8. Elbert Hubbard, *Little Journeys to the Homes of Famous Women*. New York: Putnam's Sons, 1897.
9. Harriet Martineau, *Society in America*. New Brunswick: Transaction, 1981.
10. Ibid., p 103.
11. Ibid., p 104.
12. Ibid., p 124.
13. Ibid., p 131.
14. Insert, p 217.
15. Ibid., p 223.
16. Ibid., p 261–62.
17. For further discussion of her later reflections see, Maria W. Chapman (Ed.), *Harriet Martineau's Autobiography*. Virago Press, 1983.
18. Harriet Martineau, *How to Observe Morals and Manners (HOMM)*. New Brunswick: Transaction Publishers, 1989.
19. *HOMM*, p 2.
20. Ibid., p 25.
21. Ibid., p 55.
22. Ibid., p 186.
23. Ibid., p 74.
24. See the essays focusing upon British government statistics over the past 25 years in, Ruth Levitas and Will Guy (Eds.), *Interpreting Official Statistics*. London: Taylor & Francis, 2007.
25. Ibid., p 171.
26. See the "Introduction" by Maria H. Frawley to, Harriet Martineau, *Life in the Sick Room (LISR)*. Toronto: Broadview Literary Texts, 2003.
27. Jane E. Brody, "New Insights Into Genital Pain in Women." *The New York Times*, January 29, 2008, p D7.
28. LISR, p 51.
29. Erving Goffman, *Stigma*. Englewood Cliffs: Prentice-Hall, 1963. After an extremely influential career, Goffman was elected president of the American Sociological Association in 1982.
30. A modern experiment cannot directly reflect all the variables that may have affected public attitudes in the 1840's, but the results are nevertheless relevant to consider. See Jo C. Phelan, "Geneticization of Deviant Behavior and Consequences for Stigma." *Journal of Health and Social Behavior*, 46, 2005.
31. *LISR*, op.cit., p 61.
32. The concept of "non-person" appeared in many of Goffman's writings. See the discussion in Andrew Travers, "Non-person and Goffman." In Greg Smith (Ed.), *Goffman and Social Organization*. London: Routledge, 1999.
33. Harriet Martineau, "What Women Are Educated For." In Once A Week, August 10, 1861. Reprinted in Gayle Graham Yates (Ed.), *Harriet Martineau on Women*. New Brunswick: Rutgers University Press, 1985.

34. Ibid., p 99.
35. Harriet Martineau, "Independent Industry of Women." *London Daily News*, November 17, 1859. Reprinted in Yates, p 225–26.
36. *HOMM*, pp 172–73.
37. Ibid., p 173.
38. Harriet Martineau, "On Women." *Monthly Repository*, 17, 1822. Reprinted in Yates. This was one of Martineau's early essays in which she denied women's potential for equality, but simply argued that their minds ought not to be empty vessels.
39. *HOMM*, p 182.
40. Ibid., p 178
41. Ibid., p 175.
42. Harriet Martineau, "On the Married Women's Property Bill." *London Daily News*, March 25, 1853. Reprinted in Yates, p 217.
43. Harriet Martineau, "Brutality to Women." London *Daily News*, September 8, 1853. Reprinted in Yates, p 222.
44. See, for example, Scott South, "Time-Dependent Effects of Wives' Employment on Marital Dissolution." *American Sociological Review*, 66, 2001.
45. See, for example, Terra G. McKinnish, "Sexually Integrated Workplaces and Divorce." *The Journal of Human Resources*, 42, 2007.

3

Karl Marx (1)

Philosophical Analyses

BIOGRAPHY

Karl Marx was born in 1818, about 50 years before most of sociology's other major classical theorists.[1] His birthplace was the city of Trier, in Prussia (now Germany). Until shortly before his birth, his family had been Jewish, but because opportunities for Prussian Jews were legally restricted, his family converted and became Lutheran. Like other Prussian and German ex-Jews, the Marx's family tried their best to ignore their religious background. With the exception of a short essay on whether Jews should have more legal rights, Karl Marx's references to Jews were usually brief, but hostile in tone, leading Historian Frank Manuel to infer that Marx regarded his ancestry as a stigma.[2] Another biographer, Francis Wheen, offered the opinion that Marx's estrangement from religion may have been a result of being, "a Jew from a predominantly Catholic city within a country whose official religion was evangelical Protestantism."[3]

Marx also became alienated from his parents and siblings. While in school he battled with his father who thought he lacked responsible career plans. At times the young Marx considered becoming a lawyer like his father— or a poet, a drama critic, perhaps a professor of philosophy. When he finished school he regularly wrote to his mother, who was then widowed, and to other family members, begging them for money. They almost always refused. Feeling scorned, he later wrote in a letter, "Blessed is he that hath no family."[4]

Marx's most important university experience was at the University of Berlin, which was then dominated by a group of radical scholars called the Young Hegelians. He joined their primary intellectual pursuit—analyzing the work of the philosopher, G.W.F. Hegel—and adopted their life-style: bohemian, anti-religious, debating philosophy in German beer halls. He subsequently earned a Ph.D. and married his childhood sweetheart, to the consternation of her family who felt she was marrying a n'er-do-well, who would never support her in the style to which she had been accustomed.[5] They were right. He never made more than a marginal living, though his analyses made unsurpassed contributions to social science.

Marx and his wife initially settled in Germany where he began to write, hoping to attain a university position despite the chasm between his radical positions and the country's reactionary political climate. When an offer did not materialize, the young couple moved to Paris, a logical destination because that city was attracting radicals from all over Europe. One of them was Friedrich Engels who had been managing one of his father's factories until he felt overwhelmed by the miserable living conditions of the working class. He and Marx met in a Parisian café in 1843 and immediately formed a bond. They became long-term collaborators, and Engels later became his primary benefactor.[6]

Marx spent about two years in Paris, publishing a number of articles, some of which were highly critical of Prussia and Germany; but the lengthier manuscripts he prepared there were not published during his life time. Two of the most notable of these books were:

Economic and Philosophical Manuscripts

The German Ideology

Marx's articles offended officials in Prussia, and they asked the French government to expel him. When France complied, he moved to Brussels, where he affiliated with workers' associations and the communist political party that commissioned him to write a pamphlet explaining the goals of communism. The document was co-authored with Engels, though Engels gave Marx most of the credit. Their brief document, published in 1848, ultimately had enormous political significance:

Manifesto of the Communist Party, or *The Communist Manifesto*

Marx subsequently returned very briefly to Germany, hoping to ferment a revolution like that which was occurring in France, but he was again forced into exile. He returned to Paris, but when the French government ordered him to leave the city he moved to London with his wife and children. Marx spent most of the rest of his life there, reading and writing in the British Museum. While in London he was paid to write occasional articles about European affairs for the *New York Daily Tribune*, but his family lived in poverty, barely surviving, mostly on Engels' generosity.

It was during the 1850's and 1860's, in London, that Marx produced his most detailed social, economic and political analyses. Included were:

The Eighteenth Brumaire of Louis Bonparte (a pamphlet)

Das Kapital/Capital (in three volumes—probably his most important work)

A Contribution to the Critique of Political Economy (which he only partly completed)

By the 1870's Marx attained prominence (but not wealth) as a leader in the international workers' movement, and socialists from across Europe and North America sought his advice. He was ill, however, and wrote very little more. He died in 1883, two years after his wife.

In this chapter we will examine Marx's earlier philosophical work, beginning with his writings on Hegel. Chapter 4, on Marx, focuses upon his later, more economic and political writings, done mostly in London at the British Museum. There are differences between Marx's earlier and later works, and some analysts stress them, but the continuities are also very strong.[7] Prior to turning to any of his writings, however, it is important to make a distinction between two of Marx's roles: one, the advocate of communist revolution, and two, the theoretician and analyst. One need not be in favor of a communist revolution to find much of value in Marx's insights. We will examine this distinction between the two roles of Marx's at the end of both this chapter and Chapter 4.

HEGEL AND THE DIALECTIC

As noted in the preceding biography, Marx spent several formative years as part of a group of scholars at the University of Berlin called, "the young Hegelians." As their name indicates, they were devoted to studying the works of the noted philosopher, G.W.F. Hegel. Of particular importance to Marx's theoretical development was Hegel's dialectic approach which provided Marx with both an image of society and a way of studying it.

The dialectic is, at its base, a juxtaposition of opposites, resulting in an apparent paradox. For example, one of the ancient Greek's self-contradictions that Hegel wrote about concerned whether an arrow shot out of a bow was really in motion. At any stage in its flight, the arrow must occupy some specific space. So, how can it also be in motion? Hegel's answer was that motion meant *both* to be and not to be in a particular place. It was this seeming self-contradiction that defined and explained motion. Similarly, he argued, mortal beings with finite lives are simultaneously living and ceasing to live. In a phrase that Marx would later utilize to describe the end of capitalism and its replacement by communism, Hegel wrote:

> "The nature of the being of finite things is that they have within
> them the seeds of their own destruction; the hour of their birth is the
> hour of their death."[8]

Because all phenomena are presumed to entail a unity of opposites, true knowledge requires understanding how the opposites are combined. However, political theorist Howard Williams points out that attempting to unify apparently opposite qualities—stationary and moving or living and dying—is extremely difficult.[9] It requires one to recognize that both of the apparently contradictory characteristics of some phenomenon, such as an arrow or a living being, may be attributed to it by observers who are in different positions, or by people who observed it at different points in time.

The dialectic is committed to a developmental point of view which recognizes that the properties of a phenomenon vary over time, and in the future may even become opposite of what they are at present.

Qualitative Change/Negation

The type of change that most interested Hegel and Marx entailed a process in which a phenomenon negated itself; that is, became something qualitatively different from what it had been. Marx illustrated what this entailed by describing how an acorn negated a seed, and how an oak tree, in turn, negated an acorn. At each stage, change involved a transformation into something new; something that was not directly apparent in the previous stage. (Does an acorn look like an oak tree?)

Marx's emphasis upon qualitative change was also part of his polemic against "conventional" science and philosophy. He viewed the unenlightened scholars of his day as toiling to understand how small increments in one phenomenon led to small increments in another. The correlations they were able to infer may be descriptively accurate, but he complained, they missed the larger picture. What is observed to be true, he argued, does not necessarily translate directly into real knowledge.

Let us try an example to clarify what Marx was trying to say: Suppose we want to understand how two people come to love each other. If we believe that increases in how much a person likes another eventually result in love—i.e. love represents an extremely high degree of liking—then to understand love we could examine how conditions that lead to liking wind up leading to love. If, for example, the more people interact together, the more they like each other, then some large amount of interaction could produce love. Whether increased interaction leads first to liking and later to love is contingent upon liking and loving falling along the same dimension. If they are qualitatively different, then love is not a high degree of liking, but a transformation of liking into something else, and studying the conditions that lead to liking will not clarify the nature of love. In general, Marx felt that the most important social issues had to be examined as transformations, involving phenomena or stages that were qualitatively different from each other.

Idealism

Hegel was part of a long tradition in German philosophy that emphasized idealism in opposition to materialism. The underlying issue concerns the relationship of the self to external objects, and the degree to which the reality of an external world is dependent upon a subjective conceptual framework. Almost everyone recognizes an interplay between the subjective and objective, between the self and an external condition. However, many theorists can be placed along an ideal-material continuum: some are near the middle, others are closer to one pole or the other. This continuum is illustrated in Figure 3-1.

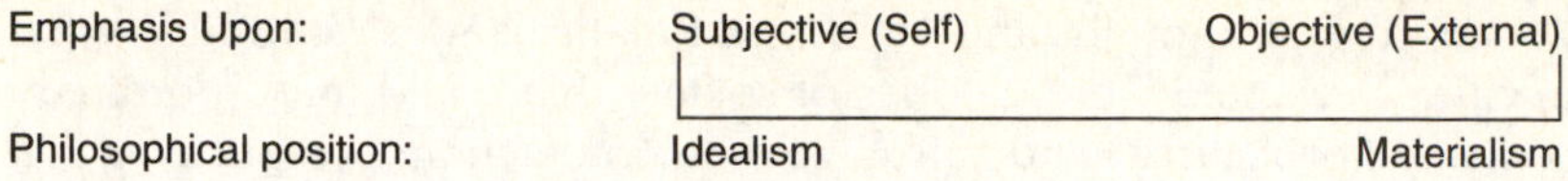

Emphasis Upon: Subjective (Self)   Objective (External)

Philosophical position: Idealism   Materialism

FIGURE 3-1 Idealism-Materialism Continuum

Philosophical Position: Idealism-Materialism

Hegel, an idealist, would be placed near the left pole of the continuum illustrated in Figure 3-1. He described social change as ultimately dependent upon people's consciousness of themselves and society. As that consciousness expanded, enhancing their ability to understand themselves and their society, the result would be both subjective and objective changes in society. Correspondingly, he stressed the importance of cultivating people's potential subjective development, believing it would ultimately provide them freedom from external conditions. Thus, freedom, for Hegel, meant a self-contained, self-conscious existence.[10]

Marx's emphasis upon historical materialism, to be described in detail later, placed him near the right end of the continuum in Figure 3-1. In an explicit reversal of Hegel's position, Marx and Engels wrote, "Life is not determined by consciousness, but consciousness by life."[11] As a result, if *real* changes were to occur, in Marx's view, they would depend upon objective changes in material conditions rather than changes in the way people thought about those conditions. "Material force must be overthrown by material force."[12]

Marx sometimes presented his materialist position in a deliberately exaggerated way, at least in part, to rectify what he believed was Hegel's exaggeration of the subjective realm. While much of Marx's writing emphasized materialism, it did not completely lose sight of idealism. Thus, in the sentence that follows the previous quotation on the necessity of utilizing material force (not ideas) to overthrow material force, Marx wrote: "But theory also becomes a material force once it has gripped the masses."[13] In other words, he believed that how people perceived and thought about the world mattered because it could influence what they did. In one of his most often quoted passages, he wrote:

> "Men make their own history, but they do not make it just as they please; they . . . make it under circumstances . . . transmitted from the past. The tradition of all the dead generations weighs like a nightmare on the brain of the living."[14]

Praxis (Practice)

Marx was also highly critical of conventional science and philosophy, and Hegel's idealism in particular, for advocating a dispassionate accumulation of knowledge. Marx dismissed most of their scholarly work as being idle speculation. He thought it was crucial to overcome the separation between theory and practice; to fuse thought and action, rationality and practicality. What Marx specifically wanted were theories of society that could inform ordinary workers (i.e. the proletariat) and galvanize them into action; perspectives that would give them new views of reality that they could put into practice. He also justified action-oriented theory by insisting that knowing the likely reaction to an intervention was a critically important part of understanding any phenomenon. For example, to really understand school systems or inheritance taxes or monogamous marriages, one must also understand what would probably happen if some group tried to change them. Hence, any theory that is divorced from practice actually distorts reality. His strongest statement on the primacy of praxis was: "The philosophers have only *interpreted* the word in various ways; the point is to *change* it."[15]

In emphasizing the importance of translating ideas into overt actions that can change society, Marx was also directly criticizing Hegel's idealism. The proper goal of knowledge, in Hegel's view, was subjective: "to make us more at home in the world."[16] In other words, as our view of a phenomenon changes, our relationship to it is changed and the phenomenon itself is thereby altered. Hopefully, Hegel wrote, we can be more comfortable with the change, and that represents progress. However, Marx was emphatic in arguing that no change in people's perceptions or understandings, in and of themselves, alters the external (material) world.

RELIGION

In confronting Hegel's idealism, Marx also addressed Hegel's view of religion. In fact, it was in a critique of Hegel that Marx wrote his most often referred to description of religion as the opium, or opiate, of the masses. Marx's view of religion was not entirely negative, though. Like all phenomena that were examined from a dialectical perspective, it had to be regarded as a unity of opposites.

Marx's writing on the place of religion began with a criticism of Hegel's extreme idealism. In Hegel's view, as previously described, the highest form of human consciousness was attained when people were able to detach themselves from the world in order to passively contemplate it. Religion, from this perspective, could play a helpful role in promoting abstract thought—*if* it provided an accurate picture of the human condition. Hegel realized it did not, but believed religion could nevertheless be useful so long as its misrepresentations were properly recognized. Marx disagreed, believing that religion was fundamentally too distorted. In his view, religion "perverted" consciousness because it was the product of a "perverted" world. It offered only illusions.

On the one hand, Marx contended that religion provided a genuine outlet for the suffering of the masses. In the mid-nineteenth-century cities that Marx was analyzing, most proletariat (i.e. ordinary working class) families barely survived because of dreadful working conditions, meager salaries and unsanitary living conditions that led to epidemics. Their distress was real and it found expression in religion. In Marx's words, "Religion is the sigh of the oppressed creature."[17] It was in that sense that he called it an opiate; that is, religion acted like a sedative to numb people's pain. On the other hand, also like a sedative, it did nothing to alleviate the underlying problem. It merely covered up the pain temporarily. Worse yet, Marx condemned religion for leading people to seek solutions to their problems in the wrong place.

To understand why Marx believed that religion led people astray, it is necessary to begin with his premise that religion reflected society. It was society that created God, in its image, not vice versa. All of religion is nothing more than a social product. Whatever power seems to inhere in religious ritual or prayer, or even in God, is due solely to what the society has attributed to them. Thus, even though the nature of religion is a reflection of a society, religion is a fantasy, a "realm in the clouds," a set of beliefs that are clung to by people who would rather believe in fantasies than face reality.

Hypothetically, if the society that religion reflected was without serious problems, then religion might be dismissed merely as an illusion. However, Marx claimed, because society, itself, is distorted, religious "fantasies" suffer from the same deficiencies. They camouflage rather than illuminate the underlying social organization. He believed it was necessary to confront religion precisely because it reflected the society that needed to be changed. Simply eliminating religion would not accomplish this objective, but eliminating religious fantasies would nevertheless be helpful in the sense that removing a veil enables people to see what is in front of themselves, and respond appropriately.

> "The abolition of religion as people's *illusory* happiness is the demand for their *real* happiness. The demand to abandon illusions about their condition is a *demand to abandon a condition which requires illusions*."[18]

Until people recognize the true role of religion, Marx continued, revolutions against religious institutions will miss the mark. For example, he noted a movement in Prussia to confiscate church property. In the larger scheme of things, what would that accomplish? he asked. Marx similarly analyzed the Reformation as a revolution that simply replaced the illusions of Catholicism with those of Protestantism. He focused in particular upon the implications of differences in church hierarchies. Protestantism—as specifically expressed in the teachings of Martin Luther—compared to Catholicism placed more responsibility on each individual to be conscientious and faithful, and relied less on an elaborate, external hierarchy. But each religion in its own way continued to delude; Protestantism by enslaving people from within, Catholicism by outside enforcement. Note the acerbic way in which Marx described this transition from Catholicism to Protestantism (as reflected in Luther's writings):

> *"Luther* . . . shattered faith in authority by restoring the authority of faith. He turned priests into laymen by turning laymen into priests. He freed man from outward religiosity by making religiosity the inwardness of man. He emancipated the body from its chains by putting chains on the heart."[19]

As Marx's campaign for a proletariat revolution moved forward, he also faced opposition from organized religion, both Protestant and Catholic. If the social principles of Christianity were only developed, he heard critics of communism contend, it would surely lead to the end of the workers' movement. If the world only followed Christian teachings, no communist revolution would presumably be necessary. His reaction was to defend communism by emphasizing the place of the church in the historical struggle of the oppressed masses. He argued that organized religion had consistently sided with the upper classes, and helped them to remain in power by encouraging those in subordinate positions to be humble and submissive.

> "The social principles of Christianity . . . had eighteen hundred years to develop, and . . . justified slavery in antiquity, glorified medieval serfdom, and . . . defend[ed] the oppression of the proletariat."[20]

Thus, organized religion not only deluded ordinary people by providing them with false illusions, it also played an active role in their oppression. The masses of people who were committed to religion were lost and confused, in his view, mistakenly looking to the heavens for answers to their earthly problems.

ALIENATION AND PRIVATE PROPERTY

Marx's analysis of alienation began with a review of the work of past German philosophers, a number of whom had examined the meanings of alienation. Hegel was an important part of this German philosophical tradition, and Marx devoted particular attention to him. The crux of alienation, in many of Hegel's writings, involved the way culture separated people from their original, or "natural," state. He recognized that for people to be fully human they must acquire knowledge and values and learn to control their drives and emotions—key elements of any culture. However, while culture was obviously necessary, at some point its cumulative growth could lead to a situation in which people regarded it as beyond their control and saw themselves as no longer fitting within it. Alienation occurs, for Hegel, when people are not able to recognize themselves in the culture, finding it foreign to their self-conceptions.[21] While he contended that alienation was wide-spread, he did not consider it necessarily inevitable, so long as the state (i.e. the political apparatus) exerted sufficient control over the culture.

Marx's critique of Hegel began in relation to the now familiar ideal-material continuum. Specifically, according to Marx's interpretation, Hegel placed too much emphasis upon alienation as a state of mind, and too little attention to alienation in relation to material social conditions arising out of a system of private property. In addition, Marx claimed that Hegel exaggerated the degree to which political institutions acted autonomously, and thereby failed to recognize the degree to which they actually served the interests of economic systems.[22] And Marx proceeded to develop a new theory that addressed these deficiencies.

One point of view that Marx most wanted to add to Hegel's perspective came from the writings of a previous generation of Scottish and English political economists, notably including Adam Smith and David Ricardo. Their writings had made important contributions to understanding the workings of capital, labor and marketplaces—the kind of materialistic forces that Marx was predisposed to emphasizing. However, while utilizing many of their insights, Marx also criticized the political economists for failing to recognize the inherent maladies of capitalism. For Smith, Ricardo, and their colleagues, unfettered marketplaces produced the best social arrangements. They expressed sympathy for the working class's terrible suffering, but felt that it was a price that had to be paid because it was not possible to rationally devise a better economic system than unrestrained capitalism.[23]

For Marx, by contrast, the human problems endemic to capitalism were so wide-spread and chronic that they had to be given priority. This meant ending capitalism by abolishing its core, private property. When ownership is not communal, in Marx's view, it produces a society in which inequality and greed flourish, and ordinary laborers are necessarily exploited and alienated. Private property creates a context in which the evils of capitalism flourish; but within this context two of the specific culprits he examined were money and systems of credit.

MONEY AND CREDIT

Money's initial function, in Marx's view, was simply to mediate transactions. It provided standardized units that facilitated stable exchanges. However, when there is private property, money's role in providing a standard—or "universal equivalent," in his terms—leads to a social environment in which "everything is exchangeable for money."[24] He was anticipating a world in which the advertisements for credit card companies could note some very limited exceptions, then claim, "For everything else . . . there's MasterCard." Or popular ceramic figurines in gift stores holding a shopping bag above the inscription: "Whoever said money can't buy happiness didn't know where to shop." The clear implication of these messages is that virtually everything worth having is for sale.

In addition, Marx believed that money became the sole arbiter of value in capitalistic societies. All objects lose their value apart from their monetary worth. In a reversal of the original relationship between objects and money, things are valued as possessions if they cost a lot! Put in contemporary terms, Marx was claiming that people would desire a Lexus or a Porsche not for their superior workmanship, design, attention to detail or other intrinsic qualities, but because they are very expensive.

In a system with private property, people who are exchanging money for objects do not relate to each other as people, Marx continued. Because no one sees past the price tag, the human effort that went into making the object is ignored: "*things* lose the significance of being human and personal property."[25] This detachment of objects from the labor that produced them creates a society in which as long as the sweatshirt with their college logo on it is priced cheaply, people would rather not be reminded that it was assembled by children in an Asian sweatshop.

When the credit system is developed it enables exchanges to occur without paper money, substituting lines of credit in particular. People make purchases without money physically changing hands at the time. With credit, it appears, Marx wrote, that people are again relating directly to each other, without the estranging effects of paper money in every transaction. In reality, though, Marx insisted that credit is even more de-humanizing because of the way it is granted. That is, it entails scrutinizing a person's past, "spying into the secrets of the private life of the one seeking credit."[26] So credit seems to be offered as a sign of trust in a person, but the entire process really emphasizes people's distrust of each other.

Credit systems, in Marx's view, are also de-humanizing in two other ways. First, a credit rating becomes *the* judgment of people's reliability and morality. How much social support they give to friends, how much they help co-workers, love their spouse or donate to charity all lose their salience relative to a person's credit rating. Second, because the recipient of credit is obligated to repay it with interest, the recipients are themselves turned into mediums of exchange. For example, financial institutions sell bundles of loans to each other, turning the people who borrowed the money (and their debts) into objects.

As the credit system continues to grow, Marx noted that the state is placed into the same position as its mass of citizens because the state becomes dependent upon selling government bonds—which is just another way of seeking credit. As one set of bonds matures, the state must sell another in order to raise the funds necessary to pay the holders of those bonds that matured. Wealthy capitalists watch fluctuations in interest and the ratings of states, then decide whether to buy or sell some particular bonds. Thus, in a credit system,

> "the state occupies completely the same position as . . . man. The game with government bonds shows how far the state has become the plaything of men of commerce."[27]

This dependence of the modern state upon capitalists was one of the reasons Marx disagreed with Hegel concerning the possible autonomy of the state in a capitalistic economy.

Objectification

With private property, Marx continued, competition (and greed) necessarily result in the accumulation and concentration of wealth. A few capitalists have tremendous holdings while the large mass of propertyless wage-workers (i.e. the proletariat) have practically nothing. Further, private property along with money economies and specialization in the division of labor separate workers from their products. Each one's contribution to the total manufacturing process is very small, and because it is measured solely in dollar terms, workers cannot feel any sense of pride in the final results. The product of labor stands apart from the effort of that labor, as though it belonged to someone else. It seems alien to its producers. Thus, Marx wrote, "The product of labor is . . . made objective in a thing. It is the *objectification* of labor."[28]

Objectification describes a process in which labor not only produces commodities, but itself becomes a commodity. Labor is a cost of production whose value is measured in monetary terms, just like the products it produces. However, on a per unit basis, labor tends to cost less the more products it produces. The more efficient a capitalist system, therefore, the poorer will be the workers as a whole; that is, the smaller will be labor's share of the economy's wealth. Marx wrote that they would be poorer not only in wealth, but in internal satisfaction as well. Because the products of labor confront labor as alien objects, workers have little opportunity to find gratification in their work. They lose out on what ought to be one of life's greatest pleasures. Work becomes only a means of subsistence, and virtually no one would continue to work (under the conditions in capitalism) given any choice in the matter.

The objectification of labor in capitalist systems, according to Marx, means that, in a sense, the process of work becomes like an object. What he meant was that workers offer hours of their effort in return for wages, and do not regard those hours of effort as a part of themselves that they are selling. They feel as though their labor exists outside of themselves: a foreign and unrecognizable entity.

> "The more the worker exerts himself, the more powerful becomes the alien objective world which he fashions against himself . . . The worker puts his life into the object; then it no longer belongs to him . . . The life he has given to the object confronts him as hostile and alien."[29]

In human functions—and Marx regarded work as a central human activity—people are like animals. Their work is entirely forced. They feel no joy. They are like oxen hitched to a wagon. Meanwhile, it is only in the functions they share with animals (i.e. eating, drinking, procreating) that people feel human because they have an opportunity to behave freely, to make choices. In capitalistic systems, Marx observed, the irony is: "The animalistic becomes the human and the human the animalistic."[30]

Alienation's Referents

Many theories of alienation have historically been criticized for their failure to specify a referent; that is, they describe people as alienated, but fail to adequately specify from what they are alienated. Marx's writings had no such shortcoming. In fact, as described in the preceding pages, he noted several distinct referents, or types, of alienation. Specifically, he analyzed how the great mass of workers was alienated:

1. From the products of their labor.
2. From the work process.
3. From co-workers, because objectification prevents people from engaging in meaningful social relationships while they are working together.
4. From their species-potential. This was Marx's conception of alienation that was closest to that previously emphasized by Hegel. Humans have the unique capacity to be fully conscious of their life's activity, Marx wrote, and to grow and develop as people. However, the mind-numbing quality of work in capitalistic systems robs them of this potential. If they could be meaningfully involved, they could "find" themselves by "losing" themselves. Here Marx was talking about the way awareness of one's self can temporarily decline when people are absorbed in an activity. For example, people often lose track of time and do not notice they are hungry or tired when they are fully engrossed in some creative endeavor. It is out of such experiences that people's human potential is realized, but that type of development is thwarted by capitalism.
5. And ultimately, from themselves.

With private property, Marx concluded, the (multiple types of) alienation of ordinary workers cannot be avoided. It is tied to their role as wage-laborers. To make this point clear, Marx speculated that even if capitalists could be forced to increase the pay of their workers— which he found impossible to imagine except hypothetically—it would not alter the basic situation of ordinary labors in a capitalistic society. More money in a weekly paycheck would only make for "a better slave salary" and the worker would still be without "human significance and dignity."[31] The only real hope for the workers was that they recognize their disadvantaged position in a capitalistic society, and collectively move to end their oppression.

Alienation from work among contemporary hotel service workers is examined in Research Box 3-1. The form of alienation they experience is a little different than that previously experienced by production workers, but from Marx's perspective, the end result seems pretty much the same.

Alienation Among Service Workers

The Publication

Margaret Zamudio, "Alienation and Resistance." *Social Justice*, 31, 2004: 60–76.

The Research Question

Marx described industrial production, under capitalism, as alienating workers by objectifying the production process and separating them from the items they produced. As a result, workers become estranged from co-workers, their products, even from themselves as they become mere commodities, just like the items they produce. Their alienation, in Marx' view, could eventually lead to class consciousness and collective resistance.

In modern, global, post-industrial economies, service jobs have largely replaced the production jobs upon which Marx had focused. However, because the transformation occurred under capitalism, workers' alienation and resistance could still be expected. What different forms might they take in a service economy?

The Data

To examine how service employment might produce alienation, Zamudio studied the hotel industry in Los Angeles. Specifically, during the mid-1990's she spent months interviewing and observing low-wage service workers—most of whom were employed as housekeepers, and laundry and kitchen workers—in one large hotel; and she also conducted lengthy interviews with union organizers and the managers of 40 other hotels in the Los Angeles area.

The Findings

From Zamudio's interviews and observations, she developed a clear picture of what managers wanted from these service workers: deference to clients. Managers and supervisors stressed that how a worker interacted with hotel guests was more important than their skill (in cleaning toilets, filling water glasses, or the like). One manager described these service jobs as ideally requiring people who could act as though they really wanted to please and serve others. Several other managers stated their belief that these ideal qualities had to be part of an employee's makeup because they could not readily be taught in a training program. Correspondingly, to hire people likely to possess these desired attributes, the managers who made employment decisions routinely selected non-citizens rather than natives, and women rather than men. The typical low-wage service worker in a Los Angeles hotel (during the time of the study) was an immigrant Latina whose gender and citizenship made her compliant to the job's humiliating demands.

Feeling like robots, these Latinas smiled and acted subserviently to guests (and supervisors), regardless of how they actually felt about them. In consequence, they felt stripped of their "real selves;" de-humanized and alienated from their true feelings. Zamudio concluded that in the low-wage service economy, "one's labor *and* identity are commodified to create and sell a product" (p 64). While they resented meager paychecks, they were most upset about how the work hurt their pride. They felt more alienated than exploited. And it was because they felt personally degraded that many of the hotel service workers joined unions in order to try to collectively resist their employers' demands.

SOCIAL CLASSES

To the general public, Marx's name is most strongly associated with communism, and in particular, the *Manifesto of the Communist Party*, or *The Communist Manifesto* (hereafter, *Manifesto*). Authored by Marx and Engels, the *Manifesto* was written for what was then a newly formed Communist League, a former trade union that became a working-class political party headquartered in London. The *Manifesto* was also published in London (in 1848), and it became, in essence, the League's party platform. Although officially co-authored by Marx and Engels, in a later German edition Engels made clear that most of the credit for the principal ideas expressed in the work belonged to Marx. It was he who deduced the political-economic principles on which the *Manifesto* rested.

After a brief preface, the *Manifesto* turns immediately to the topic of social classes. In every society there are social classes, according to Marx and Engels, and they are always arranged in a hierarchy, though the particular entities vary. It is the society's means of production that determines the specific classes. Thus, associated with the small-scale craft production of the Middle Ages were guild-masters, journeymen and apprentices, while its agricultural estates were associated with feudal lords and serfs.

In the modern capitalistic nations of their day, where large-scale factory production was becoming predominant, they described two major classes:

1. The bourgeoisie, consisting primarily of the owners of giant industry and large land-owners. They form the dominant class, and remorselessly exploit the proletariat. In pursuing its interests, the bourgeoisie has shown no mercy, stripping away all human sentiments and replacing them with cash payments. It has created a world in which money (and only money) talks. Family ties, friendships, doctor-patient and priest-congregant relationships are now all dominated by monetary considerations. Honor, respect and affection have all been stripped from the bourgeoisie-created world.

2. The proletariat, or wage-laborers who own no property capable of producing income, hence have only their labor to sell. They stand on assembly lines, clean large office buildings and work the land owned by others. As a result of their subordinate position in the system of production, their living conditions are miserable, their marriage and family life is ruined and they experience pervasive alienation. They were an immense majority of the population in terms of size, but remained disadvantaged in a system with private property.

It is important to note that class positions, according to Marx, were objectively fixed by people's relations to the means of production. Where people thought of themselves as fitting in the social hierarchy—the subjective dimension—was irrelevant with respect to class placement. With respect to the proletariat, in particular, Marx considered a difference between subjective and objective class positions as indicating "false" consciousness. (Such discrepancies were also wide-spread among the petty bourgeoisie, described later in this chapter.)

Each of these two major classes is entirely dependent upon the other in that neither could exist without the other because production results from combining the factories and land of the bourgeoisie with the labor of the proletariat. Nothing could be produced without the mix. Correspondingly, a revolution that abolished private ownership of the means of production would result in the end of the bourgeoisie, and that would necessarily mean the end of the proletariat as well. No bourgeoisie, no proletariat.

While the two classes were interdependent, like all social classes associated with differences in societies' means of production, the bourgeoisie and proletariat always stood in opposition to each other. Whatever is in the interest of one of them runs counter to the interests of the other. Occasionally their opposition is apparent to almost everyone—when, for example, there is a labor strike or a revolution—but even when there is no overt opposition, in Marx and Engel's view, the interests of different classes are never congruent.

Erik Olin Wright illustrates their fundamental opposition to each other by imagining the creation of an amazing new "device" that could provide its owner with all the basic necessities of life. Best yet, everyone could afford one. Would people in all walks of life be pleased by the innovation? Among the proletariat, Wright assumes, the device would be welcomed and viewed as bringing back the Garden of Eden. Ordinary workers and their families would all want one and probably be happy to see everyone else have it too. But what about owners and managers, the bourgoisie and those closely connected to it: How would they feel about the device? They would view it negatively, Wright assumed, because the ready availability of the device would make it more difficult to get workers to perform unpleasant tasks and take orders. Why would they, when their basic necessities would be provided anyway? The bourgeoisie would, therefore, prefer a world in which they alone had the device, or no one did! These differences in how bourgeoisie and proletariat would view a Garden of Eden illustrate the invariant antagonism between the interests of different classes.[32]

While the classes were fundamentally opposed to each other, according to Marx and Engels, the playing field on which they competed was not level. It was strongly tilted to the advantage of the bourgeoisie because with each ruthless, calculating business step, the bourgeoisie also managed to advance its political interests. The modern state is no more than a thinly disguised instrument of bourgeoisie interests; "it is but a committee for managing the affairs of the . . . bourgeoisie."[33] The proletariat is seriously disadvantaged by the role of government which acts to further the interests of the bourgeoisie. Wright provides another interesting, but not hypothetical, example. During the nineteenth century, in South Africa, peasants subsisted off small plots of land. No one was rich, but everyone got by. None of them wanted/needed to work in the mines—until the government instituted a tax on their huts that had to be paid in cash, not kind. The peasants then made their labor available to the mine owners, because there was no other way they could pay the hut tax. Thus, the government's action was designed to benefit that segment of the population that did not favor a Garden of Eden.[34]

Going Global

The bourgeoisie and proletariat were by-products of increasingly developed means of production. In Marx's day, these manufacturing plants with hundreds of employees seemed destined to dominate employment in modern nations, thereby guaranteeing a large proletariat. However, the *Manifesto* predicts that the bourgeoisie and proletariat will not end at any nation's boundaries because the development of the means of production is always associated with the growth of markets, first within and then across nations. The bourgeoisie, in pursuing its economic self-interest, is an effective champion of expanded markets. It has become increasingly international, and therefore, so too has the proletariat.

Marx and Engels were anticipating modern multinational corporations with headquarters in the wealthiest capitalist nations, employing cheap labor in Asia and Latin America; with products reaching into every corner of the world—Burger King and Levi's, for example. They also anticipated a global economic system dominated by a capitalistic ethos, so they would not be surprised by contemporary global organizations, such as the World Trade Organization and the International Monetary Fund. These organizations, from Marx's perspective, pursue the interests of the international bourgeoisie. They demand free trade everywhere in the world, even when opening a local market to cheap foreign goods that are mass produced results in the collapse of small local enterprises and their replacement with subsidiaries of foreign-owned multinational corporations. Note how, in 1848, Marx and Engels described this modern world system.

> "The bourgeoisie, by the rapid improvement of all instruments of production, by the immensely facilitated means of communication, draws all, even the most barbarian nations, into civilization. The cheap prices of its commodities are the heavy artillery with which it batters down all . . . walls. . . . It compels all nations, on pain of extinction, to adopt the bourgeoisie mode of production. . . . In one word, it creates a world after its own image."[35]

In addition to the bourgeoisie and proletariat, Marx and Engels described two other social classes in modern societies. They considered these classes relatively insignificant on the assumption that neither was likely to play more than a marginal role in the eventual revolution of the proletariat.

1. A lower middle class, or "petty bourgeoisie," consisting of small manufacturers, self-employed craft and trades people (e.g. artists, plumbers, carpenters), and the owners of small shops. Their non-reliance upon the

bourgeoisie-owned means of production sets them apart from the traditional proletariat, but Marx and Engels predicted the class would be slowly pushed down into the proletariat due to insufficient capital with which to compete with huge capitalists, or because new modes of production would make their skills obsolete. They would not be surprised that many "mom and pop" stores have been replaced by chains, such as 7-Elevens. However, the petty bourgeoisie tends to mistakenly assume its interests are the same as those of the bourgeoisie, so it supports conservative, status-quo positions instead of rallying behind the proletariat.

2. "The 'dangerous class,' the social scum, that passively rotting mass,"[36] or lumpen proletariat. Grouped here are petty criminals, vagrants, the permanently unemployed and other socially undesirable people. Marx and Engels considered them insignificant because they were not dependable. Some were too detached from society to be involved in anything, and others would temporarily give their loyalty to any group that threw them a few crumbs, hence they could not be counted upon to support the proletariat.

The Lumpen Proletariat in Jamaica

Marx and Engels were explicit about expecting little from the criminals and the permanently unemployed, who comprised the "scum" of society. The lumpen proletariat, they believed, was not a likely ally of the proletariat's because these immoral outcasts generally lacked commitments, and they were undependable in any case because they were easily distracted or bribed by a few handouts from the bourgeoisie. However, within some contemporary nations where the labor force offers relatively little conventionally proletarian work and there is wide-spread poverty because of the more-or-less permanent unemployment, segments of the lumpen proletariat have been observed to play an important role in mobilizing class consciousness and in opposing the entrenched bourgeoisie. Jamaica provides a relevant and interesting case study.[37]

In contemporary Jamaica there are two especially important (and overlapping) segments of the lumpen proletariat. One is political, originally formed by Jamaica's major political parties utilizing loosely affiliated ghetto residents. Within poor communities, support for those parties flows upward and protection and patronage flow downward. The second pertinent segment of Jamaica's lumpen proletariat is criminal. In recent years control over the local drug trade has been their most profitable activity, but they have been involved in other underworld activities as well. This segment involves gangs that have accumulated wealth, and have a very powerful presence within Jamaica's ghettos.

While the political and criminal segments of the lumpen proletariat are distinguishable from each other, there is substantial overlap between them. For example, several notable figures have moved between roles as criminals and political enforcers. Their movement has been facilitated by the fact that both segments are part of an urban subculture characterized by a strong sense of class deprivation, estrangement from conventional social norms, and a readiness to utilize violence. Further, people in Jamaica's poor communities are happy to accept help from underworld or political sources—and exactly which one is offering the assistance does not make much difference to them.

For long periods of time, due to a combination of their strength and the state's weakness, these two segments of the lumpen proletariat have been able to operate rather freely, without much direct confrontation by officials. Ghetto residents have admired their freedom and looked up to their prominent figures who have become local heroes. As a result, social rebelliousness and political awareness have been linked within Jamaica's impoverished populations, encouraging opposition to the island's ruling elites who would otherwise be unopposed. If revolutions are to occur in nations with very high permanent unemployment and a small proletariat, Jamaica's experience suggests that it may require a different role for the lumpen proletariat than Marx and Engels envisioned.

THE PROLETARIAT REVOLUTION

Engels always expressed the utmost regard for Marx's insights and scholarly analyses, but those were not the contributions for which he thought Marx would most want to be remembered. In a speech delivered at Marx's graveside, Engels stated:

> "Marx was before all else a revolutionist. His real mission in life was to contribute . . . to the overthrow of capitalist society and . . . to the liberation of the modern proletariat. . . . And he fought with a passion . . ."[38]

The bourgeoisie had determined the direction of change in society, Marx and Engels had previously written, but even as its capital accumulated it also created the means of its own destruction by creating a large, alienated working class. Work had become meaningless, even repulsive; and with high unemployment and falling wages, the proletariat was trapped in a miserable existence, both at work and at home.

> "No sooner is the exploitation of the labourer by the manufacturer . . . at an end, and he receives his wages . . . than he is set upon by the other portions of the bourgeoisie, the landlord, the shop-keeper, the pawnbroker, etc."[39]

Historical forces were on the side of the proletariat, though. Workers were growing in number and becoming more concentrated in cities, and machinery was reducing the distinctions among them. These forces were leading all workers to become more aware of how much they shared in common. They were also beginning to recognize their shared interests, and form associations, such as trade unions, to promote those interests. Their future progress may be slow, Marx and Engels cautioned. The proletariat might be sidetracked by competition for jobs, and momentarily forget that the true enemy is the bourgeoisie, not each other. In addition, by virtue of their control over the political apparatus, the bourgeoisie can see to it that obstacles are placed in the path of the proletariat. Nevertheless, the forces unleashed by the bourgeoisie, according to Marx and Engels, are too powerful to be stopped, and the proletariat movement toward solidarity and revolution will necessarily continue.

Marx and Engels predicted that a small enlightened segment of the bourgeoisie—who finally comprehended the historical movement—would eventually join in the proletariat's struggle. Some of them could be expected to contribute ideas that will help to shape the revolution. A few of the lumpen proletariat may also be swept along by the proletariat's march to freedom. However, the communist revolution was squarely on the shoulders of the proletariat. It could only be their social movement.

Marx and Engels also noted that because bourgeoisie ownership of the means of production had become global, producing a world-wide proletariat, the proletariat's revolution would also have to be global in focus. If private ownership remained anywhere in the world, a bourgeoisie would continue to exploit its workforce, and the proletariat's revolution could not succeed. Thus, the *Manifesto* concludes:

> "Let the ruling classes tremble. . . . The proletarians have nothing to lose but their chains. They have a world to win.
> Working men of all countries, unite!"[40]

Class Consciousness

The key to unleashing a proletariat movement was workers' greater awareness that they shared a class position, and that this position was the most significant factor in their lives. As previously quoted from Marx's writings, even if they were paid more, as proletariat they would still be slaves to the wages paid by the bourgeoisie. In addition to workers recognizing their common place in the class system, Marx assumed that this recognition would become an increasingly salient aspect of who or what they considered themselves to be; that other bases of identity—ethnic, geographical, familial, etc.—would recede relative to class. The result: a proletariat that has always been a class *objectively*, based upon its relation to the means of production, would be transformed into a class *subjectively*, based upon a shared identity and feelings of solidarity.

Presented in Research box 3-2 is an examination of the attitudes and values of several thousand adults working in various positions in several modern nations. The central question asked in this part of Wright's research concerned the degree to which people's views about social classes were a function of their own objective social class positions.

RESEARCH BOX 3-2

Class Position and Class Consciousness

The Publication

Erik Olin Wright, *Class Counts*. Cambridge: Cambridge University Press, 1997.

The Research Question

Marx believed that people in every social class would eventually become aware of their class position, and develop ideologies that were consistent with it. These ideologies would, therefore, reflect their material interests. He was primarily concerned with the proletariat, of course, and with the connection he hoped would occur between its class awareness and collective action. However, an important prior question concerns the degree to which groups of people in different relations to the means of production hold similar values and opinions regarding the class structure. Wright hypothesized that the contemporary bourgeoisie would hold the most pro-capital attitudes; the proletariat would express the most pro-worker attitudes, and that the petty bourgeoisie would be intermediate. In addition, he wondered whether experiences of people, other than class position, would also affect their class ideologies.

The Data

Wright and associates sampled about 3,000 employed adults in Japan, Sweden and the United States during the 1980's and 1990's. All of them were asked to agree or disagree with 5 statements that examined their perceptions, opinions and preferences regarding owners, managers and workers. The more they agreed with the anti-capital statements (e.g. "Corporations benefit owners at the expense of workers and consumers") and the pro-worker statements (e.g. "The nonmanagement employees in your place of work could run things effectively without bosses") the more their ideology was considered pro-worker. The more they disagreed with statements such as the above, the more pro-capital their ideology.

Based upon their relations to the means of production, respondents were placed into three class positions: bourgeoisie (owners and employers), petty bourgeoisie (owners, not employers) and proletariat (non-owners, employees).

The Findings

The findings were very similar in all three nations, with only small variations in the patterns. Overall, people in the bourgeoisie class held the most pro-capital attitudes and beliefs, individuals placed in the working class held the most pro-worker views, and those in the petty bourgeoisie were intermediate. Wright also found that, in addition to being an employee, pro-worker perceptions and preferences were stronger among union members and people who had previously experienced unemployment. By contrast, pro-capital attitudes were stronger among people who, apart from being in bourgeoisie positions, were home owners and had more personal income. Wright interpreted these results as indicating that people in the same class locations, primarily reflected by their relation to the means of production, tend to develop very similar ideologies about how the class structure operates.

Step one, then, entailed class consciousness, and Marx assumed that step two, a workers' social movement, would follow rather automatically from step one. However, the empirical evidence since Marx's death suggests that there is a problematic connection between collective behavior and people's self-perceptions or felt interests. Reviewing the pertinent literature, Grusky and Sorensen have concluded that, "the aggregate classes identified by Marxian theory have shown a decided reluctance to act collectively on behalf of their (presumed) interests . . ."[41] Whether people will translate their subjective identities or felt interests into concerted overt actions appears to be contingent upon the presence of organizations that could activate them: political parties, trade unions or the like. In other words, awareness of common interest may be necessary, but not sufficient, to produce collective action.

THE FAILURE OF SOVIET COMMUNISM

An intriguing question that continues to divide Marxist scholars concerns how to interpret the failure of communism in the former Soviet Union.[42] We can begin by noting that Marx did not think that a proletariat revolution was likely to occur until a society attained an advanced stage of capitalism. It was then that he expected capitalism to create the conditions under which a workers' movement would occur: a concentrated, homogeneous and alienated labor force. Quite unexpectedly, the 1917 communist revolution occurred in Russia, a nation that was far behind England, France and many other nations in capitalistic development. According to Marx, this was not where the revolution should have first occurred.

Marx also said that advanced capitalism was necessary for a workers' movement to be successful. If revolutions occurred sooner, they would be at risk because it was not until the advanced stages of capitalism that the productive forces were sufficiently developed to make adequate productivity unproblematic. Until societies were highly capitalistic, Marx did not think they could be sufficiently productive to create surpluses, and he believed that communist societies, at least initially, would require surpluses. If revolutions were premature, the need to increase production in order to ensure everyone's survival could lead to the restoration of capitalism. If there were a "struggle for necessities . . . all the old filthy business would necessarily be reproduced.[43] Did communism fail in the former Soviet Union because the revolution occurred too soon with respect to the nation's capitalistic development?

Or, did Soviet-style communism fail because it was unable to build an attractive socialist state that would inspire workers' revolutions to occur in the West? Marx had insisted upon the necessity of global revolutions, believing the capitalist epoch was not over as long as private property, and a bourgeoisie, remained anywhere in the world. If communism was to replace capitalism, as Marx hoped, it would have to be institutionalized everywhere. He would have given little hope to a communist regime in a single country, or single block of countries—and ones that had been capitalistically "backward," at that.[44]

There are, of course, no simple explanations for events as complex as those involved in the failure of communism in the former Soviet Union even though the questions (and answers) are provocative with respect to Marx's theories. It also must be recalled, however, that a roadmap for moving from capitalism to communism was only one of the many issues that Marx addressed. In Chapter 4 we will further examine Marx's political and economic critique of capitalism, a critique that remains insightful regardless of whether one would embrace communism as an alternative.

Endnotes

1. Although neither Marx nor anyone else had yet identified themselves as sociologists when he began writing, there is a clear sociological core to his analyses that has been unmistakable to later sociologists. At the same time, it is important to recognize that Marx never intended his writings to be solely sociological. For further discussion of the sociological dimension of Marx's writing, see the Introduction in Robert J. Antonio (Ed.), *Marx and Modernity*. Malden: Blackwell, 2002.

2. Frank E. Manuel, *A Requiem for Karl Marx*. Cambridge: Harvard University Press, 1995.

3. Francis Wheen, *Karl Marx: A Life*. New York: W.W. Norton & Co., 2000, p 8.

4. Ibid., p 7.

5. Marx' relationship with his wife, as indicated by letters and memos, is described in, Warner Blumenberg, *Karl Marx: An Illustrated Biography*. London: Verso, 2000.

6. For further discussion of Marx's relationship with Engels, see Manuel.

7. See the comparisons of Marx's earlier and later writings in, Allan Megill, *Karl Marx: The Burden of Reason*. Lanham: Rowman and Littlefield, 2002.

8. G.W.F. Hegel, *Science of Logic*. London: Allen & Unwin, 1969, p 129.

9. Howard Williams, *Hegel, Heraclitus and Marx's Dialectic*. New York: St. Martin's, 1989.

10. For further discussion of Hegel's idealism, and Marx's reaction to it, see G.A. Cohen, *Karl Marx's Theory of History*. Princeton: Princeton University Press, 2001.

11. Karl Marx and Friedrich Engels, "The German Ideology." In Lewis S. Feuer (Ed.), *Marx and Engels*. Garden City, NY: Doubleday, 1959, p 247.

12. Karl Marx, "Toward a Critique of Hegel's Philosophy of Right." In Lawrence H. Simon (Ed.), *Karl Marx*

Selected Writings. Indianapolis: Hackett, 1994, p 34.

13. Ibid.

14. Karl Marx, "The Eighteenth Brumaire of Louis Bonaparte. Section I." In Simon, p 188.

15. Karl Marx, "Theses on Feuerbach." Theses 11. In Simon, p 101.

16. Williams, p 176.

17. Karl Marx, "Toward a Critique of Hegel's Philosophy of Right." In Simon, p 28.

18. Ibid.

19. Ibid., p 34.

20. Karl Marx, "Social Principles of Christianity." Originally published in 1847. In John Raines (Ed.), *Marx on Religion.* Philadelphia: Temple University Press, 2002, p 185.

21. G.W.F. Hegel, *The Phenomenology of Mind.* New York: Harper, 1967.

22. For further discussion of the accuracy of Marx's interpretation of Hegel's theory of alienation, see Louis Dupre, *Marx's Social Critique of Culture.* New Haven: Yale University Press, 1983.

23. For further discussion, see Louis Schneider, *The Scottish Moralists.* Chicago: University of Chicago Press, 1967.

24. Karl Marx, *The Grundrisse.* New York: Random House, 1974. (Originally published in 1857.) In Raines, p 194.

25. Karl Marx, "Excerpt Notes of 1844." In Simon, p 42.

26. Ibid., p 45.

27. Ibid.

28. Karl Marx, "Economic and Philosophical Manuscripts." In Simon, p 59.

29. Ibid., p 60.

30. Ibid., p 62.

31. Karl Marx, "Alienated Labor." In Simon, p 67. This is sometimes translated as, "Estranged Labor." See John Raines (Ed.), *Marx on Religion.* Philadelphia: Temple University Press, 2002.

32. Erik Olin Wright, *Class Counts.* Cambridge: Cambridge University Press, 1997. Wright based this example on an old comic strip in which the "device" was actually an imaginary little being called a Shmoo.

33. Karl Marx and Friedrich Engels, "The Communist Manifesto." In Simon, p 161.

34. Wright.

35. Ibid., p 162.

36. Ibid., p 167.

37. This discussion of the lumpen proletariat in Jamaica is based upon, Obika Gray, "Rogue Culture or Avatar of Liberation." *Social and Economic Studies,* 52, 2003.

38. Friedrich Engels, "Speech at the Graveside of Karl Marx." In Robert C. Tucker (Ed.), *The Marx-Engels Reader.* New York: W.W. Norton, 1978, p 682.

39. "The Communist Manifesto," p 165.

40. Ibid., p 186.

41. David B. Grusky and Jesper B. Sorensen, "Can Class Analysis Be Salvaged?" *American Journal of Sociology,* 103, 1998, p 1205.

42. In fact, to some, Marx's entire legacy is called into question by the failure of communism, primarily in the Soviet Union. See John Cassidy, "The Return of Karl Marx." In Antonio.

43. Karl Marx, *The German Ideology,* p 46.

44. For further discussion of how to interpret the failure of communism in the Soviet Union, see Chapter 15 in Cohen.

4

Karl Marx (2)

Economic Analyses

There were a number of issues that Marx focused upon throughout his scholarly career. For example, the ways in which capitalism led to the exploitation of wage labor was never too far removed from his attention. Despite the continuities, though, one can also see some signs of a demarcation between Marx's earlier and later writings. The former tended to be a little more philosophical, while the latter contained more detailed economic analyses. This chronological change in Marx's emphasis is the basis of our demarcation between the two chapters (Chapters 3 and 4) devoted to his writings.

The particulars of several of his interpretations of economic activity have not stood up well when assessed by conventional contemporary criteria. Many economists have faulted his formulas for describing surplus value, rates of profit, the circulation of commodities, and so on. However, it must be noted that Marx was not trained as an economist, did not see himself as an economist, and his enduring contribution does not lie in technical models, but in his insight into the place of an economy within society, and its impact upon politics, in particular.[1]

His theories of economy and society are presented primarily in three volumes of *Capital (Das Kapital)*. The first volume is often considered the most important of Marx's writings, and its examination of commodities, the processes of exchange and the valorization process continue to have enormous influence upon contemporary sociology. This chapter is largely devoted to an examination of those ideas, primarily presented in volume one of *Capital*. (The last two volumes, which were edited by Engels, were published after Marx's death.)

BASE AND SUPERSTRUCTURE

In the preface to volume one of *Capital*, Marx stated that the manuscript should be read as the continuation of a book he had published eight years previously. He attributed the long hiatus between publications to several long illnesses that were apparently exacerbated by the poverty in which he was living.[2] In that earlier book he summarized his thinking as follows:

> "In the social production which men carry on they enter into definite relations that are indispensable and independent of their will. . . . The sum total of these relations of production constitutes the economic structure of society—the real foundation on which rise legal and political structures and to which correspond definite forms of social consciousness."[3]

To explain the previous quotation fully, it is helpful to begin by introducing Marx's notion of, "productive forces." They include raw materials, machinery and technology, and the skill and strength of human labor as they are *materially* necessary for production. Excluded are those tangential elements that may encourage or support production, but are not intrinsically required. To illustrate, Marx described how in an agrarian community beset with armed conflicts it might be necessary to station soldiers where they could guard field hands while they were working; but even if the field hands could not do their work without armed protection, the soldiers should not be considered a materially necessary part of the production. Similarly, he wryly observed that it was because of forgers that banknotes were perfected in the same way that the actions of thieves contributed to the development of locks.[4] Neither the forgers nor the thieves should be considered part of the productive forces, however.

The productive forces, Marx continued, do not become truly economic categories until they are socially organized; and the key feature of that organization entails their ownership, or effective control. A bull, for example, becomes a productive force when people use it to plow a field in order to grow crops. How that bull fits in the social organization is indicated by answers to questions such as: What determines who can use the bull? To what groups do the crops plowed by the bull belong? How are they distributed? Similarly, Marx contended, people become productive forces when their work is socially organized; and the key feature of that organization is reflected by whether they work independently of each other, are enslaved, kept as serfs, employed as wage-labor, or the like. These organizational arrangements are the key features of the *social relations of production*, and these relations are the base, or foundation, on which the superstructure of societies is erected.

Two of the adjectives most often used by Marx to describe the base were material and fundamental. He considered the superstructure, by contrast, to be less fundamental in that it was dependent upon the base; and its components were mental and social rather than material. Precisely what Marx meant to include in the superstructure is open to debate, though. A narrow interpretation

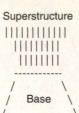

Superstructure

Social and mental components

Non-economic social
institutions, cultural values,
consciousness and ideology

Fundamental and material components   Base   Social relations of production

FIGURE 4-1   Base and Superstructure

literally takes the statement offered by Marx, in the quote presented near the opening of this section, to include only legal and political structures in the superstructure. There is also a broad interpretation that includes in the superstructure almost everything other than social relations of production: all non-economic institutions (religion, family, etc.), cultural values, science, people's consciousness and ideology.[5] The broader interpretation, which I consider more consistent with Marx's intentions, is illustrated in Figure 4-1.

While Marx viewed the superstructure as resting upon, or reflecting, the base—and in that sense dependent upon it—he also conceived of their relationship dialectically; in other words, as reciprocal, involving mutual interdependence. For example, unless a superstructure contains ideologies that are supportive of the social relations of production, those relations of production will be prone to disruptive conflicts. It would not be appropriate, therefore, to attribute to Marx an exaggerated, one-directional causal link from the base to the superstructure.

Contemporary China is a particularly interesting nation to examine in relation to base and superstructure because of the way elements of capitalism have been emerging within an otherwise controlled communist system. In 2005, columnist George Will observed that the very expensive British car manufacturer, Bentley, sold 43 cars in Beijing, mostly selling for over $200,000 each. Armani expected to have as many as 30 luxurious stores on the mainland, and China had become the world's fourth leading market for elegant products from Luis Vuitton.[6] With bourgeoning consumerism and the growth of entrepreneurship, how can a totalitarian state persist unchanged? How can the regime insulate the political system from an economic thrust that includes private property? Will calls it "Brooks Brothers Marxism," and over the long haul he bets that China's communist superstructure will be shaped by its capitalistic economic base.

For Marx to continue his earlier work—and lay bare the relations of production in capitalistic societies—Marx felt that he must analyze the core elements of their economies. He thought of these elements as being analogous to the cells of a human body; its "microscopic anatomy." He identified these fundamental units to be analyzed as commodities. Therefore, it was through a detailed examination of commodities that Marx expected to discover the essential principles of political economy.

THE VALUE OF COMMODITIES

Marx began by defining commodities as external objects that were capable of satisfying human needs. Examples would include everything from french fries to radios. To clarify further the uses and values of various commodities, the first chapter of *Capital* (volume one) introduced two important criteria for evaluating commodities: use-value and exchange-value.

Use-value is a function of the actual physical properties of a commodity in that they determine how it can be employed. The use-value of anything is realized either from: (1) the purposes to which it can be put, e.g. the use-value of an iron is a by-product of its ability to remove wrinkles from a shirt; or (2) its value in consumption, for example, the utility of a bottle of water in satisfying thirst.* In preparing an object for use, its producer would be concerned primarily with its qualitative features. In the example of the bottle of water, this could entail how it opened, whether the water was flavored, carbonated, etc.

Exchange-value, by contrast, is independent of a commodity's actual features. It does not entail direct usefulness to its producer, but entails the worth of the commodity relative to other commodities. A pound of gold may have little use-value to me—what could I do with it?—but it would have substantial exchange-value. In modern societies, exchange-value is expressed in monetary terms because money provides the common medium to which objects are reduced. Finally, while use-value emphasizes the qualitative features of a commodity, exchange-value emphasizes its quantitative features, that is, how much money or how many other commodities it can be converted into in a marketplace.

To illustrate how fundamental and long-standing the difference has been between exchange-value and use-value, Marx presented a relevant quote from Aristotle's Republic:

> "For twofold is the use of every object . . . The one is peculiar to the object as such, the other is not, as a sandal which may be worn and is also exchangeable. Both are uses of the sandal, for even he who exchanges the sandal for money . . . makes use of the sandal as a sandal. But not in its natural way. For it has been made for the sake of being exchanged."[7]

In capitalist societies, Marx continued, almost all production is directed at exchange-value rather than use-value. In addition, the capitalist producer is oriented toward maximizing exchange value and reinvesting the profit—capital accumulation—in order to attain still greater exchange value. In Marx's words:

> "Our capitalist . . . wants to produce a use-value that has a value in exchange, that is to say . . . a commodity; and secondly . . . to produce a commodity whose value shall be greater than the sum of . . . the means of production and the labor-power that he purchased . . . His aim is to produce . . . surplus value."[8]

---

*Marx defined consumption in a broad way, more-or-less equivalent to utility; hence a watch, as an object, could be consumed in the sense that telling the time has utility to a person.

By *surplus value*, Marx meant the difference between the exchange value of a commodity and its cost to the producer, including raw materials, tools or machines, and the cost of labor. However, it was the latter that he stressed, defining the value of any commodity as a function of the amount of labor required to produce it. To be more specific, he claimed that the (exchange) value of any item was determined by the *socially necessary* labor time that was required for its production. For any given society, socially necessary labor involves the assumption of workers of "average" skill levels toiling under "normal" conditions. It also takes for granted only the skill and strength of human labor as they are materially necessary for production, as explained earlier in the discussion of relations of production. (Surplus value is further examined later in this chapter.)

The emphasis upon labor time puts contested definitions of the length of the working day at the center of labor negotiations in capitalism. The greater the number of hours employees are routinely expected to work for a given wage, the cheaper are the commodities they produce, and the greater the potential upside for the capitalist. That is why negotiations over the 8-hour day, the 40-hour week and the 50-week year all involved such intense conflicts between early trade unions and capitalists. British sociologist Anthony Giddens aptly summarized the issue when he stated that, "Struggle over time is the most direct expression of class conflict in the capitalist economy."[9]

Building upon the assumption that labor was *the* cost of producing a commodity, Marx argued that commodities which require equal amounts of (socially necessary) labor must have the same value. So, if the labor costs of 100 pounds of lead were the same as those of 100 pounds of diamonds, then lead and diamonds would have the same value. They are not equal, in fact, only because diamonds are in more scarce supply, which means that to discover them requires more labor time. That is the real reason why diamonds are more valuable. Thus, the exchange values of all commodities, he concluded, represent "congealed labor-time." Under a capitalist mode of production, however, the necessarily intense tie between products and the labor necessary to produce them typically goes unrecognized. These commodities seemingly take on a life of their own, separated from the labors of the people who produced them.

THE CIRCULATION OF COMMODITIES

After an opening chapter describing commodities, volume one of *Capital* turns to the processes by which they are exchanged. Marx's initial objective here was to describe and analyze the most fundamental features of exchange. He started with nomadic societies where people owned little property, and noted that most of the items they created had use-value to the people who produced them. His analysis continued up to (then) contemporary capitalistic societies in France, England, and elsewhere. Here he observed that to the typical owners of a commodity, the item, itself, had no direct use-value. If it did, they would not offer it for sale. (Either they do not want the item at all, or they already have all of it that they can use.) Thus, it has only exchange-value for the owners, but use-value to potential purchasers. If it did not have use-values to others, then the time spent making it would have been wasted!

The owners of a commodity, Marx continued, seek to exchange it for a commodity that has at least equivalent value to them. The universal measure of equivalence is, of course, expressed in monetary terms. Money provides the social expression of a commodity's value—its value-form. However, money is only the expression, not the determinant of a commodity's (exchange) value. Remember, its value according to Marx is always a function of its socially necessary labor. However, he thought that the true source of a commodity's value was usually unrecognized, and that people tended to be confused about the role of money in setting rather than reflecting value.

In the simplest (non-monetary) situation, barter, each party trades directly with the other, and each party is in the same role as trader. When economies become more complex, and money is introduced, the process of exchange, as described by Marx, goes through a series of stages in which people continuously move from the role of buyer to seller and back again. First a commodity, which lacks use-value to the person who owns it, is sold for money; then the money is used to purchase other commodities which do have use-value to the person. However, there are multiple and overlapping networks of buyers and sellers, creating a complex system. To illustrate, suppose person A begins with some linen, sells it for cash, and buys beer. Person B begins with beer, sells it for cash, and buys books. Person C begins with books, sells them for cash, and buys linen. Marx viewed each transaction as entailing a "metamorphosis" of commodities: linen becomes beer, beer becomes books, books becomes linen, and so on.

The entire process, for Marx, described the circulation of commodities. It is fundamentally different from simple exchange, he insisted, because buyers and sellers are in a continuous state of change. The person who, in the previous example, sold the linen for cash to buy beer does not ordinarily purchase the beer from the person who bought the linen. Thus, from the circulation of commodities, "there develops a whole network of social connections . . . entirely beyond the control of human agents."[10] In more advanced capitalistic economies, ordinary people lose even the ability mentally to grasp the full complexity of the economic networks.

THE FETISHISM OF COMMODITIES

Marx began by viewing commodities merely as external objects; then he proceeded to further specify two important defining attributes. Commodities are produced when: (1) labor is organized into separate, specialized groups; and (2) these groups so transform objects that the objects' original physical nature can no longer be recognized. To illustrate, consider a group of laborers, working independently and out of public view, that fashions a table from lumber that was once part of a tree. Under these conditions, to every-one else in the society beside the furniture makers, the table is not linked, in any meaningful way, either to nature (i.e. a tree) or to the human labor that produced it. As people experience it, the table is a separate, detached entity, and that is what makes it a commodity. In an analogous way, Marx wrote, when people perceive everyday objects, they do not appreciate the subjec-tive role of their own optic nerves in producing the image, but instead regard the entity as being an objective phenomenon lying entirely outside of their own eyes.[11]

There is a tendency, Marx continued, for people to attribute various inherent qualities to commodities as though they had lives of their own or could on their own stand in direct relations to other commodities; for exam-ple, as though some wooden table was intrinsically worth $399. People went through a parallel mental process in the development of religious institu-tions. It was, Marx wrote, usually described as "fetishism" and it entailed people's attribution of special qualities to some symbolic object. Adherents of the religion believed that a totem, an amulet, or the like was not a symbolic product of human thought, but that it inherently possessed some magical healing or protective powers. Thus, a crucifix might be regarded as actually repelling malevolent creatures, or a charm might be viewed as, on its own, able to bring good fortune to its owner. It was in this sense that he introduced the *fetishism of commodities* because it similarly entailed an exaggerated detachment of objects from the human efforts that created them. However, in *Capital*, Marx insisted that the value of any commodity in exchange is always a function of the labor necessary to produce it, even though people may mistakenly believe that value results from some feature that is inherent in the commodity.

Professional athletes, entertainers and other celebrities provide an inter-esting illustration of how people, themselves, can become commodities. Professional baseball players, for example, were not very well paid prior to the middle of the twentieth century. They played, in large part, because they loved the game. However, during the latter half of the twentieth century, rev-enue and salaries dramatically increased. Players routinely hired agents to rep-resent them, and many players became limited liability corporations.

Due to extensive public relations and media coverage, professional ath-letes (like entertainers in other realms) were turned into cultural icons. Social processes created, or manufactured, celebrities, and an athlete was trans-formed into, "property," a "product," a "commodity" while the fans were becoming "markets."[12] A fundamental distinction between the authentic per-son and the commodified celebrity is clearly implied by the numerous maga-zines and television shows that promise fans a behind-the-scenes look at what the person, who became the celebrity, is *really* like.

There is, of course, a second usage of the term *fetishism*. It is psycho-sexual in origin, and describes a situation in which an inanimate object or non-genital part of a body becomes the focal point of a person's sexual desire. In such cases, primary sexual desires become fixed upon a boot, a glove, or the like, and properties of the object become indispensable to a person's sexual gratification. For example, a man with a glove fetish might be able to attain sexual release only if his partner wears a certain type of glove. The psycho-sexual fetish is also associated with compulsive needs. Thus, the man in the grip of a glove fetish is likely to feel driven by it, and his entire life may be organized about the satisfaction of this desire.[13] Marx alluded to this second type of fetishism when he described how the never-ending pursuit of commodities contributes to the false consciousness of the proletariat. He similarly analyzed how the continued existence of a global bourgeoisie was dependent upon its ability continuously to create "new wants," and how it used the "cheap prices of its commodities" to keep forcing additional nations to accept capitalist modes of production.[14]

In sum, Marx explicitly described (and emphasized) the fetishism of commodities as a function of their perceived detachment from human labor—the first usage explained earlier. He only indirectly suggested the psycho-sexual referent of the term. However, contemporary writers have often combined both of the implications of fetishism in analyzing capitalist societies. When the two are combined, people are described as focusing upon the assumed-to-be intrinsic qualities of (detached) commodities, *and* as "lusting" after these commodities in a manner that mirrors sexual desires.[15]

THE COMMODIFICATION THESIS

Because of the way labor is organized and the way goods are sold in the marketplace, the production of commodities in a capitalistic society tends to increase over time. *The commodification thesis* refers to the tendency for the products of labor in a capitalistic society to consist increasingly of commodities, as previously defined; and ultimately, for labor, itself, to become a commodity, to be purchased in a marketplace like anything else.

Poland's transition from communism to capitalism during the last decade of the twentieth century provides an interesting setting in which to examine the commodification thesis. To study the effects of the nation's economic transformation, Polish sociologist Marek Ziolkowski proposed that goods and services in any society can be examined in relation to a commodification hierarchy.[16] At the high end, more goods and services are intentionally produced for exchange, and the range of items for which they can be exchanged is very extensive. (High exchangeability would result when items were made available, in an open market, to any buyer with the requisite cash or credit.) At the low end of the hierarchy would be goods and services that are free to most people, such as welfare benefits or public radio. At an intermediate point, commodities can only be exchanged for goods of the same type, such as reciprocal tuition benefits offered by colleges to the offspring of each others' faculty.

As Poland became increasingly capitalistic, Ziolkowski observed that commodification, in most spheres of life, clearly moved to a higher point on the commodification hierarchy. To illustrate, in pre-capitalistic days, the market for cooperative flats was very limited. Only some people (with connections) had access to this market, and prices were strictly controlled by the government. These apartments were, therefore, at the low to middle end of the hierarchy. In capitalistic Poland, by contrast, more of the total stock of apartments are pure commodities, in principle available to anyone, subject only to marketplace considerations. However, while the overall trend has been toward a higher degree of commodification, much of the change has been fitful rather than linear. There is still an (access-restricted) black market for certain goods, for example, and other goods are sometimes commodities and sometimes not (e.g. there may be an admission fee for a university lecture one day, but the same lecture is free the next day).

In the United States, commodification has been examined in many social and economic realms. With respect to children's clothing, for example, prior to the 1930's, commodification was in the low to middle range. Mothers often sewed clothes for infants and children, and a lot of what kids wore consisted of hand-me-downs. When parents did purchase clothes in stores, the decisions about what to buy were based primarily upon their own tastes and preferences. Then in the 1930's, the media began to devote more attention to the child's perspective, redefining the child as a conscious consumer. Retail stores responded by creating specialized clothing departments for toddlers, children and pre-teens. Over the following decades, parents, retailers and the media came to view children of all ages as "full persons," with their own point of view, with respect to clothing. A children's consumer culture finally emerged in which children's clothing became increasingly commodified in both senses of the term; that is, both as objects detached from human labor and as "must have" items.[17]

Clothing, of course, is only one of the many types of commodities that have become fetishes for children and teenagers. Consumer goods of all types—electronics, food and drink, etc.—have become like badges that kids wear to relay information about themselves to other kids. To be more precise, who children (or adults) think they are (or aspire to be) affects what they buy, but perhaps even more importantly, what they purchase can affect who they become, because of its influence upon how others respond to them. And the opportunities to consume identity-linked commodities continue to expand within capitalistic economies. Juliet Schor, who has written a number of books on consumption patterns, notes that youngsters' slumber parties now often mimic their mothers' tupperware parties—they have turned into "marketing opportunities" for buying makeup, clothing, etc.[18]

Research Box 4-1 describes how important commodities have become to women in rural China who aspire to resemble their more sophisticated counterparts in Chinese cities. Access to these commodities appears, in fact, to be a major consideration in their decisions to migrate.

RESEARCH BOX 4-1

Commodities and Identities

The Publication

Pun Ngai, "Subsumption or Consumption? The Phantom of Consumer Revolution in 'Globalizing' China." *Cultural Anthropology,* 18, 2003: 469–492.

The Research Question

Every day in China, hundreds of young females from rural villages migrate to cities to work in factories. Most know beforehand that it means low wages and 12-hour days in sweatshops. Where is the attraction? Pun Ngai believed that the government and the media combined to present an alluring image of the contemporary woman: urban, worldly, with a lot of commodities that could only be acquired if she worked for wages. (In farming towns few commodities were available, and women lacked money of their own with which to buy things.) How important were the commodities to the migrant women? And did acquiring them alter the possessors' social identities, from backward country girls to modern urban sophisticates?

The Data

The investigator, Pun Ngai, an assistant professor, spent six months in the city of Guangdong, working in an electronics factory that employed over 500 people. About three quarters were single women, aged 16 to 24, who recently migrated from rural villages. Ngai's data came from immersing herself in their lives: working daily next to them on the assembly line, spending her nights together with them on bunks in the workers' dormitory, sightseeing and talking in their free time.

The Findings

Some case studies illustrate the importance of commodities to these women's decisions to migrate. Case #1: Jin's father would not permit her to leave their village, so she watched her girl friends go to Guangdong and have their own money to buy new jeans, fashionable T-shirts and lipstick. Finally, she could not stand it anymore, and at age 18 she used her life savings to buy a bus ticket to the city, and ran away from home. Case #2: Ying was in her 30s, a wife and mother of two sons. She saw the younger girls in her village coming back to visit wearing new clothes and carrying new electronic possessions. Ying felt she simply had to go too before she was too old. After five months she missed her sons, but figured she would soon be able to buy them some new clothes, plus a rice cooker and maybe even a sewing machine for herself.

The newcomers believed that commodities made them indistinguishable from the affluent urban middle class. However, their clothing was slightly out of fashion, and despite makeup, their faces still had a rustic look. Class and place of origin differences remained discernable. For example, one Sunday three of the women were

(Continued)

bouncing along in a park when a man, trying to take a photograph, yelled at them to get out of the way. Why are you loafing here, he asked, instead of working in the factory? The jovial mood of the women vanished. They were stunned at how easily they were put in their place. Another Sunday a security guard followed several of the women through a store until they became so uncomfortable, they just left. Ngai concluded that the women's belief in social transformation via consumption was illusory. Although they are "ready and eager to consume, they nonetheless encounter exclusion and humiliation in a myriad of little dramas occurring daily . . ." We may add that they also fail to see any irony in craving commodities made by other women being exploited in sweatshops like themselves.

THE ACCUMULATION OF CAPITAL

The circulation of commodities, as previously described, was viewed by Marx as providing the true inception of capital. Capital initially takes the form of money, but not all money will become capital. Whether or not it does depends upon where money and commodities fit in the chain of exchanges. Marx described two possibilities:

1. Selling in order to buy: A commodity, C, is transformed into money, M, then reconverted to a (C–M–C) commodity, C. In summary: C–M–C. In this form, money has been expended, resulting in use-value to the purchaser; at the end of the chain, the commodity is consumed. (This would be the case if a person sold linen, used the money to buy beer, then drank it.)
2. Buying in order to sell. It is only in this form that money can become, or be circulated as, (M–C–M) capital. In this form, the motivating force is exchange-value, rather than use-value. (Here the linen is purchased for resale in order to buy more linen, or other products that could be sold, not consumed.)

Money, unlike commodities, is distinguishable only in amount, that is, quantitatively. There are no meaningful qualitative distinctions: The color of a $5 bill, the size of a 10 Euro bill, or the like, are irrelevant. It would make no sense, therefore, for a person to sell a product at a price that was equal to its purchase price, regardless of the kind of funds involved. To buy cotton for $100 and then sell it for $100, in any currency, would be absurd, Marx wrote. We can summarize this break-even process as M1–C–M2 in which M1 = M2. When M2 > (i.e. exceeds) M1, the increment in M2 is termed, *surplus value*; and when surplus value is added, money is converted into capital.

The C–M–C transaction chain has a finite end in the satisfaction of human needs, i.e. consumption. At the end of this set of exchanges, M disappears. The M–C–M movement, by contrast, continues indefinitely. Further, not only does M not disappear, its magnitude normally increases as profit-making exchanges continuously expand; hence the old adage, money begets money. While money is being transformed into capital, the possessor of the money becomes a capitalist. "It is only in so far as the appropriation of ever more wealth . . . is the sole driving force . . . that he functions as a capitalist."[19] So, Marx contends, neither use-values nor profit from a single transaction are the typical goals of capitalists. Theirs is a "boundless drive for enrichment." The miser and the capitalist are alike, he mused, in trying to hoard wealth, however, misers seek their objective by withdrawing their money from circulation, while capitalists continuously re-enter their money into circulation. "The miser is merely a capitalist gone mad, the capitalist is a rational miser."[20]

THE ARMY OF THE UNEMPLOYED

As capital accumulation proceeds, investments in machinery and improved methods of production tend to diminish the size of the labor force required by the capitalists (i.e. bourgeoisie). At the same time, the potential size of the labor force is typically increased by population growth (due mainly to a decline in infant mortality), and to other social changes as well. Among the more important of these changes noted by Marx was mechanization that pushed farm workers off the land, forcing them to seek urban employment. In addition, many small shop owners and independent craftspeople were increasingly unable to compete with the growing capitalist firms, and they were forced to join the proletariat in offering their labor to capitalist employers. The population increase and social changes contributed to the growth of a "surplus population," or a reserve army of the unemployed. Marx used the term *army* to capture the joyless, involuntary quality of work in a capitalistic economy. He viewed the organization of work as making workers like conscripted soldiers in an army. The reserves—the unemployed who were seeking work—also resembled a (joyless, involuntary) army.

In his analysis Marx dissected the surplus population category into three distinct components, each of which was ultimately created by changes in the social organization attributable to capitalism:

1. ***Floating:*** Workers, usually in the urban centers of industry, who were temporarily unemployed; for example, between jobs.
2. ***Latent:*** A "reservoir" of potential workers, such as people in the process of being pushed off of farm lands.
3. ***Stagnant:*** People who were not motivated to work and were always irregularly employed: vagrants, paupers, criminals. (This was the lowest strata, previously referred to by Marx as the *lumpenproletariat.*)

Expansions and contractions in the overall size of this reserve were, Marx contended, the *major* variable determining general wage levels of the proletariat. The greater its relative size, the more capitalists could force workers both to increase production and to accept lower wages because they felt lucky just to have a job. By creating conflict within the ranks of the proletariat, the army of the unemployed also reduced class solidarity, making organized resistance by the proletariat less likely. As Marx described it:

> "The relative surplus population is therefore the background against which the law of the demand and supply of labor does its work. . . . Workers discover that the degree of . . . competition among themselves depends wholly on the pressure of the relative surplus population . . . and the pressure of the unemployed compels those who are employed to furnish more labor . . ."[21]

In his analysis of surplus populations, Marx took strong exception to the work of Thomas Malthus which was then very popular in intellectual circles. In his pioneering essays on population (first published in 1798), Malthus had pessimistically argued that populations always tended to increase more rapidly than their means of subsistence. The result, if unchecked, would necessarily be overpopulation and starvation. However, Malthus claimed that there were natural and necessary checks on overpopulation, such as war and disease. Societies actually benefitted from these checks because without them there would be even worse suffering.

Marx directed enormous contempt both against Malthus, personally, and at his famous writings on population. Marx referred contemptuously to Malthus's religious training (he was ordained before becoming the first professor of political economy in England, a position Marx would have certainly liked at some point in his life). He also viewed Malthus's family wealth as making him an apologist for the bourgeoisie, and he ultimately dismissed Malthus as a "shameless plagiarist."[22] What Marx perhaps objected to most was Malthus's notion that the pressure of (over)population on resources was somehow a natural process. To the contrary, Marx insisted, the scarcity of resources available to ordinary people was an artificial creation of capitalists' unquenchable desires to maximize (and horde) their wealth.

While surplus populations may provide some clear benefits to the capitalist class, there is probably an upper limit beyond which the size of the surplus population changes from an advantage into a potential threat. Specifically, if the size of the surplus population becomes excessive, there may be an increase in deviant behavior, and social control norms may become lax. If many people are starving to death, for example, the population (and even the police) are likely to become more tolerant of those who steal food from the wealthy in order to survive.

A huge excess of people to jobs can also lead to a wide-spread rejection of the status-quo and the formation of a revolutionary group, committed to radical social change. The historical analysis of sociologist Ephraim Mizruchi suggests that when, in the past, the size of surplus populations reached certain peak levels, both capitalistic and non-capitalistic societies usually responded in ways that led to the "absorption" of some of the excess population.

Expanded recruitment into monasteries or apprenticeship programs, or channeling more young people into institutions of advanced education were among the ways he found governments have historically attempted to create meaningful positions for people without places in order to reduce the size (and corresponding threat posed by) surplus populations.[23]

Research Box 4-2 examines whether jails are now used as a place to hold excess people when there are upswings in the size of a city's surplus population as a result of unemployment.

RESEARCH BOX 4-2

Unemployment and Pretrial Incarceration

The Publication

Stewart J. D'Alessio and Lisa Stolzenberg, "A Multilevel Analysis of the Relationship between Labor Surplus and Pretrial Incarceration." *Social Problems*, 49, 2002.

The Research Question

A growing labor surplus is beneficial to capitalist interests, but only if it remains within certain limits. If the surplus were to become too large, it could result in a difficult to control population of marginal people with the potential to become unruly and disruptive, challenging the status-quo. One way to control the size of surplus populations is by imprisoning a higher percentage of the thousands of defendants who are awaiting trial at any given time. If they are unemployed, incarceration could remove some of the dangerous excess labor from the market. This leads to the main research questions: (1) Are unemployed defendants in cities with high unemployment rates more likely to be incarcerated while they are awaiting trial? And (2) Is it the city's high unemployment that leads to higher rates of incarceration?

The Data

The researchers obtained the records of several thousand males who had been charged with burglary and robbery during a two year period. Included in the data set was information pertaining to whether each defendant was employed at the time of his arrest and the (then) current unemployment rate of the defendant's city. They also analyzed additional variables that could affect pretrial incarceration; for example: the defendant's race and prior convictions, type of offense he was accused of committing, etc.

The Findings

The results indicated that even when all the additional variables pertaining to defendants and their crimes were held constant, there was a much higher probability

(Continued)

that defendants would be held in pretrial confinement if they lived in a city that was experiencing a high rate of unemployment; and the probability was still higher if they were unemployed at the time of their arrest. Thus, independently of all the other variables considered, the city's unemployment rate had a strong effect upon men's pretrial incarceration, and the effect of the city's unemployment was particularly strong if the defendants were also unemployed at the time of their arrest. The investigators concluded that, "because capitalists need unemployment to engender competition for jobs, unemployed defendants should only pose a serious threat to the state during periods of deteriorating economic conditions. Our . . . analysis furnishes empirical support for this thesis" (p 190).

One of the questions that remains unanswered after the analysis concerns how the relationship between unemployment and pretrial incarceration is maintained. What is going on in the minds of judges—the people who make these pretrial decisions? The investigators did not interview any of the judges, so they can only speculate on the matter; but their conjecture is interesting, especially from Marx's perspective. Specifically, they pose the possibility that when unemployment rises in a city, judges may perceive those who are unemployed as "threatening" to the state, hence decide more often to incarcerate them prior to trial.

PURCHASING LABOR-POWER

For money to grow and become capital, Marx stated, the capitalists must find a commodity from which they can extract increased value. That commodity, in the first phase of C–M–C circulation, is labor-power. However, to obtain labor-power, in the form of a commodity, workers must be free to sell it. They cannot be slaves, indentured servants, or the like. The owners of labor-power must, therefore, sell it only for limited time periods. If the sale were open-ended, Marx noted, workers would in effect be selling themselves. They, rather than their labor-power, would become the commodity, if they were slaves, but capitalism presupposes workers that are free to contract their labor.

The sale of labor-power as a commodity further presupposes that workers have no other commodities to offer. In other words, they do not own means of production, raw materials and sufficient resources to subsist on their own, from the time they started production through the final sale. If they had these resources, they would not have to offer their labor-power as a commodity. What was distinctive about the capitalist epoch, in Marx's view, was that it brought together in a marketplace the owners of the means of production (and subsistence) and free workers who were the sellers of their own labor-power.

Recall that Marx identified the exchange-value of any commodity as a function of the socially necessary labor to produce it. So, what would then determine the value of labor-power as a commodity? Marx's answer was that the value of labor-power, like that of any other commodity, was determined by the labor time necessary for its production—and reproduction. In other words, it is the value of the means of subsistence necessary for the maintenance of those who own the labor-power, the workers. Their need for food, clothing, housing and the like must be satisfied if they are to have the health and strength required to continue to work. Norms in any historical period and particular place influenced what was considered necessary for people's subsistence, however, and this was one way in which Marx saw labor-power as somewhat different from other commodities. Nevertheless, he concluded, at any given time, in any nation, the average amount of subsistence necessary for the maintenance of free workers could be rather precisely calculated; and in this sense, labor-power was like any other commodity in a capitalistic market.

In analyzing the maintenance needs of workers, Marx took a long-term perspective corresponding with his long-term view of capital accumulation. If labor-power were to remain on the market, in fresh supply, workers would have to reproduce themselves, both biologically and socially. Therefore, the average income of workers must enable workers to adequately raise their children. How much is that? It is the sum of the value of the commodities— themselves determined by the labor-power required for their production— necessary for workers' reproduction. This would entail the labor-power required to produce the food, clothing, fuel, training and so on that is necessary to enable the offspring of workers to replace the current generation of workers.

In capitalistic societies, Marx continued, labor-power is like any other commodity in that it belongs to the capitalist who purchased it. If the capitalist pays for a day's work, then from the moment workers step through the door in the morning, their labor belongs to the capitalist who incorporates it into "the lifeless constituents of the product, which also belong to him."[24] Their labor, to the capitalist, is just another "thing," like raw materials or machines.

At the same time, the purchase of labor differs from the purchase of other commodities in a way that greatly benefits the capitalist. Specifically, it is not paid for until *after* a contractually agreed-upon period following the completion of actual work. That period may be weekly or bi-weekly, but in either case, workers give the capitalist an advance on the use-value of their labor-power. The capitalist is thereby able to "consume" it before paying for it.

> "Everywhere the worker allows credit to the capitalist. That this credit is no mere fiction is shown . . . by the . . . loss of the wages the worker has already advanced, when a capitalist goes bankrupt."[25]

Marx also elaborated upon a number of problems more commonly experienced by workers and their families as a result of advancing their labor to capitalists. One example he analyzed involved the two kinds of bakers then found in London: the full-priced and the "undersellers." The quality of the bread produced by the full-priced bakers was far superior, but its cost put their bread out of reach of most working-class families whose purchases were strictly budgeted. The undersellers added soap, chalk, stone-dust and other non-nutritious items so their flour would go further enabling them to sell their bread at a cheaper price. Many working-class families knew that the under-sellers' bread was adulterated, but they purchased it anyway, because it cost less, and they could not postpone their purchases until the end of the week, when they were paid for their work, to feed their families.

SURPLUS VALUE AND SURPLUS PROFIT

The key to the capitalist's profit, Marx wrote, lies in the difference between the use-value and the exchange-value of labor-power. Its exchange-value is based upon the historic cost of producing the means of subsistence. Its use-value (to the capitalist) is its current productivity, when added to raw materials and machinery. Labor-power's exchange-value will almost always be less than its use-value, however. Without going through a lengthy calculation, Marx thought it reasonable to assume that workers' subsistence probably required only about one-half day's labor, and that set wage rates. The other half of their day's work went to the capitalist in the form of profit. While this surplus profit seemed unjust to Marx, he recognized that the capitalists paid for labor-power exactly the way they would pay for any commodity: according to the socially necessary labor to (re-) produce it. It was a fair price, determined by the laws of economics, according to the public pronouncements of the capitalists. (In private, they sang a different tune.) At the same time, the workers, in selling their labor-power for its exchange-value and giving up its use-value, also behaved like the sellers of any other commodity.

Surplus value lands in the pockets of the capitalists because they pay the lower exchange-value for labor, but reap the higher use-value. Is this surplus value simply to be regarded as the "good luck" of the buyer, Marx asked? Of course not, he answered; it is the result of the workers' exploitation. When the capitalists are out of sight of the workers and the economic analysts, he believed, they laugh on their way to the bank and attribute their profit to their cunning, rather than either good luck or economic laws.

Marx held a different view than the capitalists, as one might expect. He began with the apparent contradiction between two observations: (1) workers and capitalists were simply following principles of commodity exchange in their dealings with each other; and (2) surplus value was a result of the capital-ist's exploitation of the worker. He reconciled the two observations by stating that the so-called "laws" of commodity exchange actually applied solely under conditions of private ownership. In other words, the behavior was normal in capitalism which, itself, was abnormal! Bourgeoisie and proletariat behaved as they must in a capitalistic society. It was capitalism that had to be transformed.

Over time, Marx anticipated that capitalists would initially try to lengthen the working day, to extract more surplus profit. That could not continue indefi-nitely, though, so the capitalists would next turn to improving labor's productiv-ity, especially through technological innovations. This means more non-human investment, but because value and profit are always determined by labor costs, in Marx's view, the *rate* of profit will tend to decline when non-human investment increases. When the rate of profit declines, capitalists try to cut labor costs by reducing employment. When unemployment increases, effective demand for commodities is lowered, firms cut back further, and the economy goes through a downward spiral. Some companies do not survive. However, labor costs have been cut in the downturn, so relative profits rebound, and the economy eventually recovers and grows again. Marx believed that such upswings and downturns were part of the intrinsic nature of capitalism; that the economy would always tend to lurch from crisis to crisis.[26]

CRISIS AND REVOLUTION

The volatile business cycles Marx expected revealed the "contradictions and antagonisms" of capitalism, but he felt that most contemporary analysts did not see this intrinsic failing because they were too busy apologizing for the economy's downswings. Marx was particularly critical of the economists who claimed that contractions of the economy were due to the capitalists' periodic over-production of commodities. He argued that these analysts incorrectly viewed the downswings as preventible miscalculations. However, it was the very notion of over-production that he found particularly absurd, given the deprived conditions of the working class.

> "If over-production could only occur when all members of a nation had satisfied even their most urgent needs, there could never, in the history of bourgeois society . . . have been a state of . . . even partial over-production."[27]

Because of the downturns in the economy, Marx believed, as previously described, that the number of firms would be reduced, so those that survived would be larger. Greater concentration of production was spurred by the economic contractions, but Marx contended that even in good times there would be a thinning of economic enterprises as a result of competition. As capitalists struggled with each other for world-wide supremacy, enormous holdings would eventually wind up in the hands of a few. For the workers, this concentration would mean more misery, oppression and degradation; but Marx stated, it would also bring them together, physically and socially, and facilitate their eventual realization of the economic situation they shared in common. Then there would be an uprising against private ownership of the means of production. Thus, toward the end of *Capital* he returned to some of the prophecies he and Engels had previously offered in *The Communist Manifesto*, and he described the bourgeoisie as their own "grave-diggers." His hope for a future revolution lay, paradoxically, in the very success of the capitalists.

Endnotes

1. Readers with some background in economics can find the views of a number of leading economists presented by Murray Wolfson, "Marx and Modern Economic Analysis." *Southern Economic Journal*, 59, 1992. For a simpler and brief discussion, see Chapter 8 (Economics) in Peter Singer, *Marx: A Very Short Introduction*. New York: Oxford University Press, 2000.

2. During this period Marx and his family lived in poverty and apparently suffered malnutrition. Three of his children died from illness related to their living conditions during this period. For further discussion, see Chapter 8 in, Isaiah Berlin, *Karl Marx: His Life and Environment*. New York: Oxford University Press, 1996. (This is the fourth edition of a classic work on Marx.)

3. Karl Marx, *A Contribution to the Critique of Political Economy*. Chicago: Charles H. Kerr and Company, 1904, Preface, p 12. When this book was originally published, in 1859, Marx was still debating Hegel's ghost, continuing after this quoted passage to state: "It is not the consciousness of men that determines their existence, but on the contrary, their social existence determines their consciousness." (Ibid.)

4. These and other examples are included in Karl Marx, *Theories of Surplus Value*. Moscow: Progressive Publishers, 1971.

5. For further discussion of productive forces in relation to base and superstructure, see pp 376–83 in G.A. Cohen, *Karl Marx's Theory of History*. Princeton: Princeton University Press, 2001; and pp 278–88 in Louis Dupre, *Marx's Social Critique of Culture*. New Haven: Yale University Press, 1983.

6. George Will, "Beijing's 43 Bentleys." *Newsweek*, March 28, 2005, p 62.

7. Aristotle, Republic, I,i.c.9. Quoted by Marx, in Lawrence H. Simon (Ed.), *Karl Marx*. Indianapolis: Hackett, 1994, p 245.

8. Karl Marx, *Capital*, vol 1. New York: International Publishers, 1967, p 186.

9. Anthony Giddens, *A Contemporary Critique of Historical Materialism*. Stanford: Stanford University Press, 1995, p 120.

10. Marx, in Simon, p 255.

11. Ibid.

12. Joshua Gamson, *Claims to Fame*. Berkeley: University of California Press, 1994. See also Chapter 6 in Charles E. Hurst, *Living Theory*. Boston: Allyn and Bacon, 2006.

13. A number of pioneering psychologists, including Alfred Binet, best known for the IQ test which bears his name, wrote about sexual fetishes during the nineteenth century. However, the most important statement of this type was Freud's. See, for example, Sigmund Freud, *Totem and Taboo*. New York: Prometheus, 2000.

14. See Karl Marx and Friedrich Engels, *The Communist Manifesto*. New York: International Publishers, 1948.

15. These two views are often combined in analyses of fashion. See, for example, Valerie Steele, *Fetish: Fashion, Sex & Power*. New York: Oxford, 1996.

16. Marek Ziolkowski, "Commodification of Social Life." *Polish Sociological Review*, 148, 2004.

17. Daniel T. Cook, *The Commodification of Childhood*. Durham, NC: Duke University Press, 2004.

18. Juliet Schor, *Born to Buy*. New York: Scribner, 2004.
19. *Capital*, p 261.
20. Ibid. p 262.
21. Ibid. pp 670–71.
22. Ibid. p 517.
23. Ephraim H. Mizruchi, *Regulating Society*. New York: Free Press, 1983.
24. *Capital*, p 166.
25. Ibid., p 156.
26. Karl Marx, *Theories of Surplus Value*. New York: Prometheus, 2000. (This is a three-volume work, originally published in 1862–1863.)
27. Ibid., p 500.

5

Max Weber (1)

Conceptual Methodology

Max Weber (1864–1920) grew up in a well-to-do suburb of Berlin, Germany, where his family's neighbors included many prominent figures in government and academics. Max Weber, Sr. was an ambitious bureaucrat who was ready to follow any party line that enabled him to get ahead. He held several positions in the Berlin and German governments. Outside of the house he was an excellent socializer who enjoyed fine food and drink. Inside the house he was a controlling despot. Weber's mother, Helene, was an educated and cultured woman, an introvert who devoted herself to her family and church. She was a devout Calvanist who felt a strong obligation to help the working poor in Berlin, even though her husband believed such social involvement was not helpful for his career. The personalities and interests of Weber's parents clashed, and they frequently fought, pulling him between two different poles: an ambitious, practical and pleasure-oriented father, and a self-sacrificing and religious mother. He was torn between these two models for much of his life, and the strain of growing up in their conflict-laced household appeared eventually to take a toll on his psychological well-being.[1]

Weber was academically precocious from the time he was a youngster, continuously excelling in school. When he graduated from college he was unable to find a suitable job so he returned home and began graduate studies, trying to decide whether to become a practicing lawyer or a professor. For the next seven years he worked at part-time jobs, feeling bitter over his inability to be self-supporting because he hated being back under his father's rule. When he was one year away from finishing his graduate studies, his cousin, Marrianne, came to live in the Weber's home. Now 22 years old, she had been raised by aunts after her own mother died. Marrianne and Helene became very close, like mother and daughter, and Marrianne and Max also grew close. There was no apparent courtship, but as Weber was completing his Ph.D. in law and history, he asked Marianne to marry him. She accepted and they left the Weber home the following year when he was offered an academic position at the University of Frieburg. The core of their marital relationship was intellectual: they studied together, attended meetings together, but had little or no physical contact. When he later had several extramarital affairs she was deeply hurt, though they remained bonded to each other as colleagues.[2]

Weber also shared a close relationship with his younger brother, Alfred. Both of them had similar graduate training in history and political economy, held similar academic positions, collaborated on research projects and participated actively together in the German Social Policy Association. This association tried to promote legislation that cut across class lines, steering a middle course between extreme forms of both capitalism and socialism. However, the brothers were separated by fundamentally different views of modern society, and it was a frequent source of tension in their relationship. Alfred was optimistic about the prospects for freedom and autonomy. Max, by contrast, tended to be fatalistic, believing there was "no way out of the cage of modern bureaucratic serfdom."[3]

Weber's early publications at Frieburg, examining business and economic policy, are hardly read today, but they earned him an appointment at Heidelberg, Germany's most elite university at the time. However, he was there only for about one year when his father visited and the two men had a nasty confrontation over the way Max thought Max Senior treated Helene. In a rage, Max threw his father out of the house. About one month passed and the two had not reconciled, when Max Senior suddenly died. The guilt led Max into a deep depression. He had to take a leave from the university, and for a period of six years he wrote almost nothing. Marianne put her own career on hold to nurse him through his illness. (In addition to authoring several books and becoming a leading feminist, she was the first woman elected to a state assembly in Germany.)

In 1903 he began to write again and completed several monographs, most notably his best known work,

The Protestant Ethic and the Spirit of Capitalism.

It was completed in 1904 and was his only book not published posthumously.

In 1907 Marianne received an inheritance from an uncle's estate, and it supported the couple so that he did not have to return to teaching, and it was many years until he took another academic position. He was active in intellectual circles, however, and in 1912 tried unsuccessfully to organize a liberal political party. When World War One broke out (in 1914) he took government administrative positions, but continued to write. Among the essays and monographs he completed during and soon after the war, several later became very important books. Included are:

The Theory of Social and Economic Organization
(Vol. 1 of Economy and Society) (1915)

Politics as a Vocation (1918)

The City (1921)

Immediately after the war he also served on some important German delegations and commissions, but felt that his writing and teaching were more important. He resumed both until he died suddenly of pneumonia in 1920. Marianne, who had also suffered from depression in the past, basically withdrew from society for several years after Max's death. She eventually worked her way out of depression, preparing many of Max's monographs for publication. She also wrote an authoritative biography of her late husband that is still widely read. In 1924 the University of Heidelberg gave her an honorary doctorate in recognition of her own impressive scholarship and her role in editing her husband's work.[4]

UNDERSTANDING SOCIAL ACTION

Like most of the pioneering sociologists, Weber had a mission for sociology. Also like most of the other pioneers, he endeavored to differentiate sociology from the already established kindred disciplines, such as history and psychology. Weber began by defining sociology's unique objective as, "the interpretive understanding of social action in order to arrive at a causal explanation."[5] There are three key phrases in this definition: interpretive understanding, social action and causal explanation. Each warrants clarification because all are central to Weber's theoretical writings.

Interpretive Understanding for Weber meant a grasp of subjective meaning rather than any kind of objectively correct conclusion based upon logical deduction or mathematics. To illustrate, television newscasts today regularly include stories of couples that have very contentious breakups when one of the parties, who did not want the relationship to end, does something "crazy:" attacks the other, attempts suicide, smashes all their possessions, etc. A subjective understanding (*verstehen* in German) would focus upon the rage or vengefulness that might have prompted such actions. The sociologist need not personally feel these emotions in order to find the conduct they produce intellectually comprehensible. "One need not have been Caesar to understand Caesar," Weber wrote.[6] A subjective understanding—verstehen—is still possible. We will have more to say about verstehen later in the chapter. For now, let us examine the rest of the terms in Weber's definition of sociology's primary objective.

Social Action entails behaviors to which the acting individual attaches subjective meaning. It consists of overt actions directed toward another, such as waiving at an acquaintance walking across the campus; or it could also involve thinking about waiving, but deciding not to. The key, according to Weber, is that the person's action (or the inhibition of the action) is oriented to another. It is meaningful conduct as long as it is consistent with the actor's intent with respect to the other person. So, for example, if the person did not want to greet or talk to the acquaintance walking across campus, then not waiving was meaningful social action. More on social action also follows later in the chapter.

Causal explanations are adequate, in Weber's view, if they meet two criteria. First is "adequacy on the level of meaning" which requires the sociologist's subjective comprehension of the relationship between social action and people's motives. He suggested that interpreting a course of conduct will likely have adequate meaning when the motive attributed to the actor is typical of the actor's time and place. If someone walking across campus wanted to talk to an acquaintance, would waiving be a typical thing to do? The second component of an adequate explanation entails being able to determine a probability that one event will be associated with another. This could involve numerical precision, such as the exact probability that someone will remarry within one year of a divorce; or it could simply involve a general sense that something is, or is not, pretty likely to occur. While considering precise probabilities desirable, Weber felt that any such statistics would be useful only if they were manifestations of a course of social action whose subjective meaning was understood by the sociologist. Therefore, he argued, statistics devoid of such meaning—death rates, amount of rainfall, or the like—were not to be regarded as sociological statistics. Correspondingly, there would be little reason for a sociologist to try to analyze them.[7]

It is only individuals whose conduct is subjectively meaningful, Weber wrote; but he added that it is often necessary for sociologists to treat the actions of various collectivities, such as corporations or states, as if they were the acts of individual people. He did not believe that there was a collective personality capable of acting because in the final analysis he insisted that only individuals could act in a subjectively meaningful way. Nevertheless, he recognized that norms of a group or organization could exert important constraints on the behavior of all individual members. Furthermore, people think about these collectivities (fraternities, political parties, religious organizations, etc.) as though they were as real as individuals. People orient their behavior to them, and therefore the collectivities have a great deal of influence over how people behave.

Weber concluded that sociological explanations frequently require situating individuals in a group or corporate context that would emphasize their shared behavioral uniformities. Analyzing the parts (i.e. individuals) in relation to wholes (i.e. collectivities) made sociology resemble the natural sciences. Biology, for example, examines the role of organs (parts) in relation to the entire body. However, Weber cautioned against taking the similarities between sociology and the natural sciences too far because,

> "We can accomplish something that is never attainable in the natural sciences, namely the subjective understanding of the action of the component individuals. The natural sciences . . . do not 'understand' the behaviour of cells . . . . This additional achievement of explanation by interpretive understanding . . . is the specific characteristic of sociological knowledge."[8]

To illustrate the kind of analysis Weber was advocating, consider some grouping of high school students, such as jocks or preppies. The uniformities in their behavior suggest that the individuals are aware of the groups in which they are placed, recognize the norms of the group, and orient their actions to the shared image of the group that exists in their minds. One could observe uniformities in the degree to which they strive for good grades or take drugs or dress fashionably, and comprehend the subjective meanings of the behavior to the individuals whose actions produced the uniformity.

IDEAL TYPES

Weber specifically addressed the analysis of uniformities and generalizations in his description of "ideal types," a concept he believed to be of great importance in sociological investigations. *Ideal types* refer to typical courses of action whose component parts are intentionally exaggerated by the analyst in order to differentiate them from other similar types of actions. To pursue the previous example, jocks and preppies may, in reality, share certain qualities, but their features in common would be conceptually de-emphasized or ignored in an ideal-type analysis, because these shared qualities do not help to distinguish the two types from each other. To be useful, the unique features of any ideal type need to be stressed in order to describe the "pure" and distinct form of the type.

Whether or not an ideal type is correct or true, by some calculation, misses the point. On the one hand, he wrote, are analytic concepts, including ideal types. On the other hand is the empirical arrangement of events. The two hands are separate, and it is only empirical arrangements whose validity can ever be shown. Efforts to establish the reality of analytic concepts, such as ideal types, are always destined to be fruitless. Weber presented Marx's "laws" as examples of mental constructs that are useful so long as they are recognized as such; but unlike observable laws, cannot be verified. It is when people incorrectly regard Marx's "laws" (or anyone else's mental constructs) as empirically verifiable that they try to conduct tests on them which are a complete waste of time. (This was apparently not meant as a criticism, but as a matter-of-fact description of the nature of concepts because in this same passage he refers to Marx as a, "great thinker."[9])

Ideal types both abstract from reality and at the same time help sociologists to understand it. They are likely to produce insights—their function—when they present conceptual models that can be compared to empirical observations. Their divergences from reality are particularly illuminating because, "It is probably seldom if ever that a real phenomenon can be found which corresponds exactly to one of these ideally constructed pure types."[10] To illustrate, Weber proposed that a totally rational course of action frequently provided a useful ideal type conception to be applied to the way some people or groups of people actually behaved. He proceeded to analyze as an example the commander-in-chief of an army waging war. A commander who is acting in a purely rational way, which is generally expected of commanders, must carefully assess each side's resources, acquire intelligence indicating the likelihood that certain strategies will defeat the enemy, and then deploy forces accordingly. Once the role of the purely rational commander has been adequately conceptualized, this ideal type becomes a yard stick against which the actions of actual commanders can be examined.

Another way to think about ideal types, with respect to roles, organizations or historical periods, is as a cluster of inter-related characteristics. Authority roles, for example, according to Andreas Schneider, contain a mixture of evaluative statuses, potency (or power) and activity. In the U.S., positions with highly evaluated status—such as surgeon or advisor—are usually expected to be high in power (controlling interaction in their social relations) and highly active as well. At the other extreme, low authority positions—such as visitor or baker— are typically expected to be subordinate and passive. Thus, in the U.S., positions form distinct authority clusters. The ideal-type high status position is high in authority, power and activity, while the ideal-type low status position would be low in all three.[11] All empirical roles could then be examined against these ideal types.

In employing the term, *ideal type*, Weber claimed he was not getting into evaluations. He wrote that he intended the term only to convey the idea of a pure, unadulterated embodiment of a type. In the same sense one could refer to a student whose study habits and work were always flawless as an ideal student; or describe the ideal beauty, the ideal athlete, or so on. In each of the preceding examples some evaluation might seem implicit because the ideal possesses desirable features. However, by the same token, one could conceptualize an ideal type of despot or a cohort of public officials so dishonest that they provide an ideal type of government corruption.

VALUE FREE

We can also assume from Weber's writings that he did not intend to convey a positive evaluation of ideal types because he went to some lengths to insist that sociologists had to be value free and objective in their scholarly research and teaching. While insisting upon a neutral position, he recognized that the issue was complex and ambiguous. The difficulty begins with ever completely separating empirical statements of fact from value judgments, because it is initially values that usually lead an investigator to select a particular problem to study. Well before they begin to analyze data, the first question social scientists must answer for themselves is: What is worth knowing? And Weber believed that the objective canons of science could not answer that question in a way that was absolutely free from presuppositions and evaluations.[12] For example, would a sociologist decide to examine growing income differences within some society if she/he were not ethically troubled by increasing economic inequality? Similarly, what leads a particular sociologist to study divorce or race relations or academic achievement except some personal feeling on the matter?

After the problem to be studied is selected, however, Weber insisted that sociologists must proceed in a neutral manner: their own values must be held in abeyance during the study and not be permitted to intrude into the analysis. If values creep in, they can affect both what the sociologist sees and what the sociologist overlooks, and ultimately distort the conclusions of a study. To illustrate, many people in the U.S. and U.K., social scientists included, have strong negative feelings about the people who, in various parts of the world, carry out suicide missions. They find the motives difficult to fathom—verstehen is difficult—and they abhor the killings. These feelings could bias how researchers examine the biographies and circumstances of people who undertake suicide missions, and lead to the prejudiced conclusion that the people willing to kill themselves are irrationally self-destructive, and should therefore be condemned and dismissed. This conclusion might feel good to the investigator, but would it further our understanding of the people who undertake these missions? Are their subjective orientations any clearer? Perhaps if preconceived notions were put aside before and during the study, might the data equally support the view that these people made rational choices from among very limited alternatives?[13]

Weber regarded the professors who believed they had a right to express their personal values in their writing or their lectures as "altogether repugnant." In the Germany of his day—highly imperialistic and nationalistic—the abuse had become so wide-spread that in Weber's view it constituted a crisis both for the society and for the careers of young academics. He likened the professors who took advantage of their position to "street corner prophets." However, he noted with scorn that they left the street corner to enter the lecture hall where these cowardly faculty members could invoke academic freedom to protect themselves against outside intervention. These protections emboldened them to feel justified in pronouncing personal evaluations on ultimate questions that they disguised as scientific conclusions so they could not be refuted. Students are also exploited in this system, Weber concluded, because the curriculum requires that they take courses with certain instructors and then be unfairly subjected to the instructor's values, disguised as facts.[14]

In looking back at the establishment of academic sociology, which Weber helped to institute, Alvin Gouldner has argued that the value-free position entailed a trade-off. By implicitly agreeing to examine only what is, and not what ought to be, sociology made itself appear less threatening both to organized religion and to the state. In return for promising to accommodate itself to the status-quo, powerful interests outside of the university acquiesced to the establishment of academic sociology.[15]

Contemporary social scientists are divided on Weber's value-free position. Many question the degree to which it is either possible or desirable. On the one hand, a value-free ideal can make researchers reflect on their assumptions and endeavor to distinguish between facts and values. Everyone is well-served when the distinction is emphasized. On the other hand, a value-free position can lead a researcher to resemble the famous fiddler who played while Rome burnt. To illustrate, Devora Davis, an epidemiologist who has studied environmentally-produced illnesses, argues that, in the name of being value free, the scientific community has been guilty of being superficial and inconsequential. Specifically, as a result of the scientists' misguided neutrality they failed to aggressively investigate and publicly report on how lead in gasoline was producing brain damage, how toxic chemicals posed a hazard to everyone's health, etc.[16] Science that is responsive to the public's interest requires value commitments rather than neutrality—though the possibility of abuses are the acknowledged downside to such commitments.[17]

In sum, Weber thought a good deal about the methodology that would best serve the new discipline of sociology, and his writings on the matter have had a strong and enduring impact upon later sociologists. The four key features of his methodology were:

1. A focus upon subjectively meaningful social action,
2. Explanations of social action that emphasize verstehen (interpretive understanding),
3. The conceptual development of ideal types, and their application to empirical situations,
4. Striving to maintain a value-free position.

We now turn from Weber's methodological positions to his substantive analyses.

LEGITIMACY AND VALIDITY

Weber observed that social action was frequently characterized by uniformities: patterns of behavior that were both wide-spread and recurrent. These uniformities range from the trivial (students refusing to carry umbrellas, even when it is raining) to the solemn (people standing and removing their hats when the national anthem is played). A general explanation for such uniformities was a central theoretical issue in most of Weber's major works. He approached the issue by noting that people acting in concert could share any number of subjective meanings. They might be oriented to the same self-interest; for example, students may fear being ridiculed if they carry umbrellas. Custom might also provide an explanation as illustrated by everyone standing for the anthem by simple force of habit. In addition, Weber wrote, uniformities may be due to people's shared belief in the *legitimacy* of the convention, norm or rule. Legitimacy implies a congruence between the pattern of behavior and people's values. For example, they think it is right for people to stand when the anthem is played.

Weber recognized that in most situations people's behavior was the product of multiple motives. Most people stand for the anthem because they think it is the right thing to do, *and* because it is a habit, *and* because they fear how others would respond if they remained seated. As long as the people whose actions produce the uniformity are at least in part motivated by the feeling that the behavior is desirable in its own right, then legitimacy is involved. Weber thought of legitimacy as a variable, as more-or-less present, and used the term *validity* to refer to the degree to which people oriented their behavior to a uniformity they considered legitimate. The greater the validity, the greater the likelihood of actual compliance because, in his view, legitimacy produces a more stable pattern than sheer expedience or custom, alone.[18]

Subsequent analyses of validity have distinguished between two dimensions that Weber often combined in his discussions of legitimacy. When he wrote that a pattern possessed legitimacy if people felt it was and should be binding upon them, he merged a cognitive assessment of what was expected (i.e. knowledge) with an evaluative (i.e. normative) standard. Some later sociologists have separated these two parts, retaining the term *validity* to refer to a recognition that a normative pattern provides the current standard, and that those who deviate from it will be punished (formally or informally). The second dimension, labeled "propriety," involves perceptions of fairness. Thus, validity can be roughly equated with people's awareness of how a pattern operates; their knowledge of what "is." If they know how others will behave and what actions will be sanctioned, then the normative pattern possesses validity. Propriety, by contrast, rests upon whether people believe that behavioral expectations and sanctions ought to operate as they do. If they seem right and fair, propriety is indicated, and some recent research has concluded that the propriety dimension has a stronger effect upon people's rates of compliance than the validity dimension.[19]

When a normative pattern has a degree of validity or propriety, no individual can simply ignore it. Even if people deviate, Weber wrote, they usually do it surreptitiously and/or find ways to justify the deviation, indicating that they feel uncomfortable going against the uniformity. He also recognized the possibility that different meanings could simultaneously co-exist, each possessing a degree of validity or propriety and thereby partially influencing people's actual conduct. In Weber's late-nineteenth century Germany, dueling provided an interesting example. On one side of the coin, it was banned and constituted a criminal offense. On the other side, if a man were insulted, he was likely to consider a duel obligatory to maintain his honor. Each side of the coin possessed a degree of validity and propriety and people could not completely ignore either side.

> "A person who fights a duel orients his action to the code of honour; but at the same time, in so far as he either keeps it secret or conversely gives himself up to the police, he takes account of the criminal law."[20]

Organizational Legitimacy

Thus far we have described Weber's analysis of legitimacy at a macro level where it involves the congruence between societal patterns of conduct and cultural values. At a more micro level, he also analyzed legitimacy of and within organizations, such as government agencies, retail firms, universities, etc. Consider any group of people who are in a hierarchical arrangement: a king and his subjects, the president of a corporation and her staff, a lieutenant and the soldiers in a platoon. When the king, president or lieutenant gives an order, will subordinates obey? Will they obey right away, or stop and think about it? If they do promptly obey, how is their compliance to be explained? Perhaps they do so out of fear of the consequences of not obeying. Maybe they want to pretend to be loyal in order to gain something for themselves. Legitimacy is involved to the degree subordinates comply because they believe the authority over them is justified.

Within and among organizations, *legitimacy* typically refers to the congruence between the organization's procedures and widely held values about those procedures. The legitimacy of an accounting firm's hiring policies or a bank's rules for approving mortgages would therefore be indicated by how well they matched values held in the larger society. These widely held values are usually embodied in industry-wide standards of evaluation, and involve licensure, accreditation, certification or the like, depending upon the type of organization. So an organization's accreditation or license provides evidence of the legitimacy of its procedures.

Weber wrote that organizations would always try to establish the legitimacy of their procedures because it would very effectively lead officials and employees of the organization to comply with its rules. That would make the authority of its leadership relatively unchallenged. For example, if during a lecture a professor turned to the class and said, "Put down your pencils, and stop taking notes for a moment," everyone would probably comply because they considered the professor's directive to be legitimate—consonant with pedagogic goals. However, what if at the same point in the lecture the professor were to say to the students, "Take off your clothes!" It is likely that no one would comply because the order would seem inconsistent with university values, hence not legitimate. If the professor persisted in asking students to disrobe, they might permanently walk out of the class, complain to the dean, transfer to another school, etc. According to Weber, the permanence and stability of an organization depend upon the legitimacy of its practices. A university in which professors went around ordering students to undress in class (or behave in other ways that lacked legitimacy) would probably not survive for long.

An analysis of the causes and effects of one particular type of organization's legitimacy is presented in Research Box 5-1. It summarizes the results of a long-term study of the permanence and dissolution of a large group of hospitals in the San Francisco Bay area.

RESEARCH BOX 5-1

Legitimacy and Permanence Among Hospitals

The Publication

Martin Ruef and W. Richard Scott, "A Multidimensional Model of Organizational Legitimacy." *Administrative Science Quarterly*, 43, 1998: 877–904.

The Research Question

The primary question posed by the investigators concerns whether they can empirically demonstrate the effects of an organization's legitimacy. Focusing upon hospitals, they examine whether indicators of "technical legitimacy" are associated with the hospital's chances of surviving. *Technical literacy*, while only one of the types of legitimacy any organization could possess, is important because it refers to the results of normative assessments of the hospital's organization and practices. These examinations are routinely conducted by professional associations, such as the American College of Surgeons, the Joint Commission on Hospitals and national organizations of medical schools. High scores for a hospital on these assessments indicate high legitimacy: that the hospital has excelled at adopting procedures that are considered appropriate and desirable according to widely held technical standards. A low score, by contrast, signifies that a hospital is not adequately complying with the procedures valued in the industry.

The Data

The investigators analyzed 143 hospitals in the San Francisco Bay Area for a period of 46 years, beginning in 1945. Of the total, 78 had continued to operate until (at least) 1990, the year the data collection ended. The other 65 hospitals either dissolved, were acquired by other hospitals, became rehab centers, etc.

The Findings

The researchers found two variables that were strongly related to a hospital's legitimacy score. The first correlate was age. Hospitals that had already been in operation for many years by 1945 were more likely to possess high legitimacy. Over time they may have become proficient at adapting to new standards; and the more established hospitals may have benefitted from having become exemplars for the assessments conducted by professional associations. The second correlate was size. Larger hospitals had higher legitimacy scores, perhaps because size was related to wealth or resources that permitted hospitals to adapt the procedures and organizational forms that were positively evaluated. To a lesser degree, the investigators also found that more focused niche hospitals (e.g. children's or tuberculosis hospitals) had higher legitimacy scores than the general hospitals. That is not surprising given that specialization is usually valued in our society.

Then the investigators turned to the question of whether the legitimacy score of hospitals had the theoretically expected effect on their permanence. The main finding of the study was that the higher a hospital's technical legitimacy the greater the likelihood that it would survive intact. In fact, those hospitals whose procedures best fit with general normative expectations (and therefore received the highest scores on their legitimacy ratings) were found to be about five times more likely to survive over the 46 years the study encompassed than the hospitals with average ratings. These findings are, of course, highly consistent with Weber's expectation that legitimacy conferred stability, and made the persistence of any organization more likely.

TYPES OF LEGITIMACY

Whether or not people would consider the authority of another to be legitimate, Weber wrote, depended upon how they viewed the person's "credentials," and that perception varied among societies. The request of an elderly relative to attend religious services, for example, might receive more respectful compliance in a small farming community than in a large modern city. The reverse might be true, however, with respect to following the legal advice of an attorney.

Weber again noted that yielding to the will of others could be a result of habit or self-interest, but he viewed neither, by itself, as providing a reliable basis for long-term compliance. The additional element that must ordinarily be present for stability and permanence is belief in the legitimacy of authority. He proposed that there were three "pure" types of legitimate authority, each of which rested upon a distinct claim to validity and propriety, and that different societal conditions made each type more-or-less likely to predominate.

Weber again noted that most actual situations in any society involve a mixture of all three types of legitimation, but the characteristics of one tend to predominate. We will very briefly define the types and then turn to a more lengthy discussion of the ideal-type features of each of the three.

1. *Traditional:* where there is an emphasis upon people's shared history and personal loyalties that have been handed down from the past. Obedience is owed to the person whose position is traditionally associated with authority.
2. *Charismatic:* where authority is based upon the special gifts a person is believed to possess, leading to compliance because of the followers' personal devotion to the charismatic leader.
3. *Rational-Legal:* where people's calculation of efficiency is emphasized, behavior is governed by formal rules and authority is impersonal, owed to the incumbent of a position rather than a specific person.

Traditional Authority

Legitimacy based upon a belief in the sanctity of tradition, in Weber's view, was the most universal and the most "primitive" type, modeled after a father's authority over his household in a patrilineal society. (Weber's formulation has been criticized for viewing traditional authority as an arrangement in which only men had power, and their domination over women was at least implicitly natural or inevitable.[21]) It is common for the traditional chief or lord to be head of a lineage with followers drawn from both his patrilineal relatives and other non-kin who are personally loyal to him. Both group members' allegiance to the chief is often an inherited obligation.

In the pure type of traditional authority, a chief makes arbitrary decisions concerning who does what, and who, besides him, gets to make certain types of decisions. The responsibilities of followers are often decided in an ad hoc way, according to the leader's preference at the moment. However, while traditional chiefs have a great deal of leeway to reach impulsive decisions, there is a tension between arbitrariness and adherence to precedent.

> "A master who violated tradition . . . would thereby endanger the legitimacy of his authority which is based entirely upon the sanctity of that tradition . . . Outside the norms of tradition . . . his arbitrary will prevails."[22]

A traditional master has no staff in the modern sense of a group of people who are technically trained for their positions, and hence specialized. Regular staff salaries also tend to be absent. In their place, a chief may dole out a variety of in-kind benefits, which can consist of: food, particular statuses (e.g. knighthood), various privileges, such as the right to collect taxes and so on.

Traditional authority, Weber continued, contains an irrational element which tends to inhibit the development of large-scale, profit-oriented economic activity. The arbitrary determination of fees and taxes, for example, makes it difficult for business people to make long range plans. They also do not know how much personal freedom they may have to engage in business dealings at any time in the future. Finally, and perhaps most importantly, it is extremely difficult to rationally calculate one's obligations. Because traditional ties have the potential to be all-encompassing, business people may not be able to buy and sell freely to anyone in a marketplace. Capitalistic enterprises are also inhibited when some relationships may require historically fixed in-kind exchanges rather than negotiated prices.

The growth of large-scale economic activity which, in turn, favors the growth of rational calculation provides one of the most important historical challenges to the legitimacy of traditional authority. Once many people begin routinely to calculate their self-interest, and act upon it, the legitimacy of a tradition-based regime is called into question. As a result, regimes built upon traditional authority are often precarious, and unlikely to permanently endure. One alternative is for entities in which traditional authority predominated to become transformed into a rational-legal mode, the third type to be discussed here. The other major alternative is a temporary conversion to charismatic authority, the next type to be considered here.

Charismatic Authority

Charismatic and traditional authority, according to Weber, shared two important features in common. The allegiance of followers and the authority of the leader are both personal characteristics tied to a particular person, not a position. Second, both types of regimes typically confront circumstances that prevent them from being permanent. Hierarchies based upon traditional authority can last for hundreds of years, however, until they are challenged by rational calculations or by the emergence of a charismatic leader. The authority of charismatic leaders, by contrast, tends not to last beyond the leader's life time.

The principal defining feature of charisma is that it is a personal characteristic that sets a person believed to possess it apart from ordinary people. The charismatic individual is usually regarded as possessing exceptional, even superhuman, powers. Throughout history such people have been prophets, magicians, war heroes, great healers, etc. Some specific examples include Jesus Christ, George Washington and Joan of Arc.

By definition, charismatic authority is outside the realm of the ordinary and routine. In that sense it is different from both traditional and rational-legal authority because the latter two types involve everyday ways of controlling actions. It also differs from both with respect to rules. Both traditional and rational-legal are more-or-less bound to rules, either by precedent or law; but Weber regarded the charismatic type as the direct antithesis of rules. The charismatic leader, to be effective, must be free to improvise in order to keep followers inspired. Their faith in a leader is crucial because charisma is a revolutionary force, spawned by crises or conflict that lead people to repudiate the status-quo, and that carries with it certain threats to their well-being. In joining a charismatically led, and therefore revolutionary, group, followers know that they may face a firing squad, if caught, be excommunicated, have their property confiscated, etc. The charismatic leader has to make sure that followers do not succumb to the pressures to come back into the fold.

It is typically a crisis that a group confronts—in a religious, military or economic realm—that leads people to "surrender" themselves to a charismatic leader. They are carried away by the hope that this person's special power can resolve the crisis that appears to be beyond the ability of ordinary mortals. It may simply be, in a sense, that exceptional times call for exceptional people. Or, does the anxiety generated by the exceptional times simply induce followers to believe that their leader possesses exceptional qualities because they are looking for reassurance? In other words, they believe because they want to believe. The effect of a crisis on a leader's charisma is the subject of Research Box 5-2.

RESEARCH BOX 5-2

Charismatic Leadership During Crises

The Publication

Stefanie K. Halverson, Susan E. Murphy, and Ronald E. Riggio, "Charismatic Leadership in Crisis Situations." *Small Group Research,* 35, 2004.

The Research Question

Weber associated the emergence of charismatic leadership with times of crisis. When faced with a stress-inducing change in circumstances, almost any leader might theoretically be expected to behave in a more charismatic manner. Confronting a new set of unanticipated expectations, or finding that procedures which worked in the past are no longer operative, are examples of such stress-inducing changes. Prior studies of changes in collectivities varying from small groups to entire nations have suggested that when they faced a crisis, more charismatic leadership apparently tended to follow. What has not been clear, however, is whether the seeming increase was entirely an attribution of followers. Perhaps because of the insecurity and stress they feel, members of groups that face a crisis are simply inclined to perceive their leaders as being more charismatic, even when there has been no change in the leader's actual behavior. Hence, the main research question: Does the behavior of leaders, in fact, become more charismatic during times of crises?

The Data

The investigators placed 168 new college freshmen into three-person groups, and one of the three was randomly selected to be the leader. (There was no reason to assume that the randomly selected person would be particularly charismatic.) All of the student-subjects were initially told their groups would have to complete a simple, but ambiguous, task. Then one-half of the leaders were surprised to discover that they would be videotaped to enable experts to evaluate their leadership and that they would also have to give an oral report on their group's experience to the faculty. No such stress-inducing directions were given to the other half of the groups.

All of the group sessions were taped, and the charisma of the leaders was rated by three coders who were not members of any group and did not know which of them were in the crisis situation so they would not be influenced in their ratings by any preconceived notions. Charisma was measured by a total of 13 indicators, including the degree to which each leader: behaved in an unconventional or nontraditional way, worked to establish personal trust with followers, offered visions of the future, etc.

The Findings

Leaders operating in the stressful condition, according to the ratings of the coders, exhibited substantially higher levels of charismatic behavior than leaders who were in the non-stressful condition. The ratings of all three coders were extremely similar to each other, suggesting that they had a very reliable measure of the leaders' behavior. The investigators also asked the members of each group to rate their own leaders' charisma, and these ratings correlated very highly with those of the coders: The followers of leaders operating in the stressful condition saw their leaders as more charismatic. Thus, it appears that stressful situations do produce charismatic leaders, as Weber expected, and that members of their groups were not simply engaged in wishful thinking when they perceived their leaders as highly charismatic.

Charisma's Impermanence

It is only at the onset of a revolutionary movement that one sees charismatic authority in its pure form. Over time, the leader's authority is at least partly transformed into another type. For example, the leader's special message may become part of a written or oral tradition. The subjects or followers then react less to their perception of the leader's exceptional qualities and more to their belief in what has become part of their tradition. Thus, charismatic authority may be replaced by traditional authority, or the two may co-exist as a mixed type.

Alternatively, the organization established under the charismatic leader may add rules, a professional staff and a hierarchy of authority, and be transformed into a rational-legal (i.e. bureaucratic) organization. To illustrate, Fidel Castro was initially the charismatic leader of a group of Cubans who wanted to topple Batista's regime which they saw as a powerful, but corrupt, puppet of the U.S. They followed Castro because of the special qualities they attributed to him. After the revolution succeeded and the new regime came into power, Castro became the President and many of his followers became officials of the new Cuban government. Castro retained a degree of charisma for many Cubans, but his authority slowly came to be based more upon his bureaucratic position (including his control of the army) than his personal charisma. To illustrate further, Jesus's authority was initially purely charismatic; but the organization he established, based upon personal loyalty, morphed from a small anti-establishment religious rebellion into a large rational-legal bureaucracy, namely, the Catholic Church. Today, any given Pope may be viewed as charismatic, but his authority would nevertheless be based largely upon his formal position in the church hierarchy.

To survive, an organization based upon the charismatic authority of its leader must change into something else. The new form could be based upon tradition, rational-legal principles, or a mixed type—or the organization will cease to exist entirely. One fundamental reason for the transitory nature of charismatically-led organizations, Weber stated, is that no matter how special the leaders may be, they are still mortal. Their death creates a very difficult to resolve succession problem for the group they leave behind. How could a replacement be selected? Charismatic leaders are rarely able to identify a likely successor before they die, and it is never clear how the survivors can find someone as gifted as their former leader.

Even during the charismatic leader's lifetime it may be difficult for him or her to hold the organization together. Ironically, the problem may be exaggerated by the leader's success as more members are attracted, and there is no staff to help the leader to govern. Furthermore, in joining an anti-establishment movement, the disciples, as previously noted, put themselves in some jeopardy. Given the dangers they are facing, they want continuous reassurance that the leader has lost none of the special qualities that attracted them in the first place. However, yesterday's miracles may seem commonplace today. As a result, the followers may push the leader to attempt feats that exceed even his or her powers, and failure usually leads to disillusionment and the disbanding of the group.

Rationality

The third pure type of legitimation in Weber's model involved rationality. He generally defined this as entailing an emphasis upon the connection between the objective of participants and the degree to which their course of conduct was tailored to meet that objective. Conduct was rational then if people selected means according to the probability the means would lead to certain ends (assuming they possessed adequate knowledge of the circumstances). In Western societies, he believed that an emphasis upon rationality was increasing, and that it cut across institutions: economics, religion, law, even architecture and music. To illustrate, in architecture he described the pointed and cross-vaulted arch as a rational means for dealing with the distribution of weight. In symphonic music, he noted that the structure of sounds could be precisely calculated, with harmonization accomplished by following a series of rules. Correspondingly, musical instruments were being standardized, in order to increase their precision and enable them to play in harmony with other instruments.[23] Thus, in every realm, there were powerful social pressures to systematically apply rules to attain explicit objectives.

In all, Weber identified at least four distinctive types of rationality. He distinguished among them according to whether people were making practical (i.e. everyday) or theoretical (i.e. abstract) decisions, and how much the ends they were seeking were valued in their own right. He termed it "substantive" rationality when the goals people were trying to attain (e.g. to promote science or seek social justice) were very highly valued.[24]

When the assessment of means entailed systematic and quantitative calculations, Weber termed it *formal rationality*. This was the type he thought was most prevalent in Western societies, and the type that has been most examined by ensuing sociologists. George Ritzer has utilized Weber's concept of formal rationality to explain and illustrate the operations of contemporary franchises, such as McDonald's or Wal-Mart.[25] The key features of the (formal) rationality of these organizations are:

- Efficiency—involving distribution centers that are serviced by their own fleets of trucks and mechanically unloaded; getting customers to do some of the work, i.e. wait in line to place orders, remove their own trash, etc.

- Calculability—which has led to an emphasis upon the size of products— "Big Mac," "Big Gulp," etc.—rather than upon their quality because size is obviously easier to quantify than more subjective aspects, such as taste.
- Predictability—making sure customers get what they have learned to expect, by having staff everywhere dress in the same "uniforms," and offer the identical products with the same guarantees of customer satisfaction.
- Control—involving the use of technology to replace people in controlling the rational system: electronic cash registers that also provide inventory control, laser scanned bar codes, automated conveyer belts, etc.

While Weber saw rationality increasing over time and across institutions, he did not believe its increase would follow a straight linear progression, due largely to the counter-revolutionary force of charismatic leaders that periodically emerge. To a large degree they claim authority on the basis of their anti-rational accomplishments; their ability to produce results that are so extraordinary they cannot be rationally explained. Over time, however, the eventual routinization of most charismatically formed organizations was further evidence, to Weber, of the triumph of rationality.

It is important also to note that even though an emphasis upon the connection between means and ends defined rationality, Weber recognized that the route people advocated would not always lead to the ends they desired. At times, in fact, means may paradoxically produce unintended consequences that are the opposite of what people intended. For example, it may be that the wide-spread use of car alarms has actually made it easier to steal cars because everyone has become so accustomed to their going off that they no longer respond as they once would have if they saw someone suspiciously moving around an automobile. Of course, no one who installs a car alarm intends to facilitate car thefts! The more rational the society, perhaps, the greater the potential for such unanticipated consequences?

Disenchantment

Weber also noted, with a degree of sadness, that there was a downside to rationality, especially when it was carried to an extreme degree. With such hyper-rationality, people become habituated to empirical, logical and systematic reasoning. It entraps them, he wrote, like an "iron cage." They expect the world to be predictable and efficient, and explicable in rational terms. Their culture coerces them into a rational way of thinking from which they cannot escape. It is as though they were in iron cages. What then happens to illusion and fantasy? To belief in magic and miracles? Weber concluded when everything that is non-rational is stripped out of the world and made implausible, it can result in wide-spread "disenchantment."

Especially in Western societies, according to Weber, extreme rationality was permeating every institution, pushing aside superstition and fantasy in favor of calculated, systematic orientations. In the economic realm, for example, this meant that people reached decisions about careers, business investments or the like by precisely weighing probabilities rather than relying upon fate or chance. Delivery from sin in modern Christianity, to illustrate further, eliminated magic as a technique for attaining salvation and replaced it with an emphasis upon a rational, disciplined approach to following God's commandments.[26]

Contemporary analysts have viewed the hyper-rationality of Western societies as creating a void, leading people to search for ways to re-introduce enchantment into their lives. Ritzer views large-scale means of consumption, such as mega-malls, the Las Vegas strip or Disneylands, as offering the fantastic settings people deprived of enchantment are seeking. To provide illusion and fantasy to the life of the jaded contemporary consumer, who may be trapped within the iron cage of rationality, they have to offer extravaganzas that present a spectacle: something so big and so incredible as to defy conventional rational explanation.[27]

To illustrate the idea of extravaganzas, consider the way flagship stores in New York City, and Manhattan in particular, describe themselves to potential consumers. Toys "R" Us in Times Square claims their store, "is a non-stop spectacular journey for children of all ages" that contains "three levels of amazing attractions." Similarly, Macy's describes their fourth of July fireworks show in New York City by claiming, "The fireworks do not get any bigger . . . With over 120,000 bursts of color, light and pyrotechnics . . . featuring our whimsical fireworks soundtrack."[28] Who could remain blase and reserved in the face of such attractions?

While rationality may be especially excessive in Western societies, as Weber forecasted, it is certainly not confined to the West. Throughout the world a growing emphasis upon rationality may seem to be creating a cultural imbalance that leads people to search for symbols and experiences that are capable of providing enchantment. A social movement that can offer such balance may thereby strengthen its appeal. An interesting illustration is provided by Michael Roberts' analysis of the standard depiction of the Liberation Tigers in Sri Lanka. This is a revolutionary band of people who see themselves as freedom fighters, and often resort to suicide missions against the Sri Lanka army. Roberts notes that they are frequently pictured with a rifle in their left hand, and a white jasmine flower in their right hand. This is an important dichotomy on several levels. It is no accident that the freedom fighter holds the rifle in his left hand because that is the hand that is culturally favored for mundane, everyday tasks. The jasmine flower, in his right hand, is a widely-used symbol in Tamil folklore; and by cultural tradition, the right hand is expected to remain clean for ritual purposes. Each object is pictured in the appropriate hand. The rifle in the left hand symbolizes practical rationality while the flower in the right symbolizes "sentiments that are beyond reason."[29] The liberation fighter thus conjoins two sources of power, the pragmatic and the magical, the rational and the enchanted, and bringing them together makes the social movement more attractive to a mass following.

RATIONAL-LEGAL BUREAUCRACY

Weber identified "legality" as a potential fourth type of legitimacy, defined by people's belief in the way a rule has been established. It specifically entails,

> "the readiness to conform with rules which . . . have been imposed by accepted procedure . . . it . . . implies a belief in the legitimate *authority* of the source imposing it."[30]

So, one might not approve of a new law passed by the Congress and signed by the President, but nevertheless regard the process that was followed as the appropriate way to establish laws, and hence feel bound to obey it. Similarly, one might not want to follow the order of a police official at the scene of an accident, but still do so because of an appreciation of the right of the officer to issue such commands. In both of the previous examples, Weber would expect people to comply regardless of their personal feelings because legalistic considerations would lead them to think compliance was appropriate.

In most of his discussions of legality, Weber combined it with rationality. The two modes were conjoined in his highly influential analysis of bureaucracy, which he considered the dominant form of organization in modern societies. When people today think about bureaucracy, they usually envision a large organization—such as a university, police department, bank, or the like—in which every situation is governed by rules, and people are required to fill out multiple forms. Weber would agree with this depiction, as far as it goes. In describing the features that comprise an ideal-type bureaucracy, however, he presented a much longer list of attributes. The major defining features are as follows:

1. The positions in a bureaucracy are arranged in a hierarchy of authority, with lower positions under the supervision of higher ones. Because there are fewer positions as one moves up the hierarchy, the organizational chart resembles a pyramid. For example, in the military, a number of sergeants report to a lieutenant, several lieutenants report to a captain, etc.

2. To be appointed to a position presupposes that people have the requisite knowledge and competence, demonstrated by their possession of a degree, or their ability to pass a test. To be an administrative assistant, for example, candidates must show their knowledge of office procedures, word processing skills, etc.

3. Each position has a specified sphere of authority, associated with the competence of the incumbent. Subordinates are correspondingly obligated only to obey orders that fall within their supervisor's rationally delineated authority. A professor would not feel obligated to marry if the Dean ordered it because such a directive lies outside of the Dean's academic authority.

4. Authority is tied to positions rather than people, hence it is exercised impersonally. The teller in a bank responds to the directives of the head

teller because of their positions, irrespective of personal feelings between them. In addition, a general spirit of impersonality pervades bureaucracies, and is reflected by the tendency of incumbents to refer to each other by formal titles (e.g. professor, captain, doctor, etc.) rather than personal names.

5. Most people are appointed to their positions, and receive a fixed salary which is their only form of remuneration. They do not own their positions nor do the position's rights belong to them, personally. Thus, when employees resign, they turn in keys, cards, uniforms, and so on.

6. Employment in the organization constitutes a career. Officials are promoted along clearly identified steps based upon their achievements, length of service, or both. To illustrate, based upon their teaching and publication records, associate professors are typically eligible for promotion after a period of five years. Corresponding with the expectation of a career, officials in a bureaucracy are protected against arbitrary dismissal. They can only be terminated for a limited number of causes which are clearly specified.

7. Abstract rules govern behavior within the bureaucracy and it is the obligation of officials to apply the rules to make decisions in particular cases. Whether or not any customer can return merchandise to a department store, for example, is determined by a set of general store rules that are publicly posted.

The preceding features, it will be recalled, constitute an ideal-type bureaucracy. Like all ideal types, Weber's analysis of bureaucracy was meant to provide a yard stick against which to examine reality rather than a description of reality, itself. The more of these features that are present in any actual organization, the more closely they resemble the ideal type. Most organizations would be expected to approximate the ideal to varying degrees. A large established organization, such as the U.S. Postal Service, would probably correspond very closely with the ideal type. A small, recently started firm, on the other hand, might be expected to display only a few of the bureaucratic features. In particular, professional "knowledge work" that requires high levels of expertise is often difficult to manage in a bureaucratic setting. The research work of scientists and engineers, for example, cannot necessarily be done in one correct way, making it difficult to standardize with fixed rules or to quantify the results of their research.[31] As professional knowledge work has grown relative to traditional employment in manufacturing firms, it has put an emphasis upon flexibility and openness, resulting in more organizations whose characteristics are further from the ideal-type bureaucracy.

Bureaucracy was, in Weber's view, the most efficient, and therefore, the most rational means of creating a permanent organization of people to manage large-scale administrative tasks: operating the social security system or maintaining student records, the kinds of large-scale administrative tasks characteristic of contemporary societies. Economic and technological developments, in his view, had brought improvements in communications and transportation that had made possible permanent and large-scale organizations, such as the Wal-Mart Corporation or the U.S. Navy. Without these technological and economic developments there would likely be neither the large-scale organizations nor the means to monitor far-flung activities from within a centralized headquarters.[32]

Also favoring the dominance of bureaucracy, according to Weber, was the fact that it provided the organizational form that was most compatible with the constraining modern emphasis upon rationality.

> "However much people may complain about the 'evils of bureaucracy,' it would be sheer illusion to think that continuous administrative work can be carried out [differently] . . . . The whole pattern of everyday life is cut to fit this framework."[33]

The inevitability of bureaucracy meant that if an organization was to endure, it would usually wind up taking a bureaucratic form, Weber claimed. For example, a charismatically-led group survives in a society dominated by rational legitimation by becoming a bureaucracy: from Jesus's small band to the Catholic Church. Weber also contended that organizations created in opposition to bureaucracies were themselves subject to the same process. Thus, a trade union might form to enable employees to protest working conditions in a bureaucracy. If the union was successful in attracting members and it grew larger, it might eventually become as bureaucratic as the organization it was initially formed to oppose.

Implications

While bureaucracy was the result of economic and technological developments along with increasing rationality, Weber thought that bureaucracy, in turn, had a number of potential effects upon society. It certainly furthered rationality, by replacing organizations based upon any other mode of legitimation. In addition, Weber's analysis suggested to him that it could be a force for or against democracy. On the one hand, a system of examinations by which people demonstrate expertise in order to be hired, could promote a meritocracy by opening positions to people who were not born into the aristocracy. Talent and achievement would trump lineage.

On the other hand, democracy would not be furthered if particular groups, such as people of limited income, were unable to obtain the education or training necessary to obtain positions in bureaucracies; and Weber feared that advantaged groups might try to use access to education to control movement into the most valued positions. In a cynical way, people who could afford education would insist upon that expertise always serving as a precondition for being hired—a viewpoint that is highly compatible with bureaucratic emphases; but democracy would not be served if those who could not afford education could not compete.

> "If we hear . . . demands for . . . regulated curricula culminating in specialized examinations, the reason behind this is, of course, not a suddenly awakened 'thirst for education,' but rather the desire to limit the supply of candidates for these positions and monopolize them for the holders of education . . ."[34]

Endnotes

1. For biographies of Weber, see Marianne Weber, *Max Weber: A Biography*. New Brunswick: Transaction Press, 1988; and Hans Gerth and C. Wright Mills, *From Max Weber: Essays in Sociology*. New York: Oxford, 1958.

2. Patricia Lengermann and Jill Niebrugge-Brantley, *The Women Founders*. New York: McGraw-Hill, 1998.

3. Eberhard Demm, "Max and Alfred Weber and the Verien fur Sozialpolitik." In Wolfgang J. Mommsen and Jurgen Osterhammel (Eds.), *Max Weber and His Contemporaries*. London: Unwin Hyman, 1987.

4. Lengermann and Niebrugge-Brantley.

5. Max Weber, *The Theory of Social and Economic Organization*. (Edited by Talcott Parsons). New York: Free Press, 1947, p 88.

6. Ibid., p 90.

7. The statistics Durkehim analyzed, most notably suicide, would not have been met Weber's criteria for sociological statistics because Durkheim explicitly excluded any consideration of the subjective motives of the individuals that produced the statistic.

8. *The Theory of Social and Economic Organization,* pp 103-4.

9. Max Weber, *The Methodology of the Social Sciences*. New York: Free Press, 1949, p 103.

10. *The Theory of Social and Economic Organization,* p 110.

11. German samples, by contrast, do not view power as related to level of authority. And surprisingly, in light of traditional German stereotypes, they view power less favorably than their American counterparts. Hence, the ideal-type authority cluster is different in the U.S. and Germany. Andreas Schneider, "The Ideal Type of Authority in the United States and Germany." *Sociological Perspectives*, 47, 2004.

12. Weber's positions are presented in David S. Owen and Tracy B. Strong, *Max Weber, The Vocation Lectures*. Indianapolis: Hackett, 2004. (Included are Weber's lectures on science as a vocation and politics as a vocation.) For a critique of Weber's position, see Basit B. Koshul, *The Postmodern Significance of Max Weber's Legacy*. New York: Palgrave Macmillan, 2005.

13. See the essays in, Diego Gombetta (Ed.), *Making Sense of Suicide Missions*. London: Oxford University Press, 2005.

14. *The Methodology of the Social Sciences,* p 4.

15. Alvin W. Gouldner, *The Coming Crisis of Western Sociology*. New York: Basic Books, 1970.
16. Devra Davis, *When Smoke Ran Like Water*. New York: Basic Books, 2002.
17. For a general assessment of the issue, see Jay A. Ciaffa, *Max Weber and the Problems of Value-Free Social Science*. Lewisburg, PA: Bucknell University Press, 1998.
18. *The Theory of Social and Economic Organization*, pp 124-26.
19. For further discussion, see Sanford Dornbusch and W. Richard Scott, *Evaluation and the Exercise of Authority*. San Francisco: Jossey-Bass, 1975.
20. Ibid., p 125.
21. R.A. Sydie, *Natural Women, Cultured Men*. New York: New York University Press, 1987, p 54.
22. Translated from *Staatssoziologie*, p 101, in Reinhard Bendix, *Max Weber*. New York: Doubleday, 1960, p 332.
23. Weber's major analysis of music is in a posthumous book entitled, *The Rational and Social Foundations of Music*. For a brief summary and analysis that relates symphonic development to rationality, see Thomas W. Segady, "Consequences of the Increasing Rationality of Music," *Sociological Spectrum,* 13, 1993.
24. Weber discussed types of rationality in Chapter 2 of, *The Protestant Ethic and the Spirit of Capitalism*. Los Angeles: Roxbury, 2002.
25. George Ritzer, *McDonaldization*. Thousand Oaks, CA: Pine Forge, 2000.
26. For further discussion, see Marcel Gauchet, *The Disenchantment of the World*. Princeton, NJ: Princeton University Press, 1999.
27. George Ritzer, *Enchanting a Disenchanted World*. Thousand Oaks, CA: Pine Forge, 2005.
28. These advertisements appeared in the New York City, *City Guide*. June 21, 2007.
29. Michael Roberts, "Pragmatic Action and Enchanted Worlds." *Social Analysis,* 50, 2006, p. 93.
30. *The Theory of Social and Economic Organization,* pp 131-32, italics in original.
31. There is a substantial literature on this topic. See, for example, Ryan W. Quinn, "Flow in Knowledge Work." *Administrative Science Quarterly,* 50, 2005; and Forrest Briscoe, "From Iron Cage to Iron Shield?" *Organization Science,* 18, 2007.
32. For further discussion of the conditions leading to centralized bureaucracies, see Edgar Kiser and Joshua Kane, "Revolution and State Structure." *American Journal of Sociology,* 107, 2001.
33. *The Theory of Social and Economic Organization,* p 337.
34. Max Weber, *Economy and Society,* vol 2. Berkeley: University of California Press, 1978, p 1000.

Max Weber (2)

On Social Organization

In this chapter we turn to several of Weber's analyses of social organization, specifically including the Protestant ethic and capitalism, city life and social stratification. In his examination of each of these topics, the reader will recognize many of the concepts and methods of analysis introduced in Chapter 5. Particularly noteworthy is his continued focus upon the subjective meanings of behavior. In addition, Weber continues to stress the importance of legitimation in shaping wide-spread patterns of behavior, and to show how distinctive forms of rationality impinge upon every aspect of social life.

THE PROTESTANT ETHIC AND THE SPIRIT OF CAPITALISM

We begin with Weber's analysis of how capitalism's development was shaped by the "new" Protestant religions (he called them sects) that emerged as part of the sixteenth century Reformation. These new religions included groups we now know as: Presbyterians, Methodists, Lutherans, Congregationalists, etc. His thesis was initially presented in a couple of lengthy journal articles, later published (under his wife's editorship) as a book entitled, *The Protestant Ethic and the Spirit of Capitalism* (*PESC*).[1] It is probably his best remembered work, the theory with which people today most associate his name.

A Non-Material Theory

Weber defined the spirit of capitalism by a number of inter-related orientations that were widely shared. At its core, it consisted of a rational, systematic, highly self-controlled commitment to accumulate wealth. In *PESC*, Weber was primarily interested in explaining the orientations that supported capitalism rather than the actual (or objective) structure of capitalism, as an economic system. This approach ran counter to the then prevailing intellectual current in Europe, which had a strong Marxian influence. Marx, 50 years earlier, had emphasized a *materialistic* approach which insisted that the most important qualities in defining capitalism were its distinctive patterns of ownership and class structure. Weber's approach, with its (subjective) emphasis upon people's attitudes and ideas, was clearly *non-materialistic*.

Weber justified his non-materialistic approach by presenting some historical evidence of how the spirit of capitalism preceded the large-scale development of capitalistic economies. The (non-materialistic) orientation often came first, but it was usually confronted by other beliefs that were hostile to it. In some societies it remained a minority view while in others it became ascendant. Which outcome occurred determined how much a capitalistic system grew. Weber explained this relationship by claiming that capitalistic development required a set of beliefs that could legitimate the capitalist spirit. This is where the Protestant Ethic's emphasis upon hard work and self-discipline entered the picture. Unless some value system—like the Protestant ethic—provided legitimation, he concluded, the capitalistic spirit was unlikely to become wide-spread in any society, and without that, a capitalistic economy could not fully develop.[2]

To illustrate Weber's argument, let us begin by briefly examining Venice around the turn of the eighteenth century. The world's first large-scale banks had recently been established in the city, and Venice's banking activities supported its extensive manufacturing and global trade in woolens, silk, glass, etc. Outside of a small merchant class, however, people looked down upon those who strongly embraced a capitalist ethos. Shylock, in Shakespeare's *Merchant of Venice*, provides a graphic depiction of the capitalist as seen through the eyes of the larger society, even though he was a bit of a caricature of the (Jewish) merchant in Venice at the turn of the eighteenth century. In act two he learns that his daughter and her boyfriend, who he disapproves of, have fled and taken some of his ducats (i.e. money).[3] Shylock's ensuing monologue equally bewails the loss of his ducats and the loss of his daughter. Nothing, including his only daughter, meant more to him than his money, which Shakespeare expected would earn him the contempt of popular audience of the time.

By contrast, consider rural Pennsylvania at about the same time. Its core economic activity was carried out by small farmers and merchants, trade of any kind was hampered by unpaved roads, and banking was very rudimentary. By comparison to Venice, material conditions would not appear to have been conducive to capitalism, but the spirit of capitalism was widely exalted. Benjamin Franklin's advice about saving and accumulating wealth was popularly embraced with a fervor usually reserved for religion. (Some of Franklin's sayings are included in the following section.) Comparing people's beliefs in places like Venice and rural Pennsylvania indicated to Weber that the economic outlooks prevalent in a society were not a reflection of people's economic situations. In other words, material conditions did not produce ideas and values as "naive historical materialism" would postulate.[4]

Over the following centuries, capitalism evolved much further in rural Pennsylvania than in Venice. So, the ideas and values that embodied the spirit of capitalism apparently acted as a precursor to material developments. In one of his clearest expressions of this position, Weber argued that the expansion of modern capitalism was not propelled by any sudden infusion of new money, but by the spirit of capitalism.

> "Whenever this spirit becomes active . . . it *acquires* the money reserves to be used as fuel for modern capitalism's activity—not the other way around."[5]

As previously noted, *PESC* may be Weber's best remembered contribution. It may also be his most misinterpreted work, though, because it is often examined outside of his other writings on religion. In *PESC* he does try to show how a set of ideas and values, embodied in the Protestant ethic, provided a crucial legitimation for the ethos of capitalism, and thereby facilitated the development of large-scale capitalistic economies. It is also true that he viewed this thesis as contradicting a "naive" use of Marx's historical materialism which would contend that it is always the economic structure of a society that ordinarily determines people's interests and outlooks. However, it is not true that he regarded the primacy of ideas and values as an absolute rule. From his other writings on religion, which involved more diverse nations and longer time periods, it appears that he did not view any one type of variable as necessarily determining social and economic organization; and he explicitly said so in the conclusion to *PESC.* This takes us ahead of the story, though. We will return to these issues, but let us begin, as Weber did, with some observations about people's wealth, occupation and religion.

Protestant–Catholic Differences

Writing at the turn of the twentieth century, Weber noted that in societies with substantial numbers of both Protestants and Catholics, on average, the Protestants were in higher status occupations, were better educated, and were more likely to own businesses and factories. (To some degree, these differences have persisted.[6]) In addition, within nations, he noted that regions and cities with large Protestant populations tended to be wealthier than those made up predominantly of Catholics. Weber recognized that the relationship between religion and socio-economic measures, such as occupation and wealth, could be very complex, and he wrestled with how best to interpret which was cause and which was effect. For example, in many of the wealthiest cities in Europe he discerned that there had been a rush of conversions from Catholicism to various Protestant denominations during the sixteenth century. Subsequently, through inherited wealth, the Protestant offspring could afford better educations plus they had more capital, so their economic advantages persisted. Their religion was not the original causal variable in this case. On the other hand, differences in religion could have consequences for people's educational and occupational aspirations, and this was his primary argument in *PESC*. The most common pattern, he wrote, was for people's early exposure to different religious philosophies to have later effects on their socio-economic status. With respect to religion and occupation, for example:

> "The causal relationship is undoubtedly one in which a *learned inner quality* decides a person's choice of occupation. . . . And this learned inner quality is influenced by . . . the religious climate in one's native town and one's parental home."[7]

The primary difference in "inner qualities," Weber continued, was that Protestants were more inclined toward economic rationalism, which led them to be more fully engaged in commerce and industry, and to place more emphasis upon obtaining an education that would be appropriate to business careers. He saw Catholics, by contrast, as more estranged from the secular world, and therefore, less concerned with trying to be successful in terms of conventional socio-economic accomplishments.

To be precise, he was not looking at Protestant and Catholic orientations as literally inscribed in religious liturgy or as preached from pulpits. One could not understand the impact of the new Protestant sects, according to Weber, from an *objective* analysis of their scripture. Rather, it required an analysis of the everyday meanings that the faithful derived from the sacred scripts, and the way those meanings were applied to work, the community and the afterlife. Here Weber is continuing to stress the importance of *subjective* interpretations: how people view their own and other's behavior, justify it and imbue it with meaning. And he explicitly denied that the major Protestant reformers (Calvin, Luther and others) had any economic intent. Their goal was the "salvation of the soul . . . and that alone;" that their writings and teachings ultimately had a profound effect upon economic development was "unforeseen and even *unwanted* . . ."[8]

The Spirit of Capitalism

To lay out the core of the spirit of capitalism, Weber presented some lengthy excerpts from the writings of Benjamin Franklin, a man he considered to be an exemplar of this spirit. A couple of these quotes are condensed in the following. The first illustrates the emphasis (in Franklin's writings and in the spirit of capitalism) upon acquiring money and the second embraces the virtue of protecting it, so it can accumulate.

1. "Remember that *time* is money. He that can earn ten shillings a day . . . and . . . sits idle, one half of that day . . . has really spent, or thrown away, five shillings."[9]

2. "keep an exact account . . . of your expenses and . . . you will discover how . . . trifling expenses mount up . . . and will discern what might have been . . . saved, without . . . great inconvenience."[10]

Franklin's writings, as the previous quotations imply, were intended to be more than an economic primer. They were meant as a blueprint for how people should organize their lives. Constantly searching for opportunities to earn and save money at every opportunity was also more than desirable, it was one's moral duty, the mark of a person's virtue. Thus, acquiring and retaining wealth was the goal; and it was to be sought in a systematic and calculating manner. These are, of course, the same qualities that, in a different time and place, earned Shylock nothing but contempt.

Strict conformity with the spirit of capitalism also made the accumulation of wealth an end in itself, rather than a means to something else. "Striving for riches becomes suspect," Weber wrote, only if it is carried out in order to lead "a carefree and merry life once wealth is acquired."[11] Thus, there was an ascetic dimension to the spirit of capitalism (and to the Protestant ethic): an emphasis upon self-denial or a distrust of the spontaneous enjoyment of the money because any hint of hedonism was to be avoided. To the subjective orientation of the capitalists, a systematic pursuit of wealth seemed rational. However, from the standpoint of personal happiness, Weber wryly observed, this way of organizing people's lives may be irrational because they, "live for their businesses rather the reverse."[12]

As the depiction of Shylock illustrated, the spirit of capitalism was easy to caricature. The Scottish, the Dutch, and New Englanders, according to British sociologist Christie Davies, have traditionally been held up as relatively universal exemplars of (Protestant) groups whose lives personify the spirit of capitalism, and correspondingly they have been the butts of jokes. "They are comic because whenever money is at stake they are unable to break out of their . . . iron cage and follow the ordinary everyday . . . pattern of life."[13] Davies has assembled a large number of jokes about these groups, and they illustrate the spirit of capitalism because the humor is based upon exaggerating the proclivities of these people to hang on to their money. (Many of these jokes have actually circulated from Weber's day to the present.) A few examples are presented next, without naming any specific group; but any of the previously mentioned Protestant groups can be inserted into the following jokes:

- There was the _____ (member of the previously mentioned group), who always valued the wristwatch his dying father *sold* him on his deathbed.
- There was a _____ who was very ill, and complained to a friend, also a _____, that only an operation would save his life, but it would cost thousands of dollars. The friend replied that such an expenditure was terribly extravagant and asked, Do you think it is worth it?
- A _____ sat at a table and was about to order a drink when the waiter told him it would cost $9. He was ready to leave when the waiter

said it would only cost $6 for the drink if he stood at the bar. How much, the _____ asked, if I stand at the bar on only one leg?

What could business people do with the money they worked so hard to accumulate, but were restricted from spending on anything that might be seen as pleasure-seeking? Save it and reinvest it, Weber noted, a perfect recipe for the growth of a capitalist economy.

The Protestant Ethic

The way the writings of Luther, Calvin and other religious leaders of the Reformation were interpreted and acted upon by their early followers (i.e. the Lutherans, Calvinists and other Protestant sects) provided Weber with the model of an ideal type Protestant Ethic. Its key features are described next, beginning with the conception of "the calling." According to Weber, it encapsulated the single most widely shared and centrally important belief among all of the Protestant groupings.

THE CALLING   When the term "the calling" is used today, it is probably most often in relation to someone entering the clergy, as in the expression, he/she was "called" to the ministry. The implication is that there was a divine intervention in people's decisions; they did not just *happen* to become members of the clergy. The term is also occasionally used to describe people who decide very early in life that they are committed to becoming a doctor, lawyer, or the like. In such cases the profession is sometimes referred to as "their calling" and again, the implication is that there was heavenly guidance in their choice.

With the emergence of the Protestant sects during the Reformation, the idea of a calling was attached to whatever work a person did; a much more general view than that taken today. The butcher, baker and candlestick maker were all following their callings. And because the Protestant interpretation of the Bible indicated that their work was God's will—they had been called to it— they had to take their work seriously; treat their job, whatever it was, with a dedication and reverence.[14] To illustrate the significance of occupation and hard work to the Protestants, Weber again quotes from Benjamin Franklin's autobiography. Though not a religious person as an adult, Franklin vividly recalled how his strict Calvinist father repeatedly drilled one maxim from the Bible into him. "Seest thou a man vigorous in his *vocational calling?* He shall stand before kings (Prov. 22:29)."[15]

In medieval Catholicism, by contrast, work had no more moral salience than eating and drinking. Furthermore, Catholicism held a monastic ideal that glorified the monks' withdrawal from society to live in cloistered monasteries. In traditional Catholicism, Weber pointed out, the more an individual adhered to religious commitments, the more the person was driven out of conventional society. Among the Protestants, however, religious devotion was translated into the pursuit of vocational callings; performing God's work, in *this* world.

Catholic monasteries and monks were not admired because they represented disavowal of one's duties in society.

PREDESTINATION ANXIETIES   A key element in the cultural conflicts of the sixteenth century involved the marked difference between the Protestant doctrine of predestination and the Catechism of the Catholic Church which contended that heaven was a reward for a lifetime of good deeds. People could presumably tally their good (and bad) deeds, and use the net result to reckon their likely hereafter. However, by virtue of people's fall from the original state of grace, according to the Protestant sects, they are no longer able to prepare themselves for salvation. Some people are predestined for eternal life, others for everlasting death. God alone decrees, and how He decides is essentially a mystery, impossible for people to fathom. For a mortal to claim to know is, "a presumptuous attempt to intrude into God's secrets."[16] Therefore, commitment to one's calling, even though it was God's work on earth, could not literally be used to "purchase" salvation.

The belief in a fixed and unknown predestination created an enormous amount of anxiety for the Protestant faithful. The advice from their religious leaders was to have faith, and assume they were among the chosen. (The devil tries to make people doubt!) Working diligently in following one's calling could completely absorb people, according to the early Protestant ministers, and that was the only legitimate way they would be able to reduce their predestination anxieties. Nevertheless, being human, they were inclined continuously to try to monitor their state of grace, looking for a "sign." Even though it was not a logical deduction, most assumed that success in their calling could be such a sign. Would God permit a person to succeed in performing His work on earth if the person had not been predestined for eternal life? In the eyes of fellow Protestants, then, the successful business people were admired for their worldly accomplishments *and* because their attainments implied their status among those destined to be saved.

COMMUNITY TIES   In contrasting the Protestant sects that emerged in the sixteenth century with traditional Catholicism, Weber was struck by the difference in social bonds they advocated. This difference was expressed in a number of ways beginning with attitudes toward the sinners among them. Catholics had been instructed to feel compassion for people whose lives were in shambles because they drank too much, were caught stealing, etc. Everyone was weak and there, but for the grace of God, goes anyone. Among Protestants, however, sin was seen as a moral failure because it indicated a lack of self-control and because it inevitably detracted from people's efforts in pursuing their callings. In place of compassion, it was appropriate to feel, "a hatred and contempt for the sinner as an enemy of God . . ."[17] Furthermore, among Protestants one was not held similarly accountable for one's relations with others, in general. The Catholic insistence that everyone was their "brother's keeper" was replaced by the belief that every person faced their Maker alone. No priest, no sacraments, no community could help the Protestant acquire salvation. Every person needed to be self-reliant because no one could help them to alter their destiny. More competitiveness, in business dealings, was a consequence according to Weber. The Protestant's view did not authorized people to stab each other in the back in an economic realm, but it did weaken Catholicism's sanctions against being too competitive.

Social ties might have been strengthened in the Protestant community if each person's work had been viewed as enhancing everyone else's well-being, and thereby warranting appreciation. However, the occupational contributions each person made to others were interpreted as indirect and impersonal. Specifically, fulfilling one's calling, of paramount importance, was seen as promoting the social order God had in mind. If people benefitted also, so much the better, but that was not its primary intent. God's plan was seen as the beneficiary, and any inadvertent contribution to people was seen as an impersonal by-product that did call for feelings of attachment to the collectivity.

One aspect of the difference Weber described 100 years ago between the community attachments of Protestants and Catholics is analyzed in Research Box 6-1. The primary question the study examines is whether a religious difference in volunteering to help others in the community has persisted, at least within a U.S. sample.

RESEARCH BOX 6-1

Are Protestants' and Catholics' Community Ties Still Different?

The Publication

Daniel Rigney, Jerome Matz, and Armando J. Abney, "Is There a Catholic Sharing Ethic?" *Sociology of Religion*, 65, 2004.

The Research Question

According to Weber, capitalism was more easily legitimated in nations with Protestant rather than Catholic majorities because of an (ideal type) tendency for Protestants to be more individualistic and self-reliant while Catholics placed more emphasis upon community and sharing. Weber offered this thesis more than 100 years ago, though. Even if he accurately described differences in his day, the key question remains whether these differences have persisted. Is there still a distinctively Catholic ethic centered about sharing and helping others in the community?

The Data

In 1996 a national survey asked a representative sample of people in the U.S. how, with respect to religion, they identified themselves. From their responses they were classified as Protestant or Catholic. (There were a small number of people who could

(Continued)

not be classified as either: Jews, Muslims, unaffiliated persons, etc. They were not analyzed in this study.) All respondents were also asked whether they were doing volunteer work—helping others for no pay. Specifically, they were given a list of 15 areas in which they might be volunteers, including organizations devoted to improving health, the environment, education, etc.

The Findings

The investigators compared contemporary Protestant and Catholic volunteering patterns, and found that they were much more alike than different. People in both religions were most likely to volunteer in religious, educational and other youth organizations, and least likely to volunteer in arts, political and international organizations. In 13 of the 15 areas, the rates with which Protestants and Catholics volunteered were not significantly different. And when there were small, but insignificant differences, Protestants were as likely to score higher as lower than Catholics within each of the volunteer areas.

Because Protestants and Catholics have different racial and ethnic profiles, the investigators wondered whether those differences might be masking religious differences in people's willingness to give of themselves; but race and ethnicity had little effect upon the results. The similarities between Protestants and Catholics continued to far exceed the differences when people's other social characteristics were held constant.

In conclusion, the investigators offered several possibilities to consider. It is possible that Weber was wrong; that there is/was nothing distinctive about Catholicism with respect to sharing. Maybe all religions value it. Alternatively, they could once have been different, as Weber believed, but in recent decades American culture may have come to be dominated by a highly individualistic materialism. Perhaps Protestants and Catholics have become more alike as everyone has moved away from sharing with and helping others because they have all been engulfed by a selfish consumer culture.

Systematic Rationality

The traditional Catholic priest, Weber wrote, was a kind of "magician" who could miraculously (through the mass) provide the means of repentance and bestow hope for salvation. The Protestant doctrine of predestination, by contrast, eliminated all appearances of invoking supernatural powers, regarding them as sacrilege. Thus, the Protestant minister, unlike his Catholic counterpart, could not "magically" reduce the predestination tensions felt by members of the congregation. The faithful had to be self-reliant, and the Protestants viewed God as requiring methodical and systematic self-reliance. They did not allow for a cycle of sin, atonement, penitence and relief (likely to be followed by additional sin).

Weber also described the Protestant–Catholic difference as though it entailed two separate accounting schemes. Weakness (i.e. sin) could be offset by good deeds, among Catholics. Admirable actions were, in a sense, credited to the believers' heavenly accounts, and could offset their evil actions.

> "Catholic's good works and duties were . . . not . . . *rationalized* into a life-*system*. Rather they remained a series of *isolated* actions . . . to atone for specific sins . . . or . . . at the end of the believer's life, to acquire insurance credits, so to speak."[18]

Salvation for Protestants, by contrast, required that their entire lives be subject to a continuous and rational monitoring. Their eternal fate would not be based upon a net balance, but upon whether they had rationally and methodically organized their entire life to control their emotions; and there was no "magician" to intervene and no community that could help.

Conclusions

In sum, Weber described the spirit of capitalism as expressed in people who were shrewd, steady and calculating as they devoted themselves to acquiring and accumulating wealth. This economic ethos was encouraged by a Protestant ethic that emphasized work as God's calling, viewed people as standing alone, and advocated a systematic and rational approach to life. In other words, the Protestant ethic provided a necessary legitimation for the spirit of capitalism which, in turn, enabled a capitalistic economic system to grow. However, Weber did not regard the Protestant ethic as having "caused" capitalism, in spirit or practice, in any conventional sense of the term. It would be "foolish," he wrote, to believe that capitalist economic systems were created by the Protestant Reformation because many forms of capitalism pre-dated the Reformation. Causes must precede their presumed effects. Where the values and ideals espoused by the Protestant ethic took hold, they enabled the pre-existing capitalistic economic ideas and practices to flourish, but did not cause them.

Furthermore, Weber did not intend to overly generalize the results of this investigation. As noted previously, he thought that attitudes and values (the non-material dimension) *could* lead to (material) social conditions, and he believed he illustrated that position in *PESC*. However, he thought that the reverse sequence—from material to non-material—could also occur. "Both are equally possible," he concluded.[19]

THE DECLINE OF HOUSEHOLDS

The most basic social unit in most societies, Weber wrote, was the household. In some ancient societies, it was the only important social unit, but as the household became incorporated into successively larger aggregations, it lost many of its functions. All of the activities that were once carried out within households, he wrote, later became associated with more specialized institutions. To be specific, the household formerly offered protection for its members, but in modern societies, protection is provided by governments and militias. Households were once organized into units of production, working together on crops or crafts. Now family members work away from the home and each other. Households once provided the setting in which people acquired education and cultural values, but these are now obtained externally, from schools, bookstores, theaters, etc.

The institutional developments described earlier ultimately deprived households and families of most of their social vitality, according to Weber. As their former functions were moved to other institutions, households faded from prominence in the larger social organization. In addition, he argued, the rational orientations that were slowly becoming pervasive were further eating away at family units from within. This was, of course, one of Weber's most persistent themes: the increase in rational calculation and its penetration into every realm of human action. Moving back a step, he (again) identified a money economy as a major source of rationality. When people worked as part of a household in a pre-money economy, the family grouping seemed "natural" to them. Everyone in the household worked in the fields, for example, and no alternative arrangements occurred to them. People did not scrutinize their contributions or rewards, and wonder whether they should be doing less or getting more. However, the rational calculations that Weber associated with money changed everything within the household unit.

"Even when the household unit remains outwardly intact, the internal dissolution of household . . . by virtue of the growing sense of calculation . . . goes on irresistibly in the course of cultural development."[20]

Money changes everything, Weber wrote, by making it possible for people to assess the precise value of their productive contributions to the household. And when they can assess it, they do. In addition, goods and services can be freely purchased in most sectors of a money economy—everything is for sale—so that money provides the medium by which (earnings from) production can be exchanged for (items for) consumption, and that exposes both production and consumption to people's rational calculation.

The epitome of rational social action, Weber wrote, occurs in the market where people are free to shop and bargain, and buying and selling commodities is the only motivation that brings them together. All kinds of distinctions among people break down because it is expected that the seller's price will not vary in relation to any of the personal characteristics (such as race or gender) of the buyer. "As the money economy expands . . . it . . . creates a steadily increasing interest . . . in the possibility of . . . exchange with the highest bidder, even though he be an outsider."[21]

Contemporary examples of what Weber meant by markets would include stock exchanges and shopping malls. Weber, thinking historically, focused upon smaller retail and commercial concentrations. All of the current and historical examples share one important quality, though: every market involves the most impersonal relations into which people can enter, being oriented solely to the products they want to buy or sell. Each party only expects every other party to behave rationally, legally and formally—nothing more. In this respect marketplaces are unique social entities in that they lack the kind of personal ties among people that are typically part of family groups, sport teams, fraternities and most other human associations.

Weber's historical research suggested a strong relationship between the dissolution of households and the development of a money economy, but it was not a perfect relationship. In China, for example, the principle of filial piety, supported by Confuscianism, led offspring to deny themselves the use of their deceased father's property and to engage in extended mourning periods. These rituals may once have fit in the society, but given the changes that occurred in China's economic conditions, associated with a money economy, Weber regarded the continuation of these traditional family practices as "irrational" exceptions to the rule.

CITY LIFE

In Weber's hierarchy of social organization, neighborhoods followed households, but he considered them of limited sociological importance. Their boundaries were generally too open, and participation in them was typically too infrequent for them to be significant. Neighborhoods are relegated to a secondary status, especially in a modern urban context, because they do not ordinarily serve economic or political functions. Furthermore, while people's close relationships to their neighbors are frequently espoused as an ideal, Weber believed it was uncommon in fact. Particularly if the neighborhood is a part of a large city, indifference toward other people in the community tends to predominate.

Turning next to cities, Weber analyzed many types of cities in different historical periods, then tried to describe them as ideal types. He found the task difficult, but concluded that the key defining features were large population size and homes built closely to each other in a settlement so extensive that inhabitants could not know much about each other as distinct individuals. Where modern cities were concerned, he added the presence of a fixed marketplace as part of the definition, and regarded impersonal orientations as so strongly associated with marketplaces that such orientations also became a feature of ideal type cities.

Weber regarded population size as a very important attribute, but he was reluctant to rely solely upon size in defining cities because his historical research had disclosed communities in which people's orientations seemed inconsistent with the size of their community. In Russia, for example, he noted some villages with thousands of inhabitants where intimate relations among residents tended to predominate. By contrast, he was aware of some communities of only a few hundred people in Poland where relations among inhabitants apparently had been much more impersonal. Exceptions could occur, he wrote, because the effects of population size upon people's orientations and relationships can be mitigated by cultural variables.[22]

Given his hesitancy to define cities exclusively according to size, Weber proceeded to add economic characteristics to the definition of cities. Specifically, he wrote that cities were dominated by trade and commerce, rather than agriculture, and correspondingly contained a fairly extensive range of occupations and trades, especially when compared to agricultural communities. The precondition for these economic characteristics is the presence of a relatively fixed market, involving regular rather than occasional exchanges of goods and services. Thus, Weber claimed, "the city is a market settlement."[23]

Many sociologists were introduced to Weber's definition of cities by Louis Wirth. The German-born Wirth emigrated to the U.S. in the 1920's, and studied at the University of Chicago. He became an important part of the group of pioneering urban sociologists collectively referred to as, "the Chicago School." One of Wirth's most significant contributions was his presentation of the first systematic definition of cities and the urban way of life attendant to them. Among the efforts to define cities that preceded his own, Wirth believed that Weber's formulation had been the most important, and he acknowledged an intellectual debt to him and then proceeded to elaborate upon the variables Weber had identified. Specifically, the distinctive demographic features of cities, according to Wirth, included their: large size, high density and extensive heterogeneity. Assumed to be associated with this demographic profile were a number of personal proclivities of urbanites, with impersonal orientations foremost among them.[24]

The large and dense settlement of cities, Wirth wrote, was associated with excessive stimulation. People in cities were bombarded with horns and lights, and by the possibility of too many potential other people with whom to interact. To adapt, they psychologically removed themselves from their surroundings. Acclimating to city life, according to Wirth, meant becoming aloof and detached. If people related at all to most of the other people they saw or passed on the street, it was only in a superficial, very impersonal manner. None of the other people's distinguishing personal characteristics were even noted, let alone taken into account. Urbanites' behavior thereby lost the subjectively meaningful quality that Weber had stressed.

The impersonality of city dwellers, as emphasized by Weber and Wirth, has been examined by numerous studies of helping behavior. The assumption behind most of the research is that if people are detached from each other in large, dense cities then they will be less likely to help each other, even if helping does not require that they really put themselves out very much. In Research Box 6-2 several different types of helping behaviors are examined across a diverse sample of cities both in the U.S. and throughout the world.

RESEARCH BOX 6-2

City Size, Culture, and Helping Strangers

The Publication

Robert V. Levine, et al., "Helping in 36 U.S. Cities," *Journal of Personality and Social Psychology*, 67, 1994; and "Cross-Cultural Differences in Helping Strangers," *Journal of Cross-Cultural Psychology*, 32, 2001.

The Research Question

People living in large, densely populated cities are confronted by an extensive number of other people in their everyday lives. They respond, according to numerous theories, by not getting involved with most strangers; keeping them, psychologically, removed. If the size and density of cities leads to de-personalization, then people in the largest and most dense cities will be less likely to help strangers. A related question, following Weber, concerns the impact of culture, and whether it mitigates the effects of size and density, as he believed.

The Data

The investigators observed randomly selected people in downtown areas of cities that varied in size and density. They tested their sample's willingness to help in a variety of ways, including: walking almost up to a pedestrian and appearing accidentally to drop a pen or a pile of magazines, wearing dark glasses and carrying a cane, waiting near a stop light at a corner as a passerby approached and so on. In each case the key question was: Did the stranger help, offer to help, or just ignore the researcher?

The first study was carried out in 36 U.S. cities, varying from small in size (e.g. Canton, Ohio and Shreveport, Louisiana) to very large (e.g. Los Angeles and New York). The second study was conducted in 23 cities around the world. These global cities varied from moderately large (e.g. Sofia, Bulgaria and San Jose, Costa Rica) to very large (e.g. Calcutta and Mexico City).

The Findings

In the largest and more densely populated U.S. cities, strangers were less likely to help people who lost a pen or dropped a pile of magazines. They were also less willing to offer change for a quarter. However, the size and density of cities did not correlate with people's willingness to help a blind person cross the street or mail an apparently lost letter. The researchers concluded that when helping requires a spontaneous reaction, then helpfulness is lower in the large and dense cities. By contrast, when strangers must think before they can act, in helping a blind person cross the street, for example, then the characteristics of cities are unimportant. A small cultural

(Continued)

effect may also have been indicated by a slight tendency for people to be most help-ful, overall, in Southern U.S. cities.

In the global study, there was only a weak and insignificant tendency for peo-ple in larger cities to be less helpful, regardless of what kind of help was involved, but cultural variables may have "overwhelmed" the effects of size. For example, in all five of the Latin and Hispanic cities, strangers were above average in helping, regardless of city size. The investigators speculated that this may be due to a cultural script in these nations that stresses amiability and helping. Further, Latinos in all cities were more likely to smile warmly when they helped the stranger, and seemed genuinely to welcome the experimenter's "thank you." Thus, as Weber anticipated, it appears that culture can condition the effects of size and density upon a city dweller's helpfulness.

STRATIFICATION

Weber's major essay on social stratification—"Class, Status and Party/Power"—was only about 15 pages long. He viewed stratification as entailing three dimensions, each of which was noted in the title to the essay. In many of his other writings, he examined these three dimensions in various historical con-texts. However, his primary analysis of how the three dimensions generally intertwined was in this enormously influential 15-page essay that was pub-lished posthumously. As a result of the essay's brevity, some questions have lingered concerning exactly how Weber conceptualized the relationship among these dimensions, and the degree to which his conceptualization was intended to refute Marx's theory. We will consider both issues in the following discussion.

Class

By a *class* Weber meant a *category* of people who more-or-less shared the same *life chances* in so far as those life chances were determined by their *market situation.* To explain what he meant, let us begin by examining life chances. They refer to the likelihood a person in any (class) category will typ-ically be able to acquire particular commodities and/or to afford certain ser-vices or experiences. Examples would include having the wealth to own a mansion, ski in the Alps or run for the U.S. Senate. He recognized that any person's life chances could be affected by a wide range of variables: luck, inherited intelligence or personality characteristics, etc. To illustrate, in run-ning for the Senate, one's chances of being elected would improve with: an attractive appearance, intelligence, a degree from a prestigious university, a prominent family name, etc. However, at least a portion of each of these vari-ables is tied to a person's economic situation. In defining class by shared life chances, Weber included only that part of life chances that was determined by people's economic (i.e. market) situations. To some degree this was a hypothetical distinction, drawn for conceptual purposes, because he was not interested in specifying the exact proportion of life chances that was due to people's market positions.

To explain how segments of the population came to share the same life chances, Weber claimed that people could typically be placed into either of two basic categories: those who owned property and were therefore in an advantaged position and those who,

> "being propertyless, have nothing to offer but their services . . . in order barely to subsist. . . . 'Property' and 'lack of property' are, therefore, the basic categories of all class situations."[25]

Weber's two class categories, it is important to note, are essentially the same as those in Karl Marx's earlier distinction between the bourgeoisie (owners) and the proletariat (laborers).

Weber, like Marx, was looking at capitalist economies in which shipping, petroleum, railroads, and so on, were in the hands of a few barons; and most people worked as laborers in factory assembly lines, in shipyards and rail yards, etc. With changes in technology and the labor force that have occurred since the theorists died, their two-class distinction based upon ownership is no longer an adequate way of summarizing class variations. Class stratification is more complex. However, stratification based upon class—meaning life chances due to market situations—remains very significant. There is even some evidence to suggest that class is becoming a more important dimension of stratification, though different ways of defining and measuring class give inconsistent pictures. In general, it appears that people's perceptions tend to underestimate the amount of class stratification or how strongly it affects life chances. Following are some illustrative studies.

Perceptions of Class

The New York Times did an analysis of class in which they first asked people how they saw themselves. In a 2005 telephone poll, the *Times* found that most people called themselves, "middle class." Among the very wealthiest (with household incomes over $150,000) it was a little more common for people to refer to themselves as, "upper middle class;" and among the very poorest people (household incomes under $30,000) "working class" was a more common self-identification. Even in the extremely high and low wealth categories, though, large numbers of people continued to refer to themselves as, "middle class."[26] If class is to be defined by people's self-conceptions, then this finding would suggest that there was relatively little class variation among Americans. If everyone's class position was pretty much the same, then it followed that their life chances could not be very different either—at least in so far as they were determined by class.

However, a very different picture of class emerged when the *Times* examined concrete trends between 1980 and 2005 rather than relying upon self-reports. The trend data indicated a clear link between life chances and class, further showing that some class differences had grown substantially. Specifically, wealth had become much more concentrated, as income in the wealthiest households grew about 10 times faster than in the rest of the society. A variety of life chances appeared to have correspondingly changed:

- Life expectancy increased overall, but was greater for the wealthiest than the middle income groups, and greater for the middle than lower income groups.
- The most affluent Americans became increasingly likely to live in economically segregated, highly advantaged, communities, "cocooned in their exurban chateaus."[27]
- The wealthiest families had fewer children and had them later in life, and therefore became even better able to "invest" in their children.
- The proportion of students in the most selective colleges who came from the wealthiest households increased.

A similar and very interesting example of how people's perceptions may not recognize class effects is provided by a retrospective study of 1958 high school graduates in New Jersey. Forty years after they graduated they were asked to recollect their experiences in what had, in 1958, been a mostly middle class school. A majority of the then middle class students, who had been the predominant group, remembered the school as generally lacking class distinctions. They claimed that they had been friends with almost everyone, and that the wealth of peers' families had been irrelevant. However, interviews with former students who had been in the minority because their families had been less well-off suggested a quite different picture. They remembered the school as being more stratified economically, and felt that class differences had affected students' life chances, such as being most popular among their peers. The 1958 graduates who came from poorer families remembered being "overlooked" by their wealthier classmates and being pushed to associate more-or-less exclusively with other students from families of similarly limited means.[28]

Weber's Criticism of Marx

Despite the agreement between Weber and Marx in some aspects of their conceptions of class, Weber went out of his way to express disagreement with Marx's analysis of class interest and class conflict. He did not mention Marx's name, but in the context Weber's reference to "a talented author" is clearly meant to be Marx.[29] Marx had previously argued that class situations produced class interests which the proletariat (i.e. the propertyless) would eventually discern, and that when they recognized their class interest it would lead them to band together in a class struggle.

One of Marx's mistakes, according to Weber, was assuming that everyone who owned property was alike, and that everyone who did not was alike. Within the two broad categories, people's perceived class situations are differentiated, according to Weber, by economic sectors. There is typically little feeling of kinship between those who own factories and those who own apartment buildings, or between those who work on ranches and those who work in mines. Because workers see themselves as miners, ranch hands, factory workers and farm laborers—not as proletariat—they will not form solidary groups.

To act in concert, Weber wrote, people must feel that they belong together; and people who have been placed in classes by sociologists do not typically share this feeling. In other words, abstract class categories do not correspond with people's actual self-conceptions, or the way they see their self-interest. Thus, Marx's most fundamental mistake, according to Weber, was in assuming that a class either was or would become a community; or to be specific, that the proletariat would act on their economic self-interest. "For however different life chances may be, this fact in itself . . . by no means gives birth to 'class action'."[30]

Status

Weber defined *status*, his second dimension of stratification, as a *style of life* associated with a distinct *social circle*. Within a society he assumed that different styles would be subject to positive or negative rankings with respect to prestige or honor. Almost anything could be ranked, but some common examples could include: the way people dress, their use (or non-use) of drugs and alcohol, the recreational activities they prefer, or any other quality generally shared by a distinguishable set of people. In every case, Weber assumed a lifestyle would be associated with a social circle that might actually be a community in which people interacted with each other. Alternatively, a social circle could be more amorphous. In the latter case, there would be little direct interaction among all the people who were in the status group, but the possibility of it would remain, and members would share a sense of belonging, or of sharing something significant. In sum, by contrast to the class dimension, which was an objective designation, status groupings did imply subjective feelings and at least the possibility of communal interaction.

Weber devoted a good deal of attention to the degree to which status was derived directly from class. If there were a 1:1 correspondence between them, then even though he could conceptually distinguish between class and status, he realized that the distinction would be of little importance. However, he insisted that class rankings did not always perfectly translate into status groupings, though in the long run he believed the two would usually be highly inter-related. (Their relationship is illustrated in Figure 6-1, at the end of this chapter.) It may be, he wrote, "that only the families coming under approximately the same tax class dance with one another."[31] (Dances, for Weber, reflected people with similar life-styles.) On the other hand, he presented examples where class and status diverged from each other. Thinking of people with very recently acquired wealth who spent it on flashy, showy, garish objects, he wrote that high status honor "normally stands in sharp opposition to the pretensions of sheer property."[32] By contrast, people of limited economic means might have higher status than one would expect if they knew how to spend their money tastefully. Thus, Weber wrote, classes are stratified by relations of *production* while status groups are stratified by their *consumption* of goods.

Status groups and especially high status groups, Weber wrote, typically restrict access to their social circle. They control the boundaries of their social circle against "incursion" by people they consider outsiders. The means by which status groups regulate access are varied, but typically include endogamous marriages, that is, a preference for marriage between persons who are within the same social circle. The principle of endogamy is sometimes supported by laws which prohibit violations. For example, in some societies, people are severely punished if they try to marry someone who is in a different racial group or caste from themselves. They might be imprisoned or forfeit any inheritance they would have otherwise received. Much more prevalent among modern societies are informal norms, in which people whose marriages violate the principle of endogamy will likely be shunned. Members of a high status group, for example, might no longer invite a former member to dinner parties if he/she married a pretentious newcomer.

In many instances it can appear that the effects of class and status, of life chances and life choices, combine in a way that makes it difficult to state where one begins and the other ends. Restaurants, and food in general, provide interesting illustrations of the interplay between classes and status groups. According to Wright and Ransom there has recently been a growing emphasis upon food as a signifier of class and/or status as part of the proliferation of television food channels, international cooking schools, celebrity chefs, etc.[33] For example, fancy "farm weekends" have, in many parts of the country, become a sought-after activity of the consumption-conscious upper middle class. The economic and symbolic dimensions are simultaneously involved as these weekends are expensive, which would tend to exclude persons of lower classes; and they appeal to certain life-styles, so the weekends enable various groups to differentiate themselves from others on the basis of group members' subjective tastes.

It is also common for people's class and status to be simultaneously distinguished by food and drink preferences generally. Consider the difference between social circles that consume caviar and imported French champagne and those who prefer salted peanuts and a keg of beer. Here again class and status overlap, which can make it difficult to identify where one begins and the other ends. The distinction between them is clarified in Research Box 6-3.

RESEARCH BOX 6-3

The Different Effects of Class and Status

The Publication

Tak Wing Chan and John H. Goldthorpe, "Class and Status: The Conceptual Distinction and Its Empirical Relevance." *American Sociological Review*, 72, 2007.

The Research Question

Weber clearly differentiated between class and status hierarchies as concepts; but can the effects of each be distinguished empirically? To answer this question, the investigators developed measures of both class and status, then examined the effects of each in various areas of people's lives. If the effects of each were different, then class and status can be empirically distinguished.

The Data

All of the data were obtained from large surveys conducted in England during 2001 and 2002, and in some instances involved reexamining a cohort that had first been interviewed in 1991. The class position of respondents was indicated by their relationship to labor markets and production units: professionals, such as doctors and lawyers, and high level managers and officials at the top; self-employed workers, small employers and technicians in the middle; and factory and agricultural workers and other general laborers at the bottom. These different class positions are characterized by different patterns of constraint and opportunity.

The status dimension was indicated by patterns of close friendships. The investigators assumed that intimate relationships, such as close friendships, typically imply social equality or, at least, that they are most likely to form between people who perceive themselves as more-or-less equal in terms of status. Status scores were given to the occupational groupings based upon the similarities of close friendships among people within them. These status scores correlated only weakly with the class scores, reinforcing the assumption that they measured different phenomena.

The Findings

To focus upon economic life chances, the investigators studied people's long-term periods of unemployment and earnings curves across their working lives. Both of these indicators correlated strongly with their class, as anticipated; and taking status also into account did not significantly increase the correlation. Thus, as Weber expected, economic life chances reflected class. The investigators then turned to cultural consumption, viewing it as expressing symbolic rather than economic distinctions. They utilized a variety of measures, including: attendance at art museums,

(Continued)

ballets, movie theaters and concerts. Across every realm they found a tendency for people to fall into one of two categories: (1) those who were interested in a wide range of activities within the genre—for example, attending rock concerts, classical music, opera and jazz performances; and (2) those whose interests were confined to a single popular type, such as rock.

Which of the two categories people were in bore almost no relationship to their class position. However, the effects of status were strong in every cultural realm. The investigators concluded that differences in life-style were expressions of status rather than class. Furthermore, the clear distinction between the class (economic life chances) pattern, on the one hand, and the status (life-style) pattern, on the other, provides unambiguous support for Weber's emphasis upon the distinction between class and status.

Party/Power

Parties, the third leg of Weber's stratification system, consist of people who, in the face of *opposition, collectively* seek to attain *power*. So intimate is the connection between parties and power-seeking that the third dimension of Weber's model is sometimes considered power rather than parties. The key feature which makes an organized group a party is that its actions "are always directed toward a goal which is striven for in planned manner."[34] A party need not be formally recognized as such, as long as its actions meet the criterion. Thus, while the Democratic Party would be recognized as a party, the National Rifle Association might not be; but because an important part of its reason for being is to influence legislation involving gun ownership, and other groups are organized in opposition to its goals, Weber would consider organizations like the NRA also to be parties.

Parties can form, Weber wrote, on the basis of class interest. Examples would include most trade unions or chambers of commerce. While people in each of these types of organizations engage in some purely social and charitable activities, seeking power over opposing groups is a central reason for the organization's existence. Parties based upon class interest can be viewed as the vehicles by which economic interest is translated into communal action.

Conceptually, separating parties and classes was important to Weber for two reasons. First, he wanted to support his argument that class not be equated with class action: an additional process was necessary to link them, and that was where parties could fit in. Second, he contended that parties could also be based upon status. In this case, it would be life-style issues that galvanized a group to take action. A right to life or pro-choice organization illustrates the conversion of a status group into a party. In most instances, Weber believed that parties tended to form on the basis of a class and status mixture, that is, partly due to the influence of each. The Republican Party, for example, brings together people on the basis of class (attracting wealthier members by advocating lower

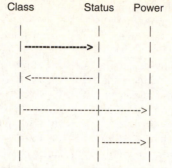

FIGURE 6-1   Class, Status and Power

taxes) and status (appealing to fundamentalists who believe the separation of church and state has been unnecessarily exaggerated).

Conclusion

It was important to Weber to expand Marx's conception of stratification with its strong emphasis upon material economic relations and interests, and that is why he stressed the potential "autonomy" of the status dimension, despite recognizing that it typically did depend upon class. Linking parties *both* to class and status, separately or together, provided him with another way in which to argue that status could not be totally reduced to class.

In sum, Weber viewed the three primary dimensions of stratification—class, status and power—as both interdependent and separate from each other, to varying degrees. Their inter-relationships, as described by Weber, are illustrated in Figure 6-1.

In this figure, the strength of the effect of one dimension upon another is illustrated by the thickness of the arrow going in that direction. So, the thicker arrow going from class to status than from status to class represents Weber's belief that class impacted status more than vice versa.

Endnotes

1. Max Weber, *The Protestant Ethic and the Spirit of Capitalism*. Los Angeles: Roxbury, 2002. This is the most modern translation of Weber's classic, translated and introduced by Stephen Kalberg. It has largely replaced the earlier translation by Talcott Parsons.

2. Collins presents an interesting parallel argument of how Buddhism in late medieval Japan provided a foundation for capitalism in Japan. See Randall Collins, "An Asian Route to Capitalism." *American Sociological Review*, 62, 1997.

3. See Act II, Scene VIII, in William Shakespeare, *The Merchant of Venice*. New York: Washington Square Press, 2004.

4. *PESC*, p 19. With the phrase, "naive historical materialism," Weber probably meant an unsophisticated use

of the theory that Marx popularized, rather than to imply that all historical materialism was naive.

5. Ibid., p 29.

6. In contemporary analyses of the relationship between religion and measures of socio-economic status, the simple distinction between Protestants and Catholics is not adequate. There are, in the U.S. for example, large differences among the many Protestant denominations. However, as recently as 2000, the education, occupation and income of mainline Protestant groups (Episcopalians, Presbyterians and others) in the U.S. continued, on average, to be substantially higher than Catholics; and between 1970 and 2000 the differences were not diminishing. See, for example, Ralph E. Pyle, "Trends in Religious Stratification." *Sociology of Religion*, 67, 2006.

7. *PESC*, p 6.

8. Ibid., p 48.

9. Benjamin Franklin, quoted in ibid., p 14.

10. Ibid., p. 15.

11. Ibid., p 109.

12. *PESC*, p 31.

13. Christie Davies, "The Protestant Ethic and the Comic Spirit of Capitalism." *The British Journal of Sociology*, 43, 1992.

14. The orientation to work associated with the Protestant Ethic continues to be widely examined. For the most part, recent research suggests that the Protestant–Catholic differences Weber described have largely disappeared. Cross-national differences are examined in F.S. Niles, "Toward a Cross-Cultural Understanding of Work-Related Beliefs." *Human Relations*, 52, 1999. Ethnic and racial differences in the U.S. are examined in Kevin Cokley, et al., "Ethnic Differences in Endorsement of the Protestant Work Ethic." *The Journal of Social Psychology*, 147, 2007.

15. *PESC*, p 18.

16. Ibid., p 64.

17. Ibid., p 74.

18. Ibid., p 69.

19. Ibid., p 125.

20. Max Weber, *Economy and Society*. Berkeley: University of California Press, 1978, p 376.

21. Ibid., p 638.

22. Max Weber, *The City*. New York: Free Press, 1966. p 65.

23. Ibid., p 67.

24. Wirth's essay, "Urbanism as a Way of Life," was originally published in 1938. The article is presented and discussed in, Jan Lin and Christopher Mele (Eds.), *The Urban Sociology Reader*. New York: Routledge, 2005.

25. Hans H. Gerth and C. Wright Mills, *From Max Weber: Essays in Sociology*. New York: Oxford University Press, 1946, pp 181–82.

26. Janny Scott and David Leonhardt, "Class in America." *The New York Times*, May 15, 2005.

27. Ibid., p 18.

28. Gender, ethnicity, and race also appeared to have been important, but frequently unrecognized, dimensions of stratification in the school. See Sherry B. Ortner, *New Jersey Dreaming*. Durham: Duke University Press, 2003.

29. From *Max Weber*, p 185.

30. Ibid., p 184.

31. Ibid., p 187.

32. Ibid.

33. Wynne Wright and Elizabeth Ransom, "Stratification on the Menu." *Teaching Sociology*, 33, 2005.

34. From *Max Weber*, p 194.

CHAPTER

7

Emile Durkheim (1)

Division of Labor and Elementary Religion

BIOGRAPHY

David Emile Durkheim was born in 1858 in the Lorraine region of Eastern France, near the German border. He was the youngest of four children in a family that was part of a close-knit and very observant Jewish community. His father was the Chief Rabbi: a position high in esteem, but low in salary. His father's father had also been a Rabbi, and he too began his early education at a rabbinical school, but soon decided not to continue in his family's footsteps.[1] Some scholars who have studied Durkheim contend that his sociological theories were shaped by his religious background—especially Judaism's traditional emphasis upon the whole community rather than the individual.[2] Most of the religion's prayers, for example, ask for the well-being of the entire collectivity rather than just the worshiper. Durkheim certainly did advocate against focusing upon individuals as individuals; but this intellectual position had much more than a religious basis. He spent much of his life trying to establish the new science of sociology as a discipline separate from psychology, and as an autonomous academic department in French universities. For this political agenda, he thought it important to steer a course for sociology that would not overlap with psychology's emphasis upon individuals.

Although young Durkheim did well in school, he always feared that he would not do well enough as a student. He was described as very serious about his studies, and everything else. This characterization of him as solemn apparently fit not only throughout his student days, but later as a professor. One sociologist who studied his life in some detail concluded, "It is not easy to picture Durkheim relaxing over a drink or laughing aloud at something funny . . ."[3]

When his formal education was completed, Durkheim taught in secondary schools for three years, studied in Germany for two more years, then took his first academic post at the University of Bordeaux in 1887. He was "officially" on the social science faculty since sociology was not yet a recognized academic discipline in French institutions.

It was during the same year in which he took a position at Bordeaux that he married. His wife devoted her life to tending the household and raising their two children so he would be free to study and write. And he surely did; colleagues described him as a workaholic.[4] He spent 15 years in Bordeaux (1887 to 1902), and they were the most productive of his career. During this period he published numerous articles, began *L'Année Sociologique* (which became one of the most influential sociology journals in the world) and completed three of his major books:

> *The Division of Labor in Society*, 1893, a revision of his dissertation; second edition in 1902.
>
> *The Rules of the Sociological Method*, 1895.
>
> *Suicide*, 1897.

Shown previously are the French publication dates. Most of his writings were not translated into English until many years later. For example, *The Division of Labor in Society*'s first English edition was in 1933—40 years after its initial publication. However, by then a number of leading American sociologists had been familiar with his work for a number of years.[5]

As Durkheim was completing *Suicide*, he wrote that he was pleased with the progress that had been made in establishing sociology as a specialty in its own right, but that the discipline's status remained precarious. What he believed necessary was an empirical study that would demonstrate "real laws" lying outside of the mental states of individuals because psychology already had a claim to that type of inquiry. But what to examine? What better than suicide?

> "Since suicide is an individual action, affecting the individual only,
> it must seemingly depend exclusively on individual factors, thus
> belonging to psychology alone."[6]

If he could demonstrate that suicide was socially patterned—that it varied in relation to societal conditions—he thought it would provide a powerful argument for the autonomy of sociology. His study of suicide, published in 1897, is generally acknowledged to be the first empirical study in sociology designed to test a theory.

In 1902 Durkheim was appointed to a position at France's leading university, the Sorbonne, but it was in education because sociology was still not an academic department. He brought the journal he had begun, *L'Année Sociologique*, with him. In Paris, along with his students and disciples he filled its pages with new studies, critiques of related work, book reviews, and essays that argued for a distinctive science of sociology. The interest in sociology that the journal created was an important source of momentum for the eventual establishment of sociology departments in the leading French universities. It was also during this period that he authored his last major book:

The Elementary Forms of Religious Life, 1912.

(Several collections of Durkheim's essays on education, socialism and other issues were later compiled and published posthumously.)

During his tenure at the Sorbonne, Durkheim attracted a group of young scholars who shared his passionate vision for the new discipline. His lectures to his students/followers were, at the time, described as resembling those of, "a prophet of some nascent religion."[7] He died in 1917, though his legacy, his books and articles, continue to be translated and read throughout the world, and *L'Année Sociologique* remains one of the most prominent sociology journals in Europe. Furthermore, many specialty areas within sociology—including social organization, religion, criminology, law and deviance—continue to rest upon a base that is strongly indebted to Durkheim's insights.

THE DIVISION OF LABOR

Durkheim's first book, *The Division of Labor in Society* (henceforward, *DoL*), was a revision of his doctoral thesis.[8] In that book he briefly sketched a theory of social change and provided a highly extensive analysis of the division of labor and its contribution to societies. Prior to describing this work, it is worth noting that in *DoL* he also outlined many of the issues he planned to explore in subsequent analyses, including suicide, religion and sociological methods. Thus, it can be read as a statement of the young Durkheim's intellectual agenda, an agenda he completed very successfully.

Social Change

Durkheim viewed social change as essentially involving an internal unfolding; that is, change that was not much influenced by events or conditions arising outside of a society, such as wars, the spread of inventions, immigration and so on. The internal change process, as he envisioned it, began with population growth, typically due to an increased birth rate. As populations grew, Durkheim noted an historical tendency for them not to expand geographically, leading to two consequences: increased physical density (the number of people per acre, mile, or the like) and increased "moral," or social, density (the rate of social interactions among people). Durkheim conceptually distinguished between the two types of density, but argued that empirically they were inseparable because neither could increase without corresponding increases in the other. Then he contended that the division of labor—the

{Physical Density}

Population Increase >>>>> { } >>>>>> Development of the Division of Labor

{Social Density}

FIGURE 7-1   Durkheim's Theory of Social Change

organization of tasks by which people in a society survive—developed as a direct consequence of the two types of density. It is not just that they "*permit a greater division of labor, but that they *necessitate* it.*"[9]

His view of change is summarized in Figure 7-1.

If we note that divisions of labor become increasingly complex over the course of time, Durkheim wrote, it is because societies continue to become physically and socially more dense.

Durkheim's theory, according to Gianfranco Poggi, rests on the ratio of the size of a population to the size of its territory. Once that ratio begins to increase, it puts pressure upon traditional arrangements in which people were largely self-sufficient and used little technology. In order for everyone to survive in a larger, denser society, people must become more specialized, hence less self-sufficient and more dependent upon each other.[10]

Durkheim's theory of societal change comprised a small part of *DoL*, just 25 pages in a book of about 350 pages. Perhaps at least partly this brevity revealed its apparent inadequacies; for example, Durkheim focused only upon two extreme types of societies: (1) very small with simple divisions of labor and (2) very large with complex divisions of labor. There are undoubtedly many other intermediate types of societies he did not consider. However, Durkheim's relative lack of interest in social change is historically significant. When he completed *DoL*, sociological theory was dominated by evolutionary theories, which of course stressed change, and the writings of Herbert Spencer, in particular. (Spencer was introduced in Chapter 1.) It was Spencer who coined the phrase, "survival of the fittest," and beginning in the 1850's he had written several influential volumes on sociology, as well as biology and psychology.[11] In these books, Spencer described evolutionary change as entailing a process of increased specialization, regardless of whether one was analyzing a society or a biological organism.

While Durkheim's frequent references to Spencer in *DoL* indicate that he was influenced by Spencer, he expressed an ambivalent view toward Spencer's writings—not because he rejected evolutionary theory, but because he did not believe that an evolutionary approach usually provided the best explanations in sociology. Instead, Durkheim advocated a functionalist perspective, in which each part of a society was examined in relation to its contribution to the society. To illustrate the difference between these two approaches, consider how each would likely examine contemporary religion. An evolutionary explanation might stress how the modern institution added specialized clergy, diverse holidays and an elaborate liturgy to simple practices that originally involved part-time shamans or witch doctors.

A functionalist explanation, by contrast, would probably note the way any religion, regardless of how complex or specialized its form, promoted solidarity within a society. Correspondingly, an evolutionary approach would devote little attention to the persistent contributions of a part (such as religion) to the whole (i.e. society), while the functionalist analysis would gloss over how the part came to evolve into its current form.

With respect to the division of labor, Durkheim argued that its major contribution to a society was to act like glue in binding people together; in other words, to promote solidarity or cohesion. While all divisions of labor serve this function, they do so in two fundamentally different ways, and Durkheim utilized the differences between them as the basis for distinguishing between two types of societies.

SOLIDARITY AND THE COLLECTIVE CONSCIENCE

The first type Durkheim identified was *mechanical solidarity*, and it was based upon a homogeneous division of labor. Typically small in size and density, societies with mechanical solidarity lack much in the way of specialization. There may be some differentiation based upon people's age or gender, but there are few differences among either adult men or adult women. Because he believed that people's outlooks were usually shaped by their positions in the division of labor, the relative absence of specialization was expected to result in a society in which each person's ideas and beliefs tended strongly to resemble those of everyone else. With mechanical solidarity, Durkheim wrote, each "individual personality is absorbed into the collective personality."[12]

In order to describe the feelings, values and ideas that most people in a society more-or-less shared, Durkheim used the term, *collective conscience*, and he specifically defined it as, "the totality of beliefs and sentiments common to the average members of a society."[13] In talking about the average members of a society, Durkheim was trying to provide a way to think about the collective conscience, perhaps even to measure it. However, he was emphatic that the collective conscience pertained to society, not to individuals. It

> "is diffused over society as a whole . . . . It is the same in north and south, in large towns and in small, and in different professions. Likewise, it does not change with every generation, but on the contrary, links successive generations to one another. *Thus, it is something totally different from the consciousness of individuals, although it is only realized in individuals.*"[14]

The second type of solidarity, *organic*, was based upon interdependence. It characterized societies that were typically larger in size and contained specialized groups. Because of occupational specialization, Durkheim expected there would be corresponding differences in the outlooks and values of butchers, bakers, candlestick makers and so on. The collective conscience recedes to the core of these societies, becoming "weaker and vaguer," though it remains capable of exerting great influence over people's actions. Put in other words, average people share less with each other, so there is greater (but not complete) individuality.

The butcher, baker, candlestick maker and so on each operate with a measure of autonomy, but none of them could be self-sufficient, though they may fail to fully appreciate how dependent they are upon each other. The reality is that none of the specialists could survive without the goods and services of the others. Problems arise in modern societies when various segments of a society fail to appreciate their interdependence, but Durkheim stressed that people's recognition of their interdependence would normally occur when they were in regular contact with each other (i.e. social density). Like many other features of societies, he thought solidarity simply occurred as a "natural" result of societal dynamics rather than due to intentional social planning. He wrote that since organic solidarity

> "is spontaneous, there is no need for any coercive apparatus either to produce it or to maintain it. Society has therefore no need to interfere in order to effect a harmony that is established of its own accord."[15]

A view of society as self-regulating and functioning without people's deliberate intervention runs throughout much of Durkheim's writing, and we will explore this issue in greater detail in Chapter 8.

Associated with each type of society are variations in social practices, beliefs and institutions. Law was the institution that Durkheim most extensively analyzed in relation to the two types of societies because he believed that the nature of law in a society was the most "visible symbol" of that society's type of social solidarity.

Law

Durkheim began his analysis of law by observing that as people enter into more relationships and interact more frequently with each other—that is, move from mechanical to organic solidarity—their new form of social organization will almost always be reflected by changes in the legal institution. Continuing, he proposed that laws be classified according to the types of sanctions that they employ. Corresponding with the two types of societies he conceptualized, Durkheim described two types of legal sanctions:

1. *Repressive:* Designed to hurt or punish the perpetrator of a crime, and serve as a warning to others, sanctions of this type may be applied by anyone in a society. (All penal laws are included here.)

2. *Restitutive:* Attempt to restore, or re-establish, the way things were prior to the actions that violated the law.* (Civil, commercial and other non-penal laws are included here.)

Durkheim looked at crimes and punishments in ancient Rome, Egypt, Germany and elsewhere, and compared them to crimes and punishments in more modern societies. His conclusion was that in societies with limited specialization—mechanical solidarity—there was a preponderance of repressive law. When the division of labor increased in complexity—organic solidarity—restitutive law came to predominate. This conclusion was not meant to imply that one type replaced the other, but rather that the ratio of restitutive to repressive law changed.[16]

In the simplest societies, where the collective conscience is least differentiated, all crimes are serious violations of shared morality. Repressive law, therefore, involves swift and direct punishment in order to dissipate the outrage that the violation created. Because this type of crime entails a violation of the collective conscience,

> "we cannot fail to react against it passionately. A mere re-establishment of the order that has been disturbed cannot suffice. We need a more violent form of satisfaction. The force that the crime has come up against is too intense for it to react with so much moderation."[17]

In complex societies, by contrast, where the collective conscience corresponds with a smaller core of shared values, not all crime offends the collective conscience so not all crime arouses people's ire. Suppose, for example, people believed that somebody was cheating on his/her income tax; or that he/she was speeding on the expressway. Would either of these acts seriously offend people's shared morality? Probably not. It would require specialized enforcement officials both to catch them (e.g. police, IRS agents) and to administer punishment (e.g. prosecutors, judges); and that punishment would likely take the form of a fine to make restitution rather than, say, a public flogging. Most crime in a complex society would be like cheating on income tax or speeding on a highway, and would involve restitutive sanctions.

In addition, the decline in normative consensus associated with the increased complexity of the division of labor may have political consequences that transcend the law. For example, in the U.S., Gibbs contends, interest groups—such as anti-abortionists, environmentalists and others—find it increasingly difficult to influence public opinion by relying upon moral or ethical appeals.[18] The electorate is simply marching to too many different tunes for any one such appeal to persuade everyone.

However, while the collective conscience has receded in modern societies, it has not disappeared, and the potential for repressive sanctions remains. To illustrate, consider how the average person would probably

---

*The legal concept, "to make whole," illustrates this objective because it is designed to redress any losses or suffering experienced by the victims of a transgression; for example, to reimburse them for damages, hence restore them to their previous condition.

respond if he/she saw a man drag a little girl into the bushes and begin to attack her. Virtually anyone who witnessed this action would feel outraged, and move to try to stop the assault: call 911 if they had a cell phone, yell for help, run into the bushes to stop the man. Everyone in the immediate area might run over, and a crowd might form, capable of severely beating the little girl's assailant. This type of collective behavior would illustrate the continuing possibility of purely repressive law, even in a large complex society, characterized by organic solidarity.[19]

The possibility of repressive law, in a segment of a contemporary society otherwise dominated by restitutive law, is examined in Research Box 7-1. The study focuses upon the sanctions that deter homeless youths from committing various types of crime in two of Canada's largest cities.

RESEARCH BOX 7-1

The Threat of Physical Harm as a Deterrent to Crime

The Publication

Bill McCarthy and John Hagan, "Danger and the Decision to Offend." *Social Forces*, 83, 2005.

The Research Question

In contemporary societies, characterized by organic solidarity, Durkheim viewed the punishment of crime as relying primarily upon the sanctions of a legal apparatus designed to dispense justice in an impersonal manner. Specialists (police, lawyers, judges, etc.) are involved, and their actions are expected to follow a technical legal code. This contemporary form of (restitutive) law largely replaced an earlier (repressive) form which relied upon ordinary people spontaneously and directly punishing perpetrators in a highly personal way. Even in a society in which restitutive law predominates, however, people's fear of being physically harmed if they engaged in certain forms of criminal behavior might act as an important deterrent. If so, it could indicate the simultaneous operation of repressive and restitutive types of law.

The Data

Over a two week period, the investigators attempted to locate all the homeless youths staying in shelters, hotels, parks and street corners in Toronto and Vancouver, Canada. They located nearly 500 such persons willing to be interviewed, and they asked each of them how frequently they had engaged in three types of crime: selling drugs, theft and prostitution. The investigators also obtained a good deal of background information from the respondents concerning their age, race, arrest history, etc. As part of the interview they also asked how dangerous the youths considered each of the three types of crime (discussed earlier) due to the possibility that in committing each they could be physically harmed by a violent reaction from a victim, bystander, vigilante, the police, etc.

The Findings

Those respondents who considered theft, selling drugs or prostitution to be very dangerous to themselves physically were several times less likely to engage in them than those who believed the acts to be relatively safe. These differences in the homeless youths' self-reported criminal behaviors remained even after differences in their backgrounds were held constant; that is, even when the researchers compared people whose backgrounds and prior criminal records were statistically matched.

The findings can be interpreted as indicating the persistence of aspects of repressive law even in a modern society, such as Canada, with fully developed restitutive law. Another possible interpretation is that a "balance" between repressive and restitutive law is maintained in any community; more of one type implies less of the other. Because homeless youths are living on the margins of society, the trappings of restitutive law may seem distant and without much relevance to them, leading to a resurgence in the significance of repressive law as the primary means of controlling behavior.

ECONOMIC HEGEMONY

As Durkheim envisioned the future, he expected that divisions of labor would continue to become more complex. With ever more specialization continuing to characterize societies, he wondered how organic solidarity could be maintained, and concluded that the division of labor would have to be the most important source of social solidarity. Economic interdependence would still be an objective fact, but it was crucial that people recognized it. He saw no alternative.

Durkheim was operating on the assumption that the economic institution was in the process of becoming the single most significant institution in modern societies. In the preface to the second edition of DoL, published (in 1902) nearly 10 years after the first edition, he wrote that while, "economic functions . . . previously . . . played only a secondary role, they have now become of prime importance."[20] He believed that the activities of all the other institutions—religion, politics, military, even the family—were simply being overwhelmed by this one institution.

The diminution of all the other institutions was occurring, he wrote, because in modern societies almost everyone spends their entire life in an industrial and commercial environment, and it fully involves them. Furthermore, he believed that economic activities had grown so specialized that no other institution remained capable of controlling them. In the past, by contrast, overlap with the family enabled it to regulate activities in all the other institutions, including the economic. For example, in a patrilineal society, the eldest male was head of the lineage, and also was automatically the chief, the military leader, etc.

Durkheim devoted a good deal of attention to the declining significance of families in general, and to their diminished ability to control economic life in particular. When the economy is simple, he wrote,

"The peasant's life does not draw him beyond the family circle. Since economic activity has no repercussions outside the home, the family suffices to regulate it . . . . But this is no longer so . . ."[21]

He also expected this trend to be even more pronounced in the future, that is, for the economy to become more ascendant in relation to the family.

In addition, when families controlled economic activity, social change was inhibited which made social integration less problematic. A very important mechanism by which families formerly maintained social stability in a society, he wrote, was inheritance. Specifically, at death, people's relatives received the wealth and possessions the deceased had accumulated, in whatever form wealth took in their society. As a result, the economic standing of families relative to each other remained the same as long as it was family members that received the wealth people bequeathed when they died.

"No change was even wrought through death, and the relationship of things to persons remained as they were, with no modification even through the accession of new generations."[22]

Research Box 7-2 examines Durkheim's prediction about the future of the family in relation to the economic institution. Following his assumptions, the study focuses specifically upon inheritance as an indicator of the standing of the familial and economic institutions relative to each other.

RESEARCH BOX 7-2
Family Inheritance Patterns

The Publication

T.P. Schwartz, "Durkheim's Prediction About the Declining Importance of the Family and Inheritance." *The Sociological Quarterly*, 36, 1996: 503–519.

The Research Question

Durkheim argued that economic activity was becoming increasingly important in modern societies, and that the salience of economic attachments might be replacing familial bonds. He did not explicitly offer a hypothesis predicting changes in inheritance. However, he did view the legacies and gifts that people bestowed in their wills as indicating the importance of relationships to them during their lives. For example, he noted the significance of the workingmen's corporations of ancient Rome to their members as follows:

> " . . . In corporations of workmen . . . they came together for the plea-sure of leading a life in common, to find outside their own home a dis-traction from their weariness and troubles, to create a less restricted form of intimacy than within the family . . . "[23]

When these workmen died, Durkheim noted that they often left their valuable pos-sessions to their corporation, and that their funeral monuments often stated their devotion to the corporation. Correspondingly, we might expect that, in modern soci-eties, as the economic institution increased in importance, the overall rate with which people left their worldly goods to family members might have declined while final bequests to co-workers, professional associations or the like might have increased. Whether inheritance patterns have changed over an extended time period is the cen-tral question of this research.

The Data

To test the hypothesis derived from Durkheim's theory, Schwartz examined a sample of 429 last wills filed in the Probate Court of Providence, Rhode Island, between 1775 and 1985. This time interval coincides with a period of substantial increase in Providence's size and density, and its occupational transformation from a pre-industrial to a modern city. If the future Durkheim anticipated has arrived and his prediction is correct, then we should expect there to have been a decrease in familial inheritance dur-ing the time period examined.

The Findings

Schwartz found that, in every time period he studied, family beneficiaries predomi-nated by a large measure. Most people left their worldly possessions to a spouse, sib-lings, their children or other kin. However, the number of non-kin who were named as beneficiaries did slightly increase over the 200 year period. Specifically, about three quarters of all wills involved a sole beneficiary, and the percentage of non-kin named in sole beneficiary wills increased from about 1% in both the eighteenth and nine-teenth centuries to about 8% in 1985, the most recent time examined. That is a small increase, but perhaps it is a harbinger of future trends. If the family, as an institution, continues to lose ground to the economy, perhaps that continuing change will even-tually be reflected by larger increases in non-kin beneficiaries. Schwarts concludes the study by reminding the reader that familial inheritance continues to predominate so "Durkheim's prediction has not been fulfilled as yet"—but, he notes, it may in fact prove true in the future.[24]

ANOMIE

The concept by which Durkheim is probably best known is *anomie*. He introduced it in relation to the division of labor to describe "breaks in organic solidarity" which occur when "certain social functions are not adjusted to one another."[25] Over-specialization of "organs"—that is, society's component parts—was frequently the culprit in Durkheim's view. Too much specialization in the economy leads to hostility between workers and owners and increased bankruptcies, he wrote, and in scientific research, overspecialization leads to the isolation of individual scientists and the fragmentation of science. Each of these problems arose because of anomie: insufficient regulation because the parts are not adequately adjusted to each other.

> "If the division of labor does not produce solidarity it is because the relationships between the organs are not regulated; it is because they are in a state of *anomie*. . . . We may say . . . that a state of *anomie* is impossible wherever organs linked to one another are in sufficient contact."[26]

Thus, Durkheim defined *anomie* as a lack of regulation due to the parts of a system not having had the opportunity to become adequately adjusted to each other. He believed it was probably a temporary condition, due largely to the transition from mechanical to organic solidarity not being complete. Some components had changed more than others and there had not been enough time for each of the components to discern their place relative to each other. For example, the economy had attained increased importance, and the family was no longer able to regulate its activities, and no other means of control had yet emerged. Over time, Durkheim expected the institutions would re-adjust to each other, but in the interim, there was anomie.

In principle, anomie could occur in a society characterized by either mechanical or organic solidarity. However, in her analysis of Durkheim, Susan Stedman Jones writes that specialized parts especially require coordination. So, close and continued contact between and among the parts is required more for organic solidarity than for mechanical solidarity. It is through repeated contact that, in a specialized society, groups of people become aware of their mutual dependence, or as Jones states, there is a "consciousness of solidarity through interdependence."[27]

In sum, anomie involves a lack of integration among the components of a system due, in Durkheim's view, to a lack of regular contact between them and an absence of normative regulation as a result of the disjunction. Many secondary sources define anomie as a lack of normative control, and that is correct as far as it goes, but to be entirely faithful to Durkheim, it is important to connect that lack of control to an insufficient melding of societal components.

Perhaps the best known application of Durkheim's theory of anomie is Merton's analysis of the relationship between two parts of the social structure: cultural goals and institutional means. By cultural goals he meant the attainments to which people generally aspire. In our society that would probably include such goals as: wealth, fame, status, etc. The *institutionalized means* refer to norms governing how people are supposed to attain the cultural goals. Depending upon the realm in which goals are sought, the generally approved alternatives could include: apprenticeships or training programs, playing in the minor leagues (or its equivalent), formal education or the like.

One of the major ways in which societies differ, Merton proposed, is in the degree to which there is a balance between these two aspects of their social structure. In American society he believed there was generally much more emphasis upon achieving success than upon the legitimacy of the methods employed. Thus, athletic teams want to win games, business firms want to make profits, and neither cares nearly as much about playing by the rules. Similarly, students tend to care more about grades than how honestly they earn them. The disjunction between means and ends, he concluded, indicates anomie, and results in "cultural chaos."[28]

Within contemporary criminology, Merton's theory has led to a theoretical emphasis upon deviance as a response to blocked opportunities. Everyone in a society is assumed to share more-or-less the same cultural goals. However, people in certain groups may lack access to the legitimate institutional means. For example, members of some ethnic groups may be excluded from certain training programs, schools or occupations. To succeed, they must then be "innovative" which often entails resorting to deviant means: selling drugs to buy expensive cars, committing fraud to attain wealth and stealing clothes to impress peers. The greater a society's emphasis upon success, and the more segments of the population confront institutional barriers, then the higher will be that society's crime rate. In the U.S., the "American Dream" encourages everyone to believe they are able to attain lofty goals, but the reality is that many people lack access to the legitimate means by which to obtain success. That is why, according to some analysts, the U.S. crime rate is consistently higher than that of otherwise similar nations, such as Canada, the U.K., etc.[29]

Note that the form of the previous explanation is highly consistent with Durkheim's preference, namely, it identifies societies' rates as the question for sociologists to examine, and seeks the explanation for those rates within societal conditions, such as the disjunction between institutional means and cultural goals. There is no place in the theory for individual qualities. For example, how people score on such personality traits as impulsiveness or level of hostility or tendency toward non-conformity may account for which of them do or do not become criminals; but, according to Durkheim, explaining such individual differences was not the sociologist's task.

ELEMENTARY RELIGION

Durkheim was primarily interested in identifying the principal elements of religion, the very core of the institution. Toward this end he focused upon some small, isolated, preliterate Australian tribes, and a few similar tribes that were native to North America. Following anthropological custom at the time, he referred to them as *primitive*. Their less complex social organization, in Durkheim's view, would offer him an unfettered view of religion and its place within societies, both primitive and modern.

> "At the foundation of all systems of belief . . . [are] . . . a certain number of fundamental representations or conceptions and of ritual attitudes which, in spite of the diversity of forms which they have taken . . . fulfill the same functions everywhere. These . . . elements . . . constitute that which is permanent and human in religion."[30]

More contemporary societies, he believed, had borrowed so much from each other that disentangling that which was original and authentic to them from that which had been taken over from other societies seemed hopeless. He wanted to move far back, to before the borrowing began, to the origins of religion where he could identify its most essential features; hence, the title of his book, *The Elementary Forms of Religious Life* (henceforward, *EFR*).

Rituals, Beliefs and Churches

Durkheim began his analysis by rejecting the idea that religions must involve the supernatural. A belief in an omnipresent power, he observed, actually occurred late in the history of religions. Furthermore, he noted that in many religions the notion of god(s) or spirits is either absent or of minor significance. Finally, and of most importance to Durkheim, the very idea of the supernatural logically required the prior conception of the natural against which the supernatural could be conceived. Given the place of religion at the very origin of societies, it seemed likely to him that elementary religion must have initially tried to explain that which was considered neither exceptional nor abnormal in society. People's concern with what they regarded as out-of-the-ordinary (i.e. supernatural) had to arise later, well after the (very early) emergence of religion, according to Durkheim's logic.

What did define the universal core of religion in his view were its three fundamental parts: beliefs (thoughts), rites (actions) and churches (followers). He defined *beliefs* as consisting of collective representations—ways of thinking about, and classifying, things that were common to everyone in a society. *Rites* involve ways of behaving. They encompass the rituals people are expected to follow in the presence of objects, people or places that they consider sacred. While distinguishing between them in this way, Durkheim contended that a society's rites and beliefs would normally match up, and operate in concert with each other. Specifically, the rites serve "to sustain the vitality of . . . beliefs, to keep them from being effaced from memory"[31] This quote makes an important point to which Durkheim repeatedly returned: Unless people continue to behave in ways that reaffirm their beliefs, the sentiments, themselves, will lose their vitality.

By a *church* Durkheim did not mean a building for worship. He meant a congregation, or group of people who share the beliefs and observe the rituals, and feel united as a result. The group may correspond with the entire society, or may be just a small cult within the society, but there must always be such a group of adherents.

> "A society whose members are united by the fact that they think in the same way in regard to the sacred world and its relations with the profane world, and . . . translate these common ideas into common practices, is what is called a Church."[32]

SACRED AND PROFANE

Within the *sacred* realm, Durkheim included: words or expressions that only consecrated (i.e. holy) people were permitted to utter (e.g. special prayers), objects thought to represent people or events of particular significance to the group (e.g. a bible or an ancestral totem) and occasions of ceremonial importance (e.g. Easter or First Communion). By *profane* Durkheim meant the ordinary and the mundane. Included here were objects that required no special handling; words or expressions that could be uttered by anyone, at any time; and everyday events lacking ceremonial significance: turning on a car radio, sharpening an ordinary pencil or the like.

Within every society, shared representations classify everything people can imagine into the sacred and the profane realms. The two domains, Durkheim wrote, are mutually exclusive. No words, objects, occasions or actions which fall into one can also fall into the other. No other dichotomy that people can imagine involves a comparable degree of separateness. Thus, compared to the sacred and the profane, the distinction between good and bad is trivial, because good and bad fall within the same class of phenomenon (i.e. morals). Similarly, sickness and health can be considered just two different aspects of life. But, Durkheim insisted,

> "The sacred and the profane have always and everywhere been conceived by the human mind as two distinct classes, as two worlds between which there is nothing in common. The sacred is *par excellence* that which the profane should not touch."[33]

Illustrative of the chasm between the two realms is the way people often think about the effects of religious initiation ceremonies. As the novice enters into the world of the sacred, via the initiation, it is as though the person he/she used to be has died, and is now re-born. This conception of a complete transformation is necessary, Durkheim wrote, to mark the absence of any type of continuity between the sacred and the profane. Thus, while the contents of the sacred and profane can be distinguished, each realm may be best described as being that which the other is not.

Durkheim's analysis of beliefs and rituals was, of course, directed primarily to religion; but he did not intend for the principles he presented to be confined to religion, and contemporary sociologists have applied them to diverse settings. To illustrate, Wallace and Hartley have examined very close friendships according to the same terms Durkheim used to describe religion. The interactions between close friends are like sacred rituals, Wallace and Hartley begin, in that the time they spend together is considered special, distinguished from ordinary time as the sacred is distinguished from the profane. The intimacy of their conversations is also set apart from the more mundane topics discussed with mere acquaintances. Further, just as a religious group's sacred rituals are not ordinarily shared with outsiders, close friends similarly feel that there are things they can share only with each other. Finally, being involved in an intimate friendship also frequently involves a transformation of people's selves, as the participants think of themselves as comprising a special "we" rather than two separate "I's," and they become a single moral unit, like a small church.[34]

Sacredness, Durkheim concluded, is not an inherent feature of things. From the variations he observed in what was considered to be sacred in different societies—various animals, trees, or the like—it seemed apparent that it was an attributed quality. In other words, sacredness was in the eyes of a group of beholders. It was due to the connection a group envisioned between objects (or expressions) and the objects or events they symbolized, so people's fear, love or respect become attached to the signs of the sacred. Durkheim illustrated the connection between symbolic objects and affect with the example of soldiers who are willing to die for their flag. Whether or not the enemy takes possession of the flag will not, in and of itself, affect the fate of their country; and yet the soldiers may be willing to die to defend it. They actually die for their country, in Durkheim's opinion, but when patriotism is inflamed by war, people embrace visible signs of their nation. In the soldiers' own consciousness, the symbol—the flag—may therefore become even more salient than the country it represents.

Research Box 7-3 examines the contemporary effect of sacred events. It focuses specifically upon the observance of religious holidays, and how such observance impacts the health of people who participate.

RESEARCH BOX 7-3
The Profane Body and the Sacred Soul

The Publication

Ellen L. Idler and Stanislav V. Kasl, "Religion, Disability, Depression, and the Timing of Death." *American Journal of Sociology*, 97, 1992: 1052–1079.

The Research Question

Most religions make a distinction between the (profane) body and the (sacred) soul, and emphasize the possibility of transcending one's body. "The first article in every creed," Durkheim wrote, "is the belief in salvation by faith."[35] It is likely that the possibility of salvation is particularly comforting for people who are elderly and/or in poor physical health. Can the relief offered by religion extend so far as to exert a protective effect on the life and well-being of those who are observant? If so, then the rate at which people die may actually be reduced during the time period before their major holidays, as they anticipate and prepare for them.

The aforementioned hypothesis concerning death rates was deduced from Durkheim's observation that sacred rituals tie people to their shared past by stressing continuity with prior generations who similarly celebrated Communion on the Thursday before Easter, recounted the exodus from Egypt at a Passover seder, or fasted daily during the month of Ramadan. Engaging in such rituals heightens the feeling of connectedness among those who observe them and provides meaning to people's lives. Thus, it is by increasing the salience of the sacred, with its comforting possibility of eternal life, that the ritual observance of holidays may exert protective health benefits.

Because of the preparations that occur during the month before a major holiday, the investigators hypothesized that death rates would be lower during this period than during the month following the ritual observance. For Protestants and Catholics, this entailed such holidays as Easter and Christmas; for Jews, it involved such holidays as Yom Kippur and Passover.

The Data

The investigators carefully selected a representative sample of nearly 3,000 people over age 65 who were living in New Haven, Connecticut. From interviews with this sample, the investigators noted their respondents' religious preference and degree of observance. People in the sample were regularly re-interviewed over a period of seven years. Each time a person in the sample died, the researchers recorded its time in relation to the religious holidays of the deceased.

The Findings

The analysis confirmed the hypothesis concerning the timing of deaths. There was a general tendency for the number of deaths among people in the sample to be substantially lower in the 30 days before their group's major holidays than in the 30 days following. No other condition seemed responsible because the mortality differences occurred only among those who celebrated the holiday: for example, among Christians, but not Jews, around Christmas; among Jews, but not Christians, around Yom Kippur. Further, within religious groups, there were large differences in rates of pre- and post-holiday deaths according to how observant people had been. The investigators note, following Durkheim, that rituals ensure the survival of the collectivity in that it is part of the group's own history that is reenacted. "The rhythm of anticipation of these holidays," they conclude, "evidently benefits the survival of the individual as well."

COLLECTIVE REPRESENTATIONS

Durkheim believed there was no such thing as unfiltered reality. The world, and all the things in it, could only be understood through approximations—representations—or mental images held in people's minds. Stating precisely what Durkheim meant by representations is difficult because he did not offer a clear definition, and according to one of the leading contemporary experts on Durkheim, W.S.F. Pickering, the French term he employed is difficult to translate into English. It appears, however, that Durkheim intended *representations* to refer to more than mental pictures. He also meant for them to include ways of thinking about objects or persons and ways of evaluating them.[36] People's division of the world into sacred and profane realms are an excellent example of collective representations.

In each person's mind is a set of representations which, Durkheim believed, would have qualities that were unique to that person. However, despite endless variations among individuals, there are also components that are widely shared, and they encompass the collective representations. Without them, neither distinctively human language nor thought would be possible. To illustrate, how can people think about time, or communicate with each other about it, except in the units that are meaningful in their society (i.e. months and hours, moons and seasons, etc.)? Thus, he concluded, those mental and verbal qualities that are uniquely human depend upon historically developed *collective* representations rather than upon personal experience. In Durkheim's words, "the individual transcends himself when he thinks and when he acts."[37]

Much of Durkheim's analysis of religion, presented both in *EFR* and in several articles published previously to it, was based upon a comparative analysis of societies. He tried to show how features of a society's own organization shaped the collective representations in that society. For example, he observed certain societies that arranged their camps in a circular form and found that they also conceived of space in that way, divided up like the tribal circle. To illustrate further, he observed that the more a primitive society contained many well-defined clans that cooperated closely with each other, the more elaborate were that society's classifications of animals, plants, objects, and so on.

> "It is because men were organized that they have been able to or-
> ganize things. . . . And if these different classes of things . . . are
> arranged according to a unified plan, it is because the social
> groups . . . themselves are unified . . . Thus . . . the essential cate-
> gories of thought [are] the product of social factors."[38]

Durkheim went on to show that the nature of religious representations followed a similar pattern, reflecting the organization of societies. However, the religious representations also served the very important function of elevating the social organization to a sacred status. Durkheim reached this conclusion from an analysis of totems: animals, plants and other objects that were associated with, and worshiped by, organized groups in primitive societies.

Membership in these groups—clans—was based upon family ties, and each kin group had its own totem from which its name was derived. The totem was like a heraldic emblem, or coat-of-arms. Members of a clan put the image of their totem on the walls of their homes, their canoes and tombs, and carved them onto their bodies.

Each clan's totem also became an integral part of the clan's religious ceremonies. What was sacred to any clan was a function of its connection to its totem. So, the totem simultaneously represented the society (clan) and the sacred (god). How could such a dual representation be possible, Durkheim asked, unless the god of the clan and the clan, itself, were the same? He concluded that when people at worship feel that something greater than themselves is involved, they are correct. It is the unity of their society or church that they are experiencing. For this reason Durkheim believed there could not really be an *individual* religion. The very notion, he claimed, misunderstood the fundamentally social nature of religion.

Given their social origins, maintaining religious beliefs—or any other collective representations—requires that people come together and actively reaffirm them. If this does not occur at regular intervals, the collective sentiments will lose their salience. The process is the same, Durkheim wrote, whether it involves Christians assembled to celebrate important dates in the life of Christ, or a gathering of citizens to commemorate a significant event in their nation's history. Thus, Easter and Washington's birthday, for example, are alike in that they require ritual observances, or the collective sentiments attached to them will recede. This principle is illustrated in an interesting analysis by sociologist Barry Schwartz.

Celebrating Washington's Birthday

At the time the Continental Congress selected Washington to lead the revolutionary army, the colonists were in awe of him, and he was unequaled as a hero and leader. Even when the war initially went poorly, Washington nevertheless was treated like a "benevolent god" wherever he went. The colonists remained optimistic, convinced victory was providential, with him in command. After the war his birthday became a national event, celebrated in every town. The only holiday of equal stature in the late eighteenth century was the fourth of July; but it was also observed as an homage to Washington, stressing his role in the founding of the nation. In addition to celebrating his birthday, people had an almost insatiable desire for any kind of likeness of Washington. Rough images of him were on dozens of coins, for example, usually lined with national emblems. People also valued even the crudest engravings of his face because they wanted some kind of representation of Washington because, like a flag or an anthem, he represented national consciousness. Between 1800 and 1860, over 400 books were written about Washington, and when the pronoun was used to refer to Him, it was frequently capitalized to suggest a sacred status.[39]

As late as the civil war, 65 years after his death, Washington's home at Mount Vernon was still considered a shrine, and armies of both the North and South respected it as neutral territory. However, after the civil war the U.S. was a different place, and more heroes crowded the national stage. Lincoln was especially notable in this regard, and over time his symbolic importance eclipsed Washington's. By the twentieth century, significant numbers of people considered Lincon "greater" than Washington because he saved the union and freed the slaves.[40] Celebrations of Washington's birthday diminished in intensity. The U.S. House and Senate no longer convened on his birthday for a reading of his Farewell Address. Eventually, many communities began largely to ignore his birthday. "From such ritual erosion . . . [came] . . . a fading of Washington's image from the collective memory."[41] Finally, his actual birthday blurred in the collective conscience when it was folded in with Lincoln's, and celebrated as Presidents' Day.

COLLECTIVE EFFERVESCENCE

The major sacred and profane representations of societies, Durkheim wrote, emanate from periods of *collective effervescence*. There is some ambiguity surrounding this term also, but he apparently meant it to refer to very exceptional periods in history when people came together to focus upon a troubling common problem: their religious organization did not seem to serve their needs, political institutions were apparently out-of-touch with the reality "on the ground," or the like. As people focus upon the problem and interact with each other more frequently and emotionally, they excite each other. There is a collective ferment. People's sentiments become particularly intense, and because they are shared they seem to take on a life of their own.

> "A man who experiences such sentiments feels himself dominated by outside forces that lead him. . . . He feels himself in a world quite distinct from that of his own private existence. Following the collectivity, the individual forgets himself for the common end . . . "[42]

Because of their power over people, these group-formulated sentiments can lead to excesses, as when a mob becomes violent or destructive. However, Durkheim viewed periods of collective effervescence as lasting longer than the typical mob and as more likely to be productive because people's shared excitement is capable of leading them to new insights into how to resolve their common problem. As a result, innovative forms of social organization are fashioned during such episodes. As illustrations of what periods of collective effervescence can produce, Durkheim pointed to the Reformation and the Renaissance.

Durkheim did not believe that the intense intellectual and emotional life associated with periods of collective effervescence could be sustained, though, as people simply found them too exhausting. Following the creation of new representations and organizations, there is a return to ordinary social life, but the ideals that emerged during the period of strong upheaval remain in people's memories. They cannot persist indefinitely, however, unless they are periodically revived in religious or secular ceremonies, feasts, rites and other events that draw people together. These subsequent events, he stated, are "minor versions of the great creative moment."[43] And so as rituals commemorating Washington's birthday diminished, Washington, himself, receded as an important symbol of the nation.

On a smaller scale, Randall Collins has examined how the creativity of intellectual communities arises from the intense solidarity created and maintained by interaction rituals. The most important of these rituals, in Collins' view, are lectures, conferences, debates and other face-to-face exchanges because in bringing members of an intellectual community together, they provide opportunities for the community to reinvest emotional energy into their sacred objects. Without such direct interaction rituals, the articles and books people write would lack any emotional energy; "they would be Durkheimian emblems of a dead religion, whose worshippers never came to the ceremonies."[44]

SOCIAL EMERGENCE

Durkheim's first three major books, written while at Bordeaux, were published during the 1890's. His last major book was *EFR* and it was not published until 1912, though he wrote a number of essays on religion in *L'Année Sociologique* in the years prior to the publication of *EFR*. This final monograph differed from Durkheim's earlier books in that it placed more emphasis upon culture, as expressed in shared ideas and values. Some analysts contend that this difference represented a dramatic—qualitative—change in Durkheim's approach, and provided an important precursor to the contemporary revival of sociological interest in culture.[45] However, Keith Sawyer argues (and I agree) that an emphasis upon the discontinuity in Durkheim occurs when analysts do not give proper weight to his consistent position as a theorist of *social emergence*.[46]

Durkheim did not employ the term, *emergence*. It was developed after his death by sociologists and philosophers, though the idea certainly applies to Durkheim's writings. The core of the idea of emergence involves a distinction between micro (i.e. individual) and macro (i.e. aggregate) units of analysis, and the contention that certain properties first—and only—appear at the macro level. This distinction was emphasized in all of Durkheim's analyses, and provided the basis for two of Durkheim's most fundamental assumptions:

1. A distinctive social reality arises from individuals' action, but is not reducible to them. To illustrate, it is individuals who are involved in the interactions that define periods of collective effervescence; but such episodes do not, strictly speaking, describe individuals. Like the collective

conscience, or anomie, or social density, they are a property of groups or societies. They "emerge" only at a more aggregate level and therefore meaningfully describe a group or a society, not individuals.

2. Causation is downward, from the social to the individual level. Although emergent properties are erected upon the actions of individuals, these properties are not only separate from individuals, they exert multiple influences upon the behavior and thought of individuals. For example, Durkheim insisted that the collective representations of a society dictate how individuals think and communicate. Neither would even be possible if individuals did not employ these representations. The contention of downward causation was important to Durkheim's political agenda, according to Sawyer, because "sociology could not be an independent science unless its objects of study could be shown to have causal powers."[47] (If collectivities could be explained as merely the results of individual actions, then there might have been little reason for the new discipline of sociology to be recognized.)

Durkheim studied a number of different phenomena: the division of labor, suicide, religion, etc., and the content of his analyses correspondingly varied. However, his arguments and explanations took a consistent form, namely, focusing upon social emergence as defined earlier, and that common emphasis provided an important bridge across all of his writings, regardless of whether he was stressing social structure or culture in any particular analysis.

Endnotes

1. For further biographical information on Durkheim, the most complete work is, Steven Lukes, *Emile Durkheim: His Life and Works.* Stanford: Stanford University Press, 1985.

2. See, for example, Donald A. Nielsen, *Three Faces of God.* Albany: State University of New York Press, 1999.

3. Frank Parkin, *Durkheim.* London: Oxford University Press, 1992, p 4.

4. Lukes.

5. See, for example, the highly critical book review of the translated work by Ellsworth Faris in *American Journal of Sociology,* 40, 1934. In the same issue, see Robert K. Merton, "Durkheim's Division of Labor in Society."

6. Emile Durkheim, *Suicide.* New York: Free Press, 1951, p 46.

7. Parkin, p 6.

8. Emile Durkheim, *The Division of Labor in Society.* New York: Macmillan, 1933. (Free Press paperback, 1997.)

9. Ibid., p 205.

10. Gianfranco Poggi, *Durkheim.* London: Oxford University Press, 2000.

11. For further discussion of Spencer's work and influence, see Jonathan Turner, "Herbert Spencer." In George Ritzer (Ed.), *The Blackwell Companion to Major Social Theorists.* Cambridge: Blackwell, 2000.

12. Durkheim, p 85.

13. Ibid., pp 38–39.

14. Ibid, p 39, italics added.

15. Ibid, p 149.
16. For further discussion of Durkheim's conclusions and the results of ensuing research, see Jack P. Gibbs, "A Formal Restatement of Durkheim's 'Division of Labor' Theory." *Sociological Theory*, 21, 2003.
17. Durkheim, p 55.
18. Gibbs.
19. The re-establishment of death penalties in many states illustrates a mixture of repressive and restitutive law. The degree of punishment seems repressive, but its administration (involving judges, appeal boards and the like) is more associated with restitutive law.
20. Durkheim, p xxxiii.
21. Preface to the second edition of *DoL*, p xlv.
22. Ibid., p lvi.
23. Boissier, *La Religion Romaine*, Vol II, pp 287–88. Quoted in the Preface to the second edition of DoL, p xii.
24. T.P. Schwartz, p 516.
25. *DoL*, p 292.
26. Ibid., p 304.
27. Page 103 in, Susan Stedman Jones, *Durkheim Reconsidered.* Cambridge, UK: Polity Press, 2001.
28. Robert K. Merton, "Social Structure and Anomie." This paper was originally published in, *American Sociological Review*, 3, 1938. A revision appears in Merton's anthology, *Social Theory and Social Structure.* New York: Free Press, 1968.
29. See, for example, Richard Rosenfeld and Steven F. Messner, "Crime and the American Dream." In Freda Adler and William S. Laufer (Eds.), *The Legacy of Anomie Theory.* New Brunswick, NJ: Transaction Publishers, 1995.
30. Emile Durkheim, *The Elementary Forms of The Religious Life.* New York: Free Press, 1965, p 17.
31. Ibid., p. 420.
32. Ibid., p 59.
33. Ibid., pp 54 and 55.
34. Ruth A. Wallace and Shirley F. Hartley, "Religious Elements in Friendship." In Jeffrey C. Alexander (Ed.), *Durkheimian Sociology.* Cambridge: Cambridge University Press, 1988.
35. Ibid., p 464.
36. W.S.F. Pickering, "Representations as Understood by Durkheim." In Pickering (Ed.), *Durkheim and Representations.* London: Routledge, 2000.
37. *EFR*, p 29.
38. Ibid., p 169–179.
39. Barry Schwartz, *George Washington.* New York: Free Press, 1987. In the preface to this book, Schwartz described himself as working from beginning to end under the influence of *EFR.*
40. Survey results from 1945 and 2001, comparing Lincoln and Washington, presented in, Barry Schwartz and Howard Schuman, "History, Commemoration and Belief." *American Sociological Review*, 70, 2005.
41. *George Washington*, p 198.
42. Emile Durkheim, *Sociology and Philosophy.* London: Cohen and West, 1965, p 91.
43. Ibid., p 92.
44. Randall Collins, *The Sociology of Philosophies.* Cambridge, MA: Harvard University Press, 1998, p 27.
45. See, for example, Jeffrey C. Alexander, *The Meanings of Social Life.* New York: Oxford University Press, 2003.
46. R. Keith Sawyer, "Durkheim's Dilemma." *Sociological Theory*, 20, 2002.
47. Ibid., p 232.

8

Emile Durkheim (2)

Rules and Suicide

I n this chapter we will examine two of the major works Durkheim wrote during the middle of his productive years. This specifically includes: *Rules of the Sociological Method* (hereafter, *Rules*), which was published in 1895, two years after *DoL (The Division of Labor in Society)*; and *Suicide*, which followed *Rules* by two years. Combined, these two volumes are largely responsible for Durkheim's legacy as a major architect of three positions that became enduring traditions within sociology: positivism, functionalism and the empirical test of social theory. (His pioneering formulations of these positions will be discussed at appropriate places within this chapter.)

Rules can be thought of as a primer; a "How To . . ." book for the serious sociological researcher. It covers the gamut of methodological issues, beginning with how to observe social phenomena and ending with how to explain them. The principles enunciated in *Rules* provided the blueprint followed by Durkheim in *Suicide*. The latter was an extremely significant book for several reasons. It was the first sociological study to systematically examine theoretically derived hypotheses in relation to empirical data. For many years it was the exemplar of such research. In addition, the study of suicide well-suited Durkheim's political agenda of boosting sociology, especially in relation to psychology. It took what appeared, at least at first glance, to be a highly individualistic phenomenon—suicide—and proceeded to explain its variations in relation to sociological variables, such as gender, occupation and marital status.

HOW TO OBSERVE

The first problem faced by the social scientist, Durkheim wrote, is the limitation imposed by "common sense." The lay public's ideas are so ingrained in everyone's thinking that they present barriers to scientific understanding. The sociologist, like anyone else, tends unconsciously to accept what common sense has generally held to be true. However, to stay with that common sense view is to forego the possibility of making discoveries, and without discoveries, of what value is a science? Furthermore, he asked, why should sociology be the only science to take common sense seriously? Does medicine or physics?

In approaching a subject matter to be investigated, the social scientist must also guard against being unduly influenced by first impressions because they are likely to be the result of common sense interpretations. For example, it may seem obvious (especially to most of the lay public) that crime is repugnant and abnormal, and societies would be better off without it. If sociologists were to stop there, however, they might not consider the implications of the fact that crime in some form is found in every society. How could it be both universal and abnormal? In addition, the punishments for crime can be useful to the society, if not the criminal. Thus, the sanctions imposed upon criminals may help to clarify the society's norms and may promote solidarity among those who disapprove of the criminal's actions. So, perhaps on second thought, societies might not be better off without crime. Do not be naive, Durkheim admonished; be rational, scientific and follow the facts rather than preconceived notions (which are probably not true, anyway).

What Durkheim had in mind for sociology was the scientific model, developed in the natural sciences. This reliance upon the scientific model and the corresponding assumption that sociological research could have the same degree of certainty as natural science research defines the major features of *positivism*. He wanted sociologists to approach their subject matter—family forms, norms, etc.—in the same way as physicists or biologists, even though the sociologists might have personal feelings about particular family forms or certain norms. Such feelings could set them apart from other scientists on the assumption that biologists, for example, do not have feelings about cells. Nevertheless, the sociologist's approach must still be the same as the physicist or chemist.

> "Our principle . . . demands that the sociologist put himself in the same state of mind . . . When he probes into . . . the social world, he must be aware that he is penetrating the unknown . . . he must be prepared for discoveries which will surprise and disturb him."[1]

To prevent being led astray by the erroneous assumptions of common sense or by first impressions, one must also be wary of everyday concepts. Democracy, family, liberty, crime—what do these concepts really imply? They are vague and imprecise, he stated, so perhaps the sociologist will have to invent new terms that are clearer and more precise. For example, he noted that the term *monogamy* was utilized, in everyday language, to describe: one husband–one wife in societies where poverty or people's relative isolation prevents them from having multiple spouses; and societies in which one husband–one wife is the legally imposed form; and non-human animals that remain more-or-less permanently with their mates. This multitude of references implied by a single term may not be a problem in everyday conversations, but the research agenda of sociologists will probably necessitate finer distinctions because each of the referents of the term may be different in sociologically important ways. As a result, sociologists may have to derive new terms/concepts. For example, *compulsory monogamy* might be employed to describe only those societies where no marital arrangement other than one husband–one wife is lawfully permitted. The usefulness of any such term cannot be fully assessed, however, until after the phenomenon has been systematically investigated, and the sociologist better understands all that the term implies.

Durkheim confronted a dilemma here: The sociologist was to be suspicious of lay conceptions, so where would the new definitions/concepts come from? Durkheim offered two answers which, on the surface, can seem incompatible with each other, but probably are not. In some recently discovered notes from Durkheim's lectures at a provincial school in Sens, presented prior to the publication of *Rules*, he stressed the importance of the scientist's creativity.[2] The only way we can know about reality, he stated, is through the use of the imagination. Everything new is initially a product of imagination. His answer in *Rules*, by contrast, was that social phenomena should be defined by their external (i.e. perceivable) characteristics, with the observer making as few assumptions as possible. Try to let things speak for themselves. That emphasis in *Rules* has led some Durkheimian scholars to view him as touting a highly inductive approach, that is, encouraging sociologists to work "robot-like" from observations to generalizations. However, if we combine the views presented in the Sens lectures with those presented in *Rules*, then a more dynamic picture emerges of a social scientist working from creative ideas to observations and back again.

One matter on which Durkheim was very insistent concerned the inclusiveness with which sociological categories, at least initially, should be defined. An investigator beginning a study could not know which of the phenomenon's properties were essential to a definition and which were peripheral. Therefore, Durkheim wrote (italics in original):

> *"The subject matter of every sociological study should comprise a group of phenomena defined in advance by certain common external characteristics, and all phenomena so defined should be included within this group."*[3]

(Later in this chapter we will see this is exactly the way he began his study of suicide.)

To illustrate how such inclusive definitions might be utilized, he noted that in every society there was a small group of people who were blood relatives and were united by legal bonds. Every aggregate of this type, he stated, should be considered a family, and the study of families should begin by including as a family every small group that possessed the aforementioned qualities. Blood relations and legal bonds were examples of what Durkheim considered observable, external characteristics in the sense that data pertaining to them were accessible and verifiable, even if the initial decision to examine them emanated from an investigator's imagination.

In likening the sociologist to the natural scientist, Durkheim was, as noted, trying to caution sociologists to avoid the preconceptions of common sense. He also had a second important concern, and it pertained to his skepticism toward the role of introspection. If sociologists looked within themselves to discover more about a phenomenon it could lead them away from the external characteristics of the phenomenon. They might invent concepts that had no empirical referent; no external counterpart. In addition, by contemplating their own thoughts, sociologists risked becoming "pop psychologists." Introspection could not be expected to lead to sociological discoveries because it put one in touch with individual, psychological states; and in his view, variables of that type could never explain sociological phenomenon. To understand why he felt this way, we turn to Durkheim's discussion of social facts, the most central idea presented in *Rules*, and then to how he insisted these social facts were to be explained.

DEFINING SOCIAL FACTS

Durkheim began the analysis of social facts by designating them as the "things" that constituted the primary objects of sociological analysis. He felt compelled, he wrote, to define them in a way that would provide sociology with a unique subject matter. He did not want its subject matter confused with that of other, previously established disciplines that also studied people, such as biology or psychology. *Social facts* consist of ways of acting, thinking and feeling that are wide-spread in any society and, with respect to individuals, have two distinctive characteristics that define them:

1. *Externality.* People often feel committed to them, and embrace them as their own, but they inherit, rather than create, the social facts.
2. *Coerciveness.* If people resist these customs or ideals they will experience sanctions, ranging from informal disapproval to confinement in a prison or mental hospital.

To illustrate these defining qualities, consider the custom of celebrating one's birth date as a social fact. It is certainly wide-spread in many societies. It is external in the sense that no one now alive invented it. The practice preceded all of us and will probably persist for future generations. Thus, everyone now and in the future could be said to inherit the practice from past generations. In that sense it does not "belong" to any of us; it is a property of the society. Coerciveness, the second defining characteristic, is indicated by the likely reactions of friends and family to a person who chose not to acknowledge, in any way, his/her birthday. When is your birthday, they might ask, Why don't you celebrate it? Isn't he/she strange, they may say to each other. The person could continue to resist, but would continue to feel pressures to conform to the custom of celebrating one's birth date. Durkheim never envisioned 100% compliance. His point was that people could not just disregard social facts with impunity.

After the first edition of *Rules* was published, there was a good deal of criticism directed at his treatment of social facts as "things." That implied, according to critics, that he thought social facts were material entities. In the second edition of *Rules* Durkheim addressed this issue, maintaining that he did not think social facts were literally things, but that he meant for social facts to be treated *as though* they were things because he believed they were every bit as real as the material things (e.g. cells, planets) studied by natural scientists. There is a difference, he wrote, between an idea, which we know from within, and a thing which is known via observation and experimentation.

> "To treat the facts of a certain order as things is . . . to assume a certain mental attitude toward them on the principle that . . . their characteristic properties . . . cannot be discovered by even the most careful introspection."[4]

But if these social facts were outside of the individual, later critics persisted, how could they exert constraints unless they really were material entities, like fences? That question, in Susan Steadman Jones' opinion, shows a failure to understand what Durkheim meant, perhaps due in part to translation difficulties. The logical quandary is resolved, she writes, by recognizing that ways of thinking and acting that individuals acquire come from social relations, with family members, teachers, religious leaders, etc. These relationships are external to individuals. Further, because the ways of thinking and acting are common to many people, the social facts are part of a shared world that is also logically external to any individual.

Despite their external origin, these ways of thinking and acting do not remain entirely outside of people, though. They are internalized; that is, people take on these ways of thinking and acting as their own, and value them in their own right. Some of any person's internalized behaviors and ideas form combinations that are relatively unique. Some of people's ideas, habits and values can therefore be thought of as personal while others, because of their wide-spread overlap with the thoughts and actions of others, represent the (external) collectivity. The constraining qualities of social facts also have this dual source: personal habits that with repetition become difficult-to-resist and external pressures to conform with the beliefs and expectations shared within a society.[5]

Most social facts are linked to an institution: kinship beliefs with the familial institution, occupational obligations with the economic institution and so on. However, wide-spread beliefs or practices are sometimes not tied to an established, enduring form of social organization; and in those instances Durkheim termed them, *"social currents."* The thoughts and actions that comprise a social current are similarly external to and coercive of individuals even though no institution is involved. Examples of social currents could include: literary or artistic standards, clothing styles or the wave of indignation that carries through a crowd right after someone has committed a heinous offense.

EXPLAINING SOCIAL FACTS

The explanation of any social fact, according to Durkheim, has two separate, but inter-related parts. First, it is necessary to show the cause that produces it, and that cause is necessarily a social fact also, because he assumed that only social facts could act as the cause of social facts. Second, the investigator must show the effects of the social fact; that is, what function does it fulfil? We will discuss each of these components of the Durkheimian explanation separately.

Causality

Durkheim began this discussion by insisting that the cause of any social fact could only be another social fact. His primary concern here was with "reductionism:" assuming that societal characteristics could incorrectly be made less abstract by equating them with individual characteristics. Society, in his view, represented a separate reality, with its own characteristics. For example, he thought it ridiculous to try to explain the types of families found in a society as due to the sentiments of parents and children, or to view a society's economic institution as resulting from people's attitudes toward wealth. Every institutionalized form, as a social fact, is external to, and coercive of, individual thought. Thus, it is the social organization that determines psychological states, and not vice versa, so people's sentiments could never be the cause of a society's characteristics.

For Durkheim, the major consideration in deciding whether one social fact caused another was that they were empirically related. He specifically advocated the method of concomitant variation: see if two social facts consistently stand in the same relationship to each other. To demonstrate concomitant variation required a sample of societies because social facts were the characteristic of societies. All proper sociological research was, therefore, comparative research. So, suppose one took a sample of 1,850 people in a society and asked them if they believed it was important to reciprocate favors or acts of kindness. The percentage who agreed that reciprocity was important could then provide a measure of the strength of that norm in the society. Readers can test their understanding of the issue by answering this question: How would Durkheim figure the size of this sample? The answer is not 1,850. It is one, because the 1,850 individuals represent *one* society.

To continue the illustration, further suppose the investigator wanted to see whether the norm of reciprocity was higher in societies that were large in population size. To test the hypothesis, the investigator would have to select a sample of societies and see whether more people agreed with the norm (a social fact) in larger rather than smaller societies (the other social fact). If there were also reason to believe the population size changed before the norm—in other words, that it was antecedent—then the concomitant variation between the social facts would indicate, to Durkheim, that one caused the other.* To conclude that an

---

*Judged by contemporary research methods, Durkheim's view of causal interpretations was not highly sophisticated. Today we know that concomitant variation and temporal ordering are not always sufficient. Several additional steps are required to infer causality.

increase in population size caused the norm of reciprocity to become stronger would be consistent with his general conclusion that, "*A given effect always has a single corresponding cause.*"[6]

Functionality

Durkheim believed that understanding the cause of a social fact was necessary for a sociological explanation, but not sufficient. To complete an explanation required that the sociologist also show the function of the social fact, that is, in what way(s) it contributed to the maintenance or stability of the society. Because he felt that his contemporaries had often blurred the distinction between cause and function, he emphasized the differences between these two aspects of sociological explanation. One reason to stress the distinction was because the analysis of cause rests primarily upon empirical observation while identifying the function of a social fact relies more upon inference. The causal relationship observed in the first step of the explanation ordinarily provides an important clue to the function, however.

To illustrate, if our hypothetical investigator found that the norm of reciprocity was stronger in large societies, why might that be? Is there something about large societies that enables them to benefit more from the norm? Perhaps in small societies people are more likely to know each others' kin and to share mutual friends. If another takes without giving, the person who feels wronged may be able to get assistance from the recalcitrant person's kin or friends. They may pressure the person to reciprocate. In larger societies, by contrast, people may lack comparable access to each others' friends and kin, and fearing a lack of reciprocity people might withhold acts that would be helpful to others. Everyone would thereby lose. A functional interpretation might propose that a strong norm of reciprocity provides assurance to people that their kindness will be returned in some form. Without such assurance, people in large societies could be less inclined to be kind or helpful. Everyone would therefore be disadvantaged. However, in small societies, the norm of reciprocity is presumably inconsequential, hence unnecessary; if present, it would serve no function.

Research Box 8-1 illustrates all of Durkheim's positions with respect to the study and explanation of social facts. Note specifically that the researcher's explanation for why many societies kept women out of warfare:

1. Focused upon characteristics of societies, not individuals;
2. Was a comparative study of societies;
3. First tried to establish a causal relationship between social facts, and then
4. Inferred the function of the social fact from its relationship to other social facts.

RESEARCH BOX 8-1

The Function of Keeping Women Out of War

The Publication

David B. Adams, "Why There Are So Few Women Warriors." *Behavior Science Research*, 18, 1983, pp 196–212.

The Research Question

Among small, pre-industrial societies that frequently engaged in warfare, men were almost invariably involved as warriors/soldiers. Women fought at their sides only occasionally, probably due to limitations placed upon women by pregnancy and the nurturance of infants. However, the question that remains unanswered by biological differences is why women were sometimes included, and sometimes excluded. What social arrangements made women's involvement more or less likely, and how might the effect of these arrangements be explained?

The Data

The investigator selected a sample of 67 pre-industrial tribes and small communities from throughout the world. Each was included in the sample because it had a history of frequent warfare, and diverse information about it was available. Two characteristics of the sampled societies (i.e. social facts) were of particular interest to the investigator: (1) whether warfare was typically *internal*, meaning it involved neighboring communities that spoke the same language, or *external*, involving distant communities where a different language was spoken; and (2) whether men remained in their village and married women who grew up in the same village (*endogamy*), or married women who grew up in a different village, requiring that the women moved when they married (*patrilocality*).

The Findings

In nine of the sampled societies, women fought alongside men, at least sometimes. All nine of these societies were the same with respect to type of warfare (it was external) and marital arrangement (it was endogamous). There were a total of 33 societies that had both external warfare and endogamous marriage, so the chances of women engaging in combat was better than one in four (9/33) in societies of this type. By contrast, in the sample's 34 remaining societies, where warfare was internal and marriage was patrilocal, there were absolutely no societies that had women warriors. Furthermore, when women were kept out of battle, they were also prevented from owning weapons, and they were excluded from all of the tribe's military preparations, such as war councils. Was it almost as though the men did not trust them?

(Continued)

The explanation for the relationship between the frequency of women warriors and the society's type of warfare and marriage, according to Adams, pivots about the potential problem of split loyalties. If a tribe was battling its neighbor (internal) and married women in the tribe were raised in that neighboring village (patrilocality), then their husbands could be fighting against their fathers and brothers. If their allegiance is thereby divided, the women are, at best, security risks in their current community of residence. That is probably why they are excluded from both war planning and actual battlefield engagement. And it is because both patrilocal residence and internal warfare were so prevalent in early human history, Adams concludes, that the pattern of totally excluding women from warfare was first widely institutionalized.

During the middle of the last century there were a large number of studies, like the analysis of women's exclusion from warfare, designed to test functional hypotheses derived from Durkheim and other theorists. Most of the studies presented data that seemed consistent with functionalist interpretations of phenomena as diverse as religious beliefs and baseball players' salaries. By the latter part of the century, however, there were very few studies of this type. There were many reasons for the change in research interests, but one is of particular importance to us here and it concerns the link between these studies and a more abstract theory of functional integration.

FUNCTIONAL INTEGRATION

Durkheim felt that showing the function of any social fact was an important part of its explanation because of his conception of societies as functionally integrated. To be more concrete, he envisioned society as comprised of inter-related social facts, each of which contributed to the stability and maintenance of the entire society. This view is generally termed a theory of functional integration or functional unity, and it leads to the expectation that every social fact will have a function, and correspondingly, research can disclose those functions.

At the core of the theory of functional integration is the assumption that the elements of society (e.g. social facts) are functionally inter-related. This means that the normal operation of one practice or institution requires the normal operation of the others. If they are not so attuned, it will be recalled, Durkheim referred to a *state of anomie* (because the parts did not fit together). However, he considered the malintegration among parts of a society to typically be a temporary condition that society—as a self-adjusting, functionally integrated system— would correct. Within an integrated society, each societal component is assumed, ordinarily, to make a positive contribution to the society. It is such contributions, or consequences, that must be explained, and it is this emphasis upon consequences, defined as functions, that earned functionalism its name.

Under the broad umbrella of functional integration, theorists differed in how unified they viewed the elements of a society. At one extreme, anthropologist Bronislaw Malinowski assumed that every element of a culture made an indispensable contribution to the culture. At the opposite extreme were numerous analysts who, like Warren Schmaus, prefer functional explanations of cultural representations, but consider them totally unrelated to any assumptions about the functional unity of society.[7] While Durkheim fits between these extremes, he is closer to the high end than the middle. He considered the possibility of disruptive elements, "dysfunctions," but paid very little attention to them. He also considered the possibility of "survivals;" that is, social facts that could persist without making a contribution.

> "A fact can exist without being at all useful, either because it has never been adjusted to any vital end or because, after having been useful, it has lost all utility while continuing to exist by . . . inertia . . ."[8]

However, he regarded survivals as depleting the resources of a society, because to continue them required collective effort, but they did not provide a payoff. How many such drains could a society afford, he rhetorically asked?

More recent criticism of the functional theory of integration occurred on many fronts. One of the most telling involved the re-analysis of earlier studies of small, preliterate societies. Robert Edgerton notes that because of the theory of functional integration, researchers often ignored theoretical anomalies: instances in which functional practices appeared to be absent, or dysfunctional practices seemed to predominate. The researchers felt pressured to assume that practices such as: cannibalism, torture, witchcraft and genital mutilation must serve some useful social ends. To illustrate, among the traditional Navaho Indians, witches and ghosts were believed to cause illness, requiring men to spend hours everyday in ceremonial "sings." Early ethnographers talked about how the fear of witches and ghosts helped to maintain traditional Navaho society—its presumed function. However, in Edgerton's view, these beliefs provoked anxiety and made people hypochondriacs. That was hardly functional; and neither, he added, was the enormous amount of (unproductive) time they felt obliged to spend in sings.[9]

Durkheim (and most other functionalists) assumed that as societies became larger and more complex, the degree to which practices and beliefs were functionally integrated would probably decline. Therefore, when the re-examination of many small, pre-industrial societies suggested that *their* degree of functional unity may have been exaggerated, one could only imagine how much analysts may have overly emphasized functional integration in contemporary societies. Interest in discovering whether every causal relationship might serve a function correspondingly waned.

DEFINING SUICIDE AS A SOCIAL FACT

Many years before Durkheim began to study suicide, some scholars were statistically describing the rates of various types of crime and illness. Still others were offering elaborate theories of social organization. Durkheim's distinctive contribution was to combine the two: to present a theory, derive hypotheses from that theory and then statistically test the hypotheses using data that he either found or prepared. More than 100 years after the original publication of *Suicide*, sociologists still regard it as a classic, a model for social research. And contemporary studies, utilizing better data than Durkheim had access to continue not only to replicate many of his findings but to provide robust support. Nevertheless, his analysis opened a methodological hornet's nest, eliciting stinging criticisms and provocative questions that have defied closure. In the course of this section we will consider the most important of these issues as we describe his pioneering research.

The first problem Durkheim confronted in analyzing suicide was how to define the phenomenon. He followed his own advice, as previously described in *Rules*. Specifically, he had written that the sociologist should initially define a phenomenon broadly, so that all cases could be included, and to avoid prior assumptions as much as possible so the phenomenon's observable features could "speak for themselves." The alternative, he feared, would be to allow common sense to dictate a typology, and that could stifle creativity. Therefore, he began with a broad, almost assumption free, definition of suicide as: *all cases of death resulting directly or indirectly from a positive or negative act of the victim himself, which he knows will produce this result.*[10]

What Durkheim meant to include were deaths resulting from both acts of omission (e.g. failure to get off the railroad tracks when a train is coming) and acts of commission (e.g. taking poison). Interpreting what Durkheim meant by the deceased's knowledge of the end result is more problematic. What is clear is that he did not mean the person's intent, in the ordinary use of the term, because he felt that people's motives could not be readily inferred.

> "Intent is too intimate a thing to be more than approximately interpreted by another. It even escapes self-observation. How often we mistake the true reasons for our acts!"[11]

Thus, it appears that when Durkheim said the person who commits suicide "knows" the act will result in death, he meant "know" in a purely cognitive sense; that is, I know the train will kill me if I do not get off the tracks, but whether or not I wish for that result, and why, are moot points. Maybe I am despondent and the train seems to me to be an efficient way to end my life and that is what I desire; or perhaps I am regrettably willing to be run over only to protect someone I believe is immobilized behind me on the tracks. Durkheim wanted sociologists to avoid trying to decipher motives because he thought they could never be inferred with any certainty; and even if they could be, he doubted that they could explain variations in suicide rates. There are probably as many reasons for suicide as there are suicides, he noted, but none of them provides the sociological explanation.

Durkheim's argument against individualistic interpretations of suicide rates had two parts. First, he showed that psychological variables, such as rates of insanity and alcoholism, did not correlate with rates of suicide. The absence of such a relationship was taken by Durkheim as evidence that the suicide rate was a societal, rather than individual, characteristic. Second, he presented data showing that the rate of suicide was stable over time within most societies, but that it varied across societies. This pattern indicated that the suicide rate was a nonreducible characteristic of societies, themselves, and that it would be best explained in relation to other social facts. We will review each of Durkheim's arguments, in turn.

To demonstrate that individual characteristics could not explain suicide rates, Durkheim looked for indicators of such variables and then examined whether they were related to the suicide rate. To illustrate, for a sample of a dozen European nations, he was able to obtain data on insanity (the number of people confined to mental institutions), alcoholism (per capita consumption of alcohol), seasonal temperatures, etc. Each of these variables was popularly viewed as psychologically affecting people's predisposition to take their own lives. He proposed that if any of these variables actually caused the suicide rate to vary, it would have to correlate with the suicide rate.[12] However, his analysis of the data showed no consistent relationships, leading Durkheim to conclude that none of these psychological inducements were responsible for a society's suicide rate. This interpretation strengthened his contention that no psychological variable could, "account for so definite a social fact as the suicide-rate."[13]

The second, and more important part of Durkheim's argument contended that suicide rates should be viewed as a social fact because they were explained by other social facts. Here he took samples of societies, and examined suicide rates within them in relation to religion, family status, gender and other sociological variables. The particulars of several of his analyses have been subject to extensive scrutiny, leaving some unanswered questions. It appears, for example, that Durkheim was highly selective in choosing cases that fit his theory. In *Suicide* he presented numerous tables with data pertaining to various European countries, taken mostly from government publications. Whitney Pope re-examined the data in the original publications, and he found that sometimes Durkheim conveniently overlooked cases that would have weakened his findings. For example, there were instances in which Durkheim selected from tables only those nations whose rates were consistent with his hypothesis.[14] Pope did not claim that Durkheim's findings were therefore bogus, but they did seem to be somewhat exaggerated. Nevertheless, more recent attempts to replicate Durkheim's original findings, using more complete data, have most often been successful.

Suicide and Social Integration

One of the first social facts Durkheim studied in relation to suicide rates were religious affiliations. Examining the religious composition of nations and provinces within nations, he found that suicide rates in Protestant areas were invariably higher than in Catholic areas. Jewish area suicide rates were sometimes higher and sometimes lower than Catholic areas, but they were always well below those of Protestant areas. On further examination, he found that when Catholics were in the majority in a nation or province, the Protestant–Catholic difference in suicide rates diminished. So, some of the low rate of Catholic suicides was due to their typically minority status. As a minority group facing hostile outsiders, they "are obliged to exercise severe control over themselves" (p 156), and Durkheim argued that the resulting cohesion in Catholic communities reduced their suicide rates. Similarly, he regarded historical persecution as having led Jews to form highly cohesive groups, and he attributed the relatively low rate of suicide in their communities to that cohesion.

Durkheim pursued an analysis of the difference in Protestant–Catholic suicide rates, and found that while the difference fluctuated in relation to the relative size of each religious grouping, it never disappeared. Rates in Protestant areas invariably exceeded those of Catholic areas. Therefore, Durkheim concluded, the generally lower rate of suicide among Catholics must primarily be due to their more extensive body of doctrine and more elaborate church hierarchy than Protestants. Because of these differences, Catholicism tends more than the Protestant denominations to dominate the entire life of adherents, resulting in a more strongly integrated group. This analysis of religious group differences provided Durkheim with the first evidence for a general thesis that suicide rates were a function of social integration. He proceeded to examine the relationship between suicide rates and political solidarity (created by revolutions, electoral crises and so on) and the strength of kinship ties. The importance of any collectivity's social integration, as a "buffer" against suicide, was continually reaffirmed by his analyses, leading Durkheim to conclude that there was nothing special about religion. Social integration in any institutional realm had a comparable effect in reducing suicides.

Research Box 8-2 presents one of several studies of social integration and suicide reported by Jack Gibbs. His research, over a period of many years, has consistently tried to systematically test Durkheim's theory of suicide by examining the effects of status integration.

RESEARCH BOX 8-2
Social Integration and the Suicide Rate

The Publication

Jack P. Gibbs, "Status Integration and Suicide." *Social Forces*, 79, 2000, pp 363–384.

The Research Question

Durkheim proposed that the social integration of a collectivity was a major determinant of its members' suicide rate, but he never specified precisely how social integration should be measured. The investigator proposed that social integration could ordinarily be indicated by the proportion of a population that engages in long-term, stable relationships. What can generally interrupt orderly relationships, according to

Gibbs, is the number of people who simultaneously occupy statuses that rarely occur together; for example, a teenager (age status) who is also a widow (marital status). When people occupy these incongruent statuses others are unsure of what to expect from them. Will the person in the previous example behave like a teenager or a widow? And the person with this unusual combination may also be unsure of which status to look to for cues. Thus, the more people that occupy incompatible statuses, the lower the degree of status integration, and the more uncertain expectations will disrupt social relationships. Gibbs proposed that this measure of status integration be viewed as the indicator of social integration, and he hypothesized that suicide rates would be a function of status (i.e. social) integration.

The Data

Data on marital and occupational statuses came from the U.S. Census, and Census figures permitted occupational and marital statuses to be examined in relation to six age groups as well as race and gender. After viewing all the combinations, Gibbs calculated the percentage of people who were in statistically unusual status configurations, assumed those categories represented people with the lowest degree of social integration, and hypothesized that their suicide rates should be higher than those whose statuses were more compatible (i.e. integrated).

The Findings

The initial analysis separately examined the correlation between suicide rates and marital and occupational statuses, configured in relation to age, sex and race. Both marital and occupational status integration were negatively related to suicide, as expected, meaning the higher the degree of integration in an age-race-occupational category or an age-race-marital status category, the lower the suicide rate of people in that category. When people's marital and occupational integration scores were combined, it gave a better measure of their overall status integration, and the magnitude of the differences in suicide rates between people in (overall) integrated versus incongruent combinations of statuses was found to be still larger. Thus, the greater the amount of status integration, the lower the suicide rate.

In related studies, Gibbs and various colleagues have also examined historical fluctuations in the overall status integration of various societies and compared status integration across different societies. Their findings have been essentially the same, consistently reporting a negative relationship between social (status) integration in a society and its rate of suicide.

In the years since the publication of *Suicide*, social integration has been a very widely studied phenomenon by sociologists and social psychologists. A large number of published studies have reported that whether social integration is measured by religion, marital status or friendship ties, it seems to protect individuals from feeling the full effects of stressful situations, such as loss of a job, death of a spouse or the like. As generally explained, it is the social support that is associated with social integration that apparently alleviates how much adverse circumstances disrupt people's sense of psychological well-being.[15]

SOCIAL FACT OR SOCIAL CONSTRUCTION?

Questions about Durkheim's research on suicide began with his definition. What was missing, according to critics, was any examination of the social meanings of people's behavior. The problem was that he treated suicides as "obvious," while skeptics considered consensus about such acts to be very problematic. Some analysts believe that social meanings must be explicitly examined because they shape people's decisions concerning whether any death ought to considered a suicide, versus an accident, a homicide, or something else.[16] Of particular relevance are the judgments of attending physicians, coroners and medical examiners who make official suicide determinations. That is, they ultimately decide whether to label a death a suicide, and it is their collective decisions that produce the official suicide rates that sociologists examine. The problem, according to Jack Douglas, is that sociologists do not know whether the definitions and meanings utilized by these officials correspond with what Durkheim may have had in mind, because he did not say enough about what he had in mind.[17]

To be faithful to Durkheim's legacy, the best way to resolve any uncertainty about social meanings and official statistics may be to ask what difference they make, from a research standpoint. Do varying assumptions about which ambiguous deaths should be classified as suicides substantially alter the results of empirical investigations? Do they change the essential pattern of relationship between suicide rates and other social facts? The answer is: sometimes they do. The mixed findings of studies are illustrated by the two following examples.

Let us begin with a study reported by van Poppel and Day. They were able to obtain complete death records for the Netherlands between 1905 and 1910, a time and place not too dissimilar from Durkheim's own data. They began by examining Protestant–Catholic differences in deaths that physicians had explicitly labeled as suicides. Like Durkheim, they found Protestant rates to be substantially higher. Then they examined two more ambiguous categories: sudden death and deaths due to "ill-defined or unspecified causes." Either of these categories could be used to hide suicides. Who might want to hide a suicide? Their answer is, Catholics, because of the greater stigma that suicide carries in the Catholic community. If there is any reason to doubt the cause of a death, a Catholic family might put more pressure on the attending physician to call it something besides a suicide. And if the cause of death is in any way ambiguous, a Catholic doctor may be more inclined to go along with the deception requested by the family. As a result, when deaths occur in Catholic communities, or the deceased is Catholic, a number of deaths that were actually suicides may officially be placed in a different category.

When the investigators compared Protestants to Catholics solely in relation to the deaths in the ambiguous categories, Catholic rates were found to be much higher than Protestant's. The most logical interpretation, they assumed, was that many Catholic deaths that were really suicides had incorrectly been given a different classification. If the apparently uncertain deaths were added to the deaths that had been labeled as suicides, then the excess of Protestant to Catholic suicides would disappear. Although they acknowledged the impossibility of knowing exactly how many of the ambiguous deaths should be re-classified, the investigators concluded that they believed the difference between Protestant and Catholic suicide rates was entirely due to the way many deaths had been mistakenly recorded.[18]

On the other hand, Pescosolido and Mendelsohn obtained data on religious affiliations and suicide rates for U.S. counties, and reported a strong confirmation of Durkheim's findings with respect to the county's number of Protestants and Catholics, and its rate of suicide. Of most relevance to us here, they also considered the possible effect of recording errors, namely deaths which had been put into unclear accident and illness categories; deaths that could really be hidden suicides. However, they found that the number of such ambiguous deaths in counties tended to correlate highly with the number of suicides; that is, there were more of these questionable deaths in counties that had higher suicide rates. Therefore, they proposed that the effect of excluding deaths whose causes were open to interpretation may in reality mask the true excess of Protestant to Catholic suicides. Furthermore, the investigators note, coroners complain of "cross pressures." While some families may push the coroner to hide a suicide, there are other interest groups, like insurance companies, that pressure them to label ambiguous deaths as suicides. In the end, interest group pressures may be a wash. In sum, when it comes to classifying deaths as suicides or due to other causes, there are probably errors going in both directions, and Durkheim's use of official statistics, they conclude, may actually have led him to understate the magnitude of differences in suicide rates.[19]

MARITAL STATUS AND GENDER

Durkheim continued his analysis of suicide by reporting that married persons, between the ages of about 20 and 40, tended to have lower rates of suicide than single persons of the same age. Among older people, the benefits of marriage with respect to suicide declined, but its salutary effects never disappeared. Even widows and widowers were found to commit suicide less than never married persons, but more than currently married persons (again, of the same age). Further, married people with children were found to have lower rates of suicide than married people who were childless. And when married couples had many children or/and it was social practice for children to continue to live with their parents, the suicide rate of the parents was particularly low. So, children might be a burden, but having such obligations could have positive consequences with respect to suicide.

> "Facts thus are far from confirming the current idea that suicide is due especially to life's burdens, since, on the contrary, it diminishes as these burdens increase."[20]

The number of offspring who remain in the household has the effect of reducing suicidal tendencies, Durkheim surmised, because collective sentiments are strengthened in direct proportion to the number of people involved. These collective sentiments, which act as buffers against suicide, become stronger when,

> "the force with which they affect each individual conscience is echoed in all the others, and reciprocally. The intensity they attain therefore depends on the number of consciences which react to them in common."[21]

As Durkheim further examined marital status's effects within various nations and provinces, he found that marriage and widowhood had especially protective effects for both men and women, but not equally for both. Why should it vary, he wondered? Adding to the puzzle was his finding that the "protective effect" of marriage (and widowhood) was typically stronger for men than for women. In fact, in some age groups, married women (without children) had higher suicide rates than nonmarried women. This was a total reversal of his expectation that women would find fulfillment in marital roles, hence married women would be less prone to suicide. "But," comments R.A. Sydie, he finds that, "domesticity produces unhappy women . . . a real sociological contradiction."[22]

To explain the apparent anomaly, Durkheim asserted that both biological and social differences were operating. For men, marriage exerts a social control, he argued. It restricts men's sexual objects, making them less likely to experience the kind of "agitation and discontent" that would arise without marital restraints, and make suicides more likely. The sexual needs of women, by contrast, were more tied to biological than social mechanisms, in Durkheim's view. Therefore, marriage was not as important a restraint for women as it was for men, and that is why it had less of a protective effect (against suicide) for women. And given the fundamental differences between men and women, he concluded, no one institution, like marriage, could be expected to have the same effects upon both.

Along the same line he proposed that women's lower overall rate of suicide occurred because they were less attached than men to non-familial institutions, hence less exposed to the potentially suicide-producing strains of contemporary societies. "Organic" differences between men and women were again seen as responsible for this difference in their social roles, and he regarded the gendered division of labor that resulted as indispensable to any smoothly functioning society. If women were able to fill the same jobs as men, it would cause social turmoil.

Conservative Positions

If we accept as the criterion of a conservative viewpoint a fearful attitude regarding change (so liberals would be defined by a more welcoming stance toward change), then there is ample reason to consider Durkheim's theoretical position conservative; but the case is not clear cut. His view of women, with respect to marriage and work, clearly supported the status-quo. On the other hand, he considered it possible that women would have more options in the future. Perhaps, some day, women would not be excluded from certain occupations, he conjectured, and would be free to choose the kind of work that interested them. For the turn of the twentieth century, this was not a conservative prediction.

Perhaps the strongest argument for classifying Durkheim as conservative stems from his theory of functional integration with its view of societies as self-regulating, and therefore, not requiring deliberate change efforts. Further, he counseled against people trying to improve social conditions because he feared that their well-meaning intentions were likely to backfire. He believed that society was so poorly understood that people's efforts to alleviate social problems might actually make matters worse.

At the same time, in classifying Durkheim's political leanings it is important to consider his position on the most defining issue of his day: the Dreyfus affair. Albert Dreyfus, a captain in the French army, was accused of treason. Many leading French intellectuals believed the government targeted him in the first place because he was Jewish. He was found guilty in a trial that was very poorly conducted. Years later he was exonerated and re-instated in the army at a higher rank, but in the interim, his case divided the French public. Liberal intellectuals who spoke out in his favor were called, *Dreyfusards*, and the term became shorthand for France's left-liberal intellectuals. Because of his strong criticisms of the government's trial of Dreyfus, Durkheim was considered part of the Dreyfusard group.[23]

TYPES OF SUICIDE

In Durkheim's analysis of marital status and gender, he confronted more complexity in the rates of suicide than in his analysis of religion, and he felt that he could not explain the patterns he observed solely in relation to social integration. In some instances, differences in external restraints seemed as important as social integration in causing suicide rates. He concluded that both of these causal factors had to be combined, resulting in different types of suicide. They differed from each other according to the mix of social conditions (i.e. social facts) that produced them. Examining high and low degrees of external restraint in combination with high and low degrees of social integration produced four types of suicide, but he focused only upon three major types: egoistic, altruistic and anomic.[24]

Egoistic Suicide

Egoistic suicide refers to suicides that occur when there is excessive individuality in a society; too much emphasis upon the individual rather than the collectivity. Because organized human life has a social origin, Durkheim argued, when the bonds that tie people to a society are weakened, individuals do not retain any meaningful goals. People "lose themselves in emptiness," and suffer feelings of despair with nothing to prevent them from ending their lives.

A distinctive feature of egoistic suicide, in Durkheim's account, was the social environment from which it principally "drew its recruits:" people in intellectual careers. In a separate essay on individuality and intellectuals, published around the same time as *Suicide*, he explained that contemporary intellectuals had been cultivating an "egoistic cult of the self." The writings of Kant, Rousseau and other modern thinkers accorded a sacred status to individuals' free inquiry. But, Durkheim asked, if all reason is free and autonomous, as the intellectuals believe, how are people going to take each other into account? An incoherent intellectual anarchy will be the obvious result, he feared, in which people will have nothing in common except their individuality, and all authority of the collectivity will be undermined.[25]

An integrated collectivity, Durkheim noted, holds people "under its control . . . and forbids them to dispose willfully of themselves."[26] They feel an obligation to a collectivity that transcends themselves. When social integration is weak, however, the disintegration of collectivities permits people to indulge their private interests, putting them before the community's. They then find themselves without any reason to "endure life's sufferings." Thus, excessive individuality not only leaves people vulnerable to suicide from any cause, but the meaningless that it generates is, itself, a cause of suicides.

Altruistic Suicide

While egoistic suicides result from a weakening of social integration, *altruistic suicides* are a consequence of its excess. In these social circumstances, people commit suicide because they feel it is their obligation to do so. Failure to take one's life would bring overwhelming dishonor or unbearable shame. Thus, social demands weigh very heavily, and correspondingly, there is insufficient individuation to resist what the person sees as society's imperatives.

The conditions which call for altruistic suicide vary from society to society, and in some societies there are no such conditions. Where present, they can include any personal shortcoming or misbehavior that causes embarrassment to one's family, peers, or other group of significance to the person. It could involve an academic failure, being unsuccessful in battle, or the like. In any case, with respect to altruistic suicide, it is society that "is the author of conditions and circumstances making this obligation coercive."[27] However, for individuals to be willing to carry out their own death sentences they must be completely absorbed into the collectivity which, in turn, must be highly integrated. Such societies, Durkheim wrote, tolerate no loose ends.

Anomic Suicide

In introducing *anomic suicide*, Durkheim acknowledged that this type could not be distinguished solely in relation to degree of social integration versus individuation. The new dimension he considered most relevant was the regulation that was imposed by collective authority. In his earliest book, *DoL*, he had asserted that only social norms could set limits on people's aspirations and that without such controls people's urges would become insatiable and a source of torment. In *Suicide* he returned to these ideas and linked them to a distinct type of suicide.

It was in the economic realm that Durkheim believed anomie was especially problematic because (in a statement that could have been made by Marx) he claimed that, "government, instead of regulating economic life, has become its tool and servant."[28] His evidence that anomie was a problem in the economic realm included the high rate of suicide of people working in industry compared to the low rate of suicide among people working in agriculture. The former were dependent upon new forms of regulation that had not yet emerged while old regulatory forces persisted in agriculture. The different careers from which they drew people was an important part of the distinction between anomic and egoistic suicides: anomie "recruited" from industry, egoism from among the ranks of intellectuals.

Durkheim also showed that among provinces and nations, there was a consistent relationship between suicide and divorce; both were high or both were low. Anomie was the common antecedent to both, he argued. First, the absence of normative regulations encourages insatiable longings not only for wealth, but for sexual gratifications which can lead to divorce and then to suicide. However, he noted that the relationship between suicide and divorce held strongly for men, but not at all for women. To explain why he claimed it was men whose sexual passions most needed the regulation accorded by marriage. Therefore, divorce led to "agitation and discontent" for men, not women, and that is why men's (and not women's) suicide rate was increased by divorce.

Endnotes

1. Emile Durkheim, *The Rules of Sociological Method*. New York: Free Press, 1966. This quote is taken from the author's preface to second edition, p xiv. Durkheim's assumption that the sociologist is male is unfortunate, but I do not want to clutter the quote with a (sic) following each "he."

2. Neil Gross and Robert A. Jones (Eds.), *Durkheim's Philosophy Lectures*. New York: Cambridge University Press, 2004.

3. *Rules*, p 35.

4. Ibid., Preface to second edition, p xliii.
5. Susan Steadman Jones, *Durkheim Reconsidered*. Cambridge, UK: Polity Press, 2001.
6. *Rules*, p 128. Italics in original.
7. For further discussion, see Warren Schmaus, *Rethinking Durkheim and His Tradition*. Cambridge, UK: Cambridge University Press, 2004.
8. *Rules*, p 91.
9. Robert B. Edgerton, *Sick Societies*. New York: Free Press, 1992.
10. Emile Durkheim, *Suicide*. New York: Free Press, 1951, p 44. Italics in original.
11. Ibid., p 43.
12. He measured these psychological variables as rates, at the societal level. So, the absence of a correlation between any of them and rates of suicide would not necessarily prove that mentally ill persons or alcoholics were not more likely to take their own lives. To assume otherwise would be to commit what has come to be termed, *the ecological fallacy*. It involves the assumption that a correlation which is found between two variables at one level (i.e. individual or collective) will similarly hold at another level.
13. *Suicide*, p 77.
14. Whitney Pope, *Durkheim's Suicide*. Chicago: University of Chicago Press, 1976.
15. For a review of studies, see Peggy A. Thoits, "Stress, coping, and social support processes." *Journal of Health and Social Behavior* (Extra Issue), 1995.
16. See the examination of cultural differences in the meaning of suicide in, Lisa Lieberman, *Leaving You*. Chicago: Ivan R. Dee, 2003.
17. Jack D. Douglas, *The Social Meanings of Suicide*. Princeton, NJ: Princeton University Press, 1967.
18. There was another difference between this study and Durkheim's. These investigators obtained information on the religious affiliation of each of the deceased people, while Durkheim relied upon the religious composition of geographical areas. These contemporary investigators were, therefore, less likely to commit the ecological fallacy. See, Frans van Poppel and Lincoln H. Day, "A Test of Durkheim's Theory of Suicide." *American Sociological Review*, 61, 1996.
19. Bernice A. Pescosolido and Robert Mendelsohn, "Social Causation or Social Construction of Suicide?" *American Sociological Review*, 51, 1986. See also, Bernice A. Pescosolido and Sharon Georgianna, "Durkheim, Suicide and Religion." *American Sociological Review*, 54, 1989.
20. *Suicide*, p 201.
21. Ibid.
22. R.A. Sydie, *Natural Women, Cultured Men*. New York: New York University Press, 1987.
23. See Robert A. Nisbet, *The Sociology of Emile Durkheim*. New York: Oxford University Press, 1974.
24. He very briefly noted a fourth type, *fatalistic*, but offered very little description.
25. Emile Durkheim, "Individualism and the Intellectuals." In Robert N. Bellah (Ed.), *Emile Durkheim on Morality and Society*. Chicago: University of Chicago Press, 1973.
26. *Suicide*, p 209.
27. Ibid., p 220.
28. Ibid., p 255.

CHAPTER

9

Georg Simmel

BIOGRAPHY

Georg Simmel was a prolific writer, mostly of essays rather than books, and the range of topics he addressed was very impressive. Many of his essays focused upon sociology, and his ideas concerned how the new discipline ought to proceed; and he also wrote extensively in philosophy, religion and art, examining Leonardo da Vinci, Rembrandt and others. His work was very well received in his lifetime, and many of his essays were translated into English and other languages very soon after they appeared.[1] However, compared to the other major theorists described in this book, we know relatively few of the intimate details of Georg Simmel's life. He did not write an autobiography, his contemporaries did not offer many biographical insights, and most of his personal papers did not survive. We do know that he was born in 1858, the youngest of seven children in an upper middle class family supported by his father's factory. He spent much of his life in the center of Berlin, Germany—a bustling and cosmopolitan city—and that probably influenced his view of how living in cities shaped people's relationships and outlooks. One of his enduring essays was entitled,

"*The Metropolis and Mental Life*" (originally published in 1902).

The death of Simmel's father (when he was a teenager) created temporary economic hardships for the family, but his mother soon remarried. Her new husband had been a family friend who the children had referred to as "*Uncle Dol.*" When Simmel's mother remarried, all of the older siblings had left home. Uncle Dol and 15-year-old Georg became very close, and when Uncle Dol died he left Georg a very large inheritance. It permitted him to travel widely and to live in the most exclusive residential areas, even though throughout almost his entire life his university salary was very meager.[2]

Both of Simmel's biological parents had been born into Jewish families, but they converted before he was born, and he was baptized. Nevertheless, to those anti-semitic Germans who looked very closely at everyone for any evidence of Jewishness, he seemed Jewish. Apart from his family's origins, many of the intellectuals he associated with, and most of his students, were Jewish. Mariane Weber (Max's wife), who admired his work, described his appearance as, "typically Jewish" (and she added, "ugly").[3] Colleagues and students also commented on Simmel's frequent use of (Eastern European) Jewish gestures and idioms.

His social identity as a Jew greatly slowed his academic career, despite his well-regarded publications. Especially notable was his analysis of how money assigned value to things and altered people's outlooks. Max Weber's copy of this book, for example, was replete with notes in the margins, and he considered it a very important work.[4]

The Philosophy of Money (originally published in 1900).

Weber and other leading scholars tried for many years to help him to obtain a major academic position, but such positions eluded him for most of his life.

The discrimination Simmel faced must have created quite a dilemma for him because he did not consider himself to be Jewish.[5] Perhaps it made him sensitive to the role of people who, like himself, stood at the margins of groups or societies, and it may have influenced his essay on strangers as outsiders.

The Sociological Significance of the Stranger (originally published in 1908).

He was part of a creative and unconventional circle in Berlin: philosophers, painters, academics, etc. They met in each other's homes, and sometimes in a beer hall, usually on Friday nights. One such group that Simmel regularly met with expressed their bohemian leanings by referring to themselves as, *The Society of the Unbridled*. One member of the group was Sabine Graef, and she considered Simmel her mentor and friend. She described him as someone who was more disposed to sadness than to joy in life. He always shared her disappointments and offered comfort, she wrote, but when things were going well he could not share her joy. He almost seemed incapable of being upbeat and optimistic.[6]

Sabine Graef's roommate was a young painter and writer named Gertrud Kinel. She was also part of their intellectual circle and she and Simmel wound up marrying. It was an unusual marriage for the time because of their commitment to an equalitarian relationship in which they wrote, traveled and studied together. Simmel became very interested in the complexity of women's roles, and wrote a number of essays exploring the issue. Several of these essays are included in a volume later translated and edited by Guy Oakes.

Georg Simmel: On Women, Sexuality and Love. New Haven: Yale University Press, 1984.

Along with Max Weber and others, Simmel was a founder of the German Sociological Association, and he examined questions about what ought to be the focus of the new discipline in a large number of papers. He emphasized the form of relationships—how they were configured or patterned—as constituting the distinguishing feature of sociological analysis. One of the great advantages of focusing upon form is that it permits the sociologist simultaneously to examine phenomena at a micro (i.e. individual) and macro (i.e. institutional) level because the same (or nearly the same) concepts can be utilized. What Simmel meant by form will be examined in detail in this chapter; for now we merely note a few of the many essays he wrote that presented his focus upon form.

"The Problem of Sociology." *Annals of the American Academy of Political and Social Science*, 3, 1895.

"The Number of Members as Determining the Sociological Form of the Group." *American Journal of Sociology*, 8, 1902.

"The Intersection of Social Circles"/"The Web of Group-Affiliations" (originally published in 1908).

Shortly before Simmel's death in 1918 he wrote, "My legacy will be . . . distributed to many heirs."[7] With respect to intellectual contributions his words were prophetic. With respect to personal artifacts, however, little survived, for an ironic reason. George and Gertrud Simmel had one son, Hans, who wound up custodian of his father's papers. During the 1930's, as the Nazis were coming to power in Germany, Hans was considered Jewish enough to be briefly interred in a concentration camp. Just before World War Two broke out he was able to flee to the U.S., but most of his possessions, including boxes of his father's papers, were lost forever in the trip.[8]

SOCIOLOGY AS THE STUDY OF FORM

Like many of the classical theorists, Simmel proposed an agenda for sociology that was designed to carve out a distinct area of inquiry for the new discipline. Sociology's establishment as a separate discipline required, they all believed, that it find a niche that would distinguish it from economics, history, psychology and other related fields of inquiry. The theorists differed in specifics, though; that is, what special and exclusive quality they advocated for sociology. In Simmel's case, the unique feature of sociology was to be its conceptual emphasis upon the form of interaction.

By *form* he meant the pattern that characterized a specific type of interaction. To illustrate, "play" as a form of interaction typically includes: some kind of search or hunt, attempts to fool or trick an opponent, competition and some dependence upon luck or chance. Consider, as examples of play, games of: monopoly, hide and seek, tag, chess, etc. The defining features of play, as noted earlier, can be inferred from the elements common to all of the games.[9]

Another way to approach the question of form is by noting that which it does not include. Simmel, himself, examined it this way, after posing a dichotomy consisting of content and form. Each subsumed everything excluded by the other. To be specific, *content*, in Simmel's scheme, had two referents:

1. Institutional contexts, pertaining to an economic, political, religious or other context in which the interaction occurred; and
2. Psychological motives, involving the greed, anger or other interests that motivated people to interact with each other.

Put differently, Simmel recognized that institutional contexts influenced interaction. The hierarchical relationship between a priest and a bishop would probably differ in some ways from the hierarchical relationship between a player and a coach by virtue of the different institutional contexts in which each occurred. In addition, the people's motives in these relationships would also be different, and these differences would also have consequences. However, transcending these variations Simmel believed it would be possible to identify similarities in how people in superordinate and subordinate roles interacted with each other. These similarities constituted form. Thus, when one eliminated institutions and motives from an analysis, what remained was pure form.

Academic politics probably also played a part in Simmel's theoretical strategy. In identifying these two aspects of content, Simmel was acknowledging, first, that the major institutions had already been spoken for, by: political science, religious studies, economics, etc. If sociology were to be recognized, it could not duplicate the disciplines that preceded it, so focusing upon institutions was not an option. He acknowledged, second, that the study of people's motives was already taken also, by psychology; so focusing upon the psychological dimension was not likely to be a winning strategy either. That left form as the unique subject matter for sociology.

The Significance of Numbers

Simmel believed that the size of a group typically exerted an important influence upon forms of interaction. Smaller groups have certain qualities, he wrote, that disappear when the group grows larger. Could there be the same degree of cohesion in a group with 700 members as in a group with 7? Further, certain forms of interaction only appear when a group reaches a certain size. Coalitions, for example, in which two or more people form an alliance in opposition to someone else, could not occur in a two-person group.

The lowest possible number, in this sense, would be one: the isolated individual. Simmel began his analysis of numbers with one, noting that others continue to have an effect on the isolated individual's feeling of aloneness. When a solitary individual is in the presence of others who are interacting with each other—at a party, on a train or the like—feelings of aloneness and loneliness are typically more pronounced than when the solitary individual is alone.

Although Simmel was intrigued with the situation of the isolated individual, he recognized that such a person was primarily of psychological interest.

The minimal size with true sociological significance, he wrote, is two: the dyad. It is the two sided *form* of interaction that distinguishes dyads. They need not be literally comprised of two persons. Thus, each party in a dyad could consist of individuals, families, organizations, nations, etc. This is a feature that makes Simmel's approach so amenable to different levels of analysis, i.e. macro to micro. (We will return to this issue at the end of this section.)

Dyads

Regardless of the number of persons within each party in the dyad, all such relationships tend to have certain distinguishing features. Each party's tie to the other, Simmel noted, is direct rather than mediated through others. If either party leaves, it terminates a dyad. Recognizing this, neither party is likely to perceive the dyad as though it were a superstructure beyond themselves. If the dyad represents an institutionalized relationship, however, then the parties sometimes do attribute an independent-of-themselves existence to the relationship. Thus, a married couple may refer to the "sake of the marriage," or two business partners may think about the "good of the partnership" as though either the marriage or the partnership had an existence that was somehow external to its participants. As the size of a group increases, the sense of superstructure becomes more salient and people respond by worrying less about shirking responsibilities, assuming there are plenty of others around to pick up the slack.

Simmel also considered the parties in a dyad particularly susceptible to extreme emotional fluctuations. At one pole of the continuum, each party grows sick of the other, and despises the very sight of the other. At the other pole, dyads offer people the greatest potential attraction and intimacy. Simmel described these extremes as the "all or nothing" feature of dyads.[10] The parties tend to love each other or hate each other, and both states tend quickly to change to the other. Popular dramas have frequently been built about the tendency-to-extremes that characterize dyads. In *The Odd Couple*, or *Who's Afraid of Virginia Woolf*, for example, the drama focuses upon a couple—roommates in *The Odd Couple*, a husband and wife in *Virginia Woolf*—in which each party's feelings toward the other continuously swing from intense rage to great closeness. These oscillations are an important feature in defining the form of the dyad.

Triads

The addition of a third party dramatically alters the form of a relationship. One possibility is that it may unite the parties in the dyad. To illustrate, the birth of a child (third party) provides a common bond to husband and wife. As mother and father, they are bound to each other directly and through the tie of each to the child. From the mother's standpoint, he is not only her husband, but the father of her child. In addition, the third party can restrain the level of conflict within the dyad. If there are three business partners (rather than two), for example, whenever two are quarreling the third party can be a voice of reason and moderation. In the absence of a third party (i.e. in a dyad), part of the reason conflicts can spin out of control is due to the absence of anyone who could play a mediating role.

The third party also separates the former two-some because the presence of a third party lessens the possibility of intense intimacy characteristic of dyads. Two can feel as one, Simmel noted, but three cannot.

> "No matter how close a triad may be, there is always the occasion on which two of the three members regard the third as an intruder."[11]

Thus, the triadic form "flattens" the extreme highs and lows of a dyad, pushing both extremes toward an emotional middle ground.

In addition, the triad introduces emergent properties: forms of relationship not possible with smaller numbers. One such form that Simmel analyzed at length was the coalition of two against one. He viewed triads as inherently unstable, that is, as regularly tending toward such coalitions, but varying in terms of who was coalesced against whom. Perhaps it is business partners one and two against partner three today, but one and three against two tomorrow; mother and child against father today, but mother and father against child tomorrow. If the composition of the coalition within the triad did not vary, it would cease to be a triad—it would become a dyad. Remember, Simmel was talking about parties, not people. Thus, if mother and father, for example, permanently remained in a tight coalition vis–à–vis their child, then the two of them would comprise a single party. The relationship would be dyadic, between parents (party one) and child (party two).

Another distinctive feature of triads, in Simmel's analysis, was the possibility of *tertius gaudens*, literally defined as third party benefit. The type of situation he described occurs when two members of a triad are quarreling or competing, and the third chooses not to play a mediating role. In order to induce the third party into a coalition, each of the competing parties might (without intending to) bid up what the other is willing to offer. Here the third party benefit is direct. It can also be indirect, as when the conflict between two parties so preoccupies each of them that the third party is free to act in ways that would otherwise be challenged. If parents are arguing, for example, they may not notice when their teenager came home at night; and if they did, each might prefer to let it go, fearing that a negative reaction would drive the teenager closer to the other parent. In order to continue to obtain tertius guadens benefits, the third party must ordinarily keep the two parties in conflict from re-uniting. If they come together, the form of interaction will change, and third party benefits will be terminated.

In recent analyses of social networks in work settings, tertius gaudens has been equated with a disunion strategy: keep contending or quarreling parties apart. While maintaining the separation between others can sometimes be in a third party's interest, that strategy may have harmful consequences for a work organization. It can be dysfunctional for the firm because innovation often requires new combinations of people; that is, bringing others together rather than keeping them apart. The way different third party orientations influence innovations is examined in Research Box 9-1.

RESEARCH BOX 9-1

To Separate Others or to Unite Them

The Publication

David Obstfeld, "Social Networks, The Tertius Lungens Orientation and Involvement in Innovation." *Administrative Science Quarterly*, 50, 2005.

The Research Question

Tertius gaudens is a "disunion" strategy: keep protagonists apart because potential third party benefits end if they unite. Following this separation strategy may be in the third party's short-term interest, but it may adversely impact an employing organization, because the innovations on which companies depend often require new combinations of people. In other words, creative ideas commonly arise when people with different viewpoints are brought together rather than kept apart. It is, of course, third parties who could bring them together. Obstfeld termed this uniting strategy, *tertius lungens*, meaning the third party connects; and he predicted that people's involvement in innovations would correlate positively with a tertius lungens, rather than tertius gaudens, orientation.

The Data

The investigator spent 12 months studying the engineering department of a Detroit automotive manufacturer. From his interviews with management, he identified 73 important innovations in design that had occurred in the firm over the preceding three years. From discussions with experts familiar with each of the 73 innovations, he assigned all potential participants a score that reflected their degree of involvement with each of the innovations. A high score was given when a person played a major role, a low score for a minor role, and zero for no role. He also had nearly 200 professional employees in the division fill out questionnaires dealing with their professional and educational backgrounds and, most importantly, whether they were personally more inclined to bring people with different perspectives together (i.e. tertius lungens) or to keep them apart.

The Findings

The results indicated that an employee's degree of involvement in innovative designs correlated highly with the employee's tertius lungens orientation. Conversely, the more people were predisposed to keep protagonists apart, the less was their involvement with innovations. Even after people's education, organizational rank, years in the firm and other background variables were held constant, this predisposition to bringing people together remained a very strong predictor of people's roles in innovations. Thus, while keeping other people apart—especially if their views clash with each other—may serve the immediate interests of a third ¬party, if this tertius gaudens approach is wide-spread in a company's work force, it will likely result in fewer creative ideas for the employing firm.

Two against one coalitions and tertius gaudens provide ways of looking at relationships that can also characterize nations. Suppose, to illustrate, the U.S. (party one) is fighting against groups in Iraq (party two). Then other nations (e.g. North Korea, Iran, Saudi Arabia, etc.) can become party three in a tertius gaudens arrangement. That is, the third party—in this case, a nation rather than an individual—may be able to aggress against another without provoking a response from party one; or the third party might receive aid from party one that would not be offered if party one was not engaged in a conflict with party two. (As a result of the conflict, party one may be more concerned with having party three as an ally; or at least, not becoming an ally of party two.) Third party benefits can thereby accrue to nations as well as individuals.

Corporations can similarly be the beneficiaries of a third party configuration. If two corporations are competing to buy a third corporation, for example, the price eventually paid by the winner will likely be greater than it would have been in the absence of competition. The shareholders of the purchased corporation—the third party—reap the benefits. The fact that international relations or corporate take-overs can be described according to the same tertius gaudens analysis as a three-person family illustrates the way Simmel's emphasis upon the form of interaction can provide a model that provides insights into relationships among both micro and macro entities.

As group size increased beyond three, according to Simmel, each addition had a decreasing effect. The third party changed a dyad more than a fourth party changed a dyad, and so on. When groups grow very large, the form of interaction tends to revert back to a dyad; that is, the people divide themselves into two groupings: blacks and whites, men and women, Republicans or Democrats. Everyone must be in one or the other grouping, and no in between status is permitted.

Simmel also contended that certain types of groups had to restrict their growth. Among the examples he noted were religious sects and aristocracies. The ties of solidarity among members that are required for groups of this type to persist cannot be maintained if their size exceeds some upper limit. In addition, the group cannot become so large that members lose the ability to survey every single other member. "Each element must still be personally acquainted with every other."[12] He did not specify the precise size of the upper limit of such groups, but he was certain that it could be deduced.

THE STRANGER

A wanderer who just passes through the midst of a group and keeps going could be considered a stranger, but such a person would be of little sociological significance because there would be no opportunity for any kind of meaningful relationship between the wanderer and members of the group. Of more interest to Simmel was the person who was a stranger because he or she came from elsewhere and, despite staying, nevertheless remained an outsider as viewed by insiders.

The stranger, as a sociological type according to Simmel, is defined by a combination of both nearness and remoteness. Because the stranger is from somewhere else and therefore brings new qualities to the group, the stranger is always set apart in the minds of group members. At the same time, the stranger lives among and within the group, hence is near. It is this mixture of distance and closeness that makes the stranger in, but not of, the group that most distinguishes the social role of the stranger.

Unlike everyone else, the stranger lacks ties to members of the group that they share with each other. Therefore, the stranger is the only one who could really leave at any moment, and recognition of this fact is usually in the back of everyone's mind. The classic example of what he meant by a stranger, Simmel wrote, was the Jewish trader in the Middle Ages. Even if he stayed in a village for years, he remained unconnected to everyone else in the village in the sense that he, alone, did not share with other villagers any important quality, such as a place of birth, a kinship, an occupation, etc.

The lack of ties, Simmel continued, means the stranger lacks entanglements, which always gives the stranger a unique objectivity. Simmel thought that probably explained why, in relations with a stranger, members of any group or community tended to be surprisingly candid, revealing confidences to the stranger that they would ordinarily withhold from anyone else. Contemporary strangers who happen to find themselves sitting next to each other on an airplane, for example, will often tell intimate details of their lives to each other that they would not disclose even to close friends.

When there are multiple strangers in a group, it is common for members of the group to emphasize some similarity among the strangers. This leads the group to develop a category based upon: where the strangers are from, their race, religion, occupation, or the like—even though the emphasized quality may not be especially salient to the strangers, themselves. Thus, group members handle the differentness of strangers by transforming them into specific *types* of strangers. To illustrate, Simmel again turned to the experience of Jews in Medieval German cities. Municipalities charged all of them the same fixed tax. Unlike the tax of everyone else in the city, which was a percentage of their wealth, the tax on Jews did not vary. All Jews, rich or poor, were outsiders and, as such, were taxed the same fixed amount which demonstrated to Simmel the fact that, "the Jew had his social position as a *Jew*, not [an] individual."[13]

The study summarized in Research Box 9-2 analyzed contemporary American communities according to whether minority groups that lived within their boundaries possessed the combination of closeness and remoteness with which Simmel defined strangers. When they did, the investigators asked, were the minority groups more likely to be the targets of hate groups? Note how the research moves from a conception of relations with strangers as individuals, to a conception of large groups as constituting strangers.

RESEARCH BOX 9-2

The Targets of Hate Groups as Strangers

The Publication

Rory McVeigh and David Sikkink, "Organized Racism and the Stranger." *Sociological Forum*, 20, 2005.

The Research Question

The primary objective of the study was to determine the characteristics of communities in which racist hate groups were active. The investigators reasoned that these hate groups would be most likely to operate in communities whose demographic profiles put minorities into the social position of "strangers," as described by Simmel. Specifically, they hypothesized that communities in which non-whites were present in significant numbers would provide the "closeness" Simmel described; the concentration of non-whites in poor, segregated neighborhoods would provide the social "distance" Simmel specified. Then they expected that the combination of both closeness and distance would, following Simmel, make non-whites analogous to strangers, from the point of view of whites in the community.

The Data

The investigators began with a list of over 3,000 counties in the U.S., then took information about each from the 2000 U.S. Census. Included were such variables as: race, income, unemployment, region of the country, etc. The Southern Poverty Law Center (SPLC) provided a list of active hate groups, designating any organization as a hate group from reading and analyzing its publications, and also by relying upon a number of other sources, including reports from law enforcement agencies and the news media. In 2001, SPLC identified a total of about 600 active hate groups in the U.S.: neo-Nazi organizations, Klan chapters, racist skinhead groups, etc.

The investigators took the 600 hate groups and placed each into its home county. They found that all of the groups were located in only 13% of the counties; thus, almost 87% of all counties had no active hate groups in 2001. The question of interest: How did the 13% of counties that had hate group differ from the 87% that did not?

The Findings

The probability that there was an active racist group in the county was found to be highest when, as expected, there was a large non-white population *and* it was separated from the white population, both geographically and socially. The large size of the non-white group apparently led to stereotyping, rumors and the formation of hate groups in the white community; meanwhile, the physical and social separation between the white and non-white segments of the population prevented people in the white community from recognizing the inaccuracies of the stereotypes that encouraged the formation of hate groups.

It was the combination of closeness and separation, rather than either alone, that was associated with hate groups; and this same combination of variables that defined strangers, wherever it was present, similarly produced hate groups in all regions of the country.

WEBS OF AFFILIATION

One of the most distinguishing features of any society, Simmel believed, was the number of different social groups with which most individuals participated, and the way those groups were arranged relative to each other. He approached the issue historically, showing how patterns of group affiliation changed over time. Simmel also analyzed the psychological implications of different patterns, focusing in particular upon degrees of individualization (i.e. personal uniqueness). Here again his analysis blended the micro and the macro.

During earlier periods in history, a common pattern involved societies in which individuals had a single group affiliation. Because they belonged to one and only one association, the demands that could be placed upon people were neither mediated nor compromised. For example, in the Roman Empire, Simmel noted, officers in the army were expected, like Roman Catholic priests, to remain celibate. In the Middle Ages, journeymen who were hoping to move ahead in their trade were discouraged from marrying. In each case, marriage was partially or completely prohibited on the assumption that a familial group could make a competing claim upon the loyalty of the Roman officer or the Medieval journeyman (or others). Members' affiliation with any other group is incompatible to a group that wants its participants "to become absorbed unconditionally in its activities."[14]

Simmel proposed, as previously noted, that there was a close correspondence between the pattern of group affiliations and the degree of individual differentiation. When one group absorbs its members entirely, the result is great personal similarities among everyone that shares that single affiliation. All the Roman army officers were entirely officers—engulfed by that one role—and only officers—nothing else. The experiences and outlooks of each officer were completely shared by every other officer. Thus, there were few individual differences among the officers or among Medieval journeymen, or within any other group whose members shared only a single affiliation.

Historically, when people belonged to several groups there tended to be a sequential arrangement among the groups based upon how and when people entered them. For example, in a preliterate society, the extended family into which people were born might provide everyone with a central role throughout their lives. Children might be educated by a grandparent (who was also the political chief, religious leader, etc.), and as the children grew into adults they took on roles in the political, religious, and other groups as determined by their position in the kinship system. Simmel described this as a concentric pattern with groups added like the rings of a tree. The congruence among concentrically added groups would ordinarily result in few opportunities for people to experience conflicting pulls in their group affiliations.

Most contemporary societies, by contrast, are characterized by multiple affiliations among groups that are not usually arranged concentrically. Most individuals belong to the family in which they were born, a family created by marriage, an occupational group, religious organization and so on. The demands of each could be in conflict, but every group's claim upon the individual's time and allegiance is typically limited by virtue of the obligations to other groups that each individual is understood to have. No group can ordinarily expect to engulf its members and absorb them entirely.

Seventy years after Simmel presented his theory of group affiliations, an American-trained sociologist, Lewis Coser, described how laws developed to confine the claims that groups and institutions could make upon people. These laws, he wrote, help to maintain a balance in the social structure.[15] (Coser was born in Berlin a few years before Simmel died.) Illustrating Coser's argument: the amount of time employees can (or can be expected to) work is limited by employment laws, insulating non-work roles from being overwhelmed by work demands; husbands and wives cannot be compelled to testify against each other, restricting the ability of a state or judicial system to intrude into marriage and family roles; child labor laws protect the educational institution from being overwhelmed by occupational demands; and so on. These regulations play an important part in enabling modern people to maintain multiple affiliations.

Despite structural constraints to inhibit them, Simmel recognized that there was a persistent tendency for certain groups to encroach upon the time and energy people had to devote to other groups. He believed that religion had a particular inclination to crowd out other (secular) groups because, "the disavowal of all social ties . . . is evidence of deep religiosity."[16] To demonstrate the potential strength of religious ties, Simmel pointed to historical relations between the Protestants of England and Ireland who, despite animosities between their nations, periodically formed a unifying bond. (They also provided an interesting example of the instability of coalitions: one month the Protestants of England and Ireland united against the Catholics; the next month the Protestants and Catholics of Ireland united against England, and so on.)

Coser similarly recognized that even with modern structural barriers to engulfment, institutions and groups still had the potential to absorb people. He utilized the term, *greedy institutions*, to describe organizations and groups that go against the prevailing trend, make excessive claims on members, seek their undivided loyalty, and attempt to encompass the person, in totality. The spouses of soldiers fighting in Iraq, according to Ender and others, provide an interesting contemporary example of people confronting greedy institutions. For the spouse of a deployed soldier, there are typically new role demands to take over familial responsibilities formerly handled by the now absent spouse: child care, shopping, home maintenance, etc. Thus, the family role greatly expands and threatens to engulf the spouse. At the same time, media coverage of the war (especially in its early stages) was omnipresent. The spouse left at home felt pulled to watch CNN all day, every day. Some spouses felt anxious whenever they turned off the news, so they slept with the television on, and forced themselves awake periodically at night to monitor events. They were caught between two greedy institutions: their families and the news media, each of which threatened to absorb them completely.

Affiliations and the Person

The differences among societies in their patterns of group affiliations correspond directly with opportunities for individualization. In modern societies, where multiple and balanced affiliations are the norm, each person's pattern of attachments tends to be unique. No individuals therefore share exactly the same experiences, have the identical orientations and so on. Simmel conceptualized these patterns geometrically, thinking about groups as represented by circles. (We still talk about the group to which a person belongs as constituting the person's social circle.) Some ancient societies could be described by a number of non-overlapping circles because most of the individuals in the society would be contained within one and only one circle. Other historical societies could be configured by a series of concentric circles, some of which might be larger in circumference, reflecting their greater importance in people's lives. Finally, the partially overlapping circles in modern societies describe individuals who are not interchangeable, and whose singular characteristics can develop because the structure of modern society enables them to stand, "at the intersection of social circles."[17]

Pescosolido and Rubin note that the distinguishing pattern of multiple affiliations in contemporary societies is also associated with a potentially distinctive problem of under-commitment.[18] Individuals, in effect, can fall through the cracks in a way that would not be possible if they were expected to be engulfed by a single group or institution. Thus, the freedom and flexibility of modern society also means a potential for alienation and isolation because people's ties to all groups may be temporary and ephemeral.

SECRECY

Simmel introduced his essay on the role of secrecy in social life by claiming that "the hiding of realities" was one of humanity's greatest accomplishments. In preliterate societies or among young children, everything is manifest: accessible to everyone. And in Simmel's view, that made social life simple and uninteresting. The secret, he wrote, enlarges life because it makes possible other conditions, such as betrayal, protection and confidence. Secrecy, in effect, creates a second social world alongside of, and mutually effecting, the manifest social world.

All relationships, Simmel wrote, can be ranked according to the amount of knowledge that people in the relationship have about each other's total personality. At the low end of the continuum, an interest group, such as a chamber of commerce or a trade union, does not require that participants have *any* intimate knowledge of each other. "Its members are psychologically anonymous."[19] Similarly, among acquaintances, one knows only who or what the other is on the outside. The essential, or intrinsic, characteristics of each are not known to the other; if they were, then by definition the parties would no longer be mere acquaintances—they would be friends. To maintain the acquaintance relationship, Simmel noted, each party must respect the privacy of the other, and be very discrete about probing beyond what the acquaintance chooses to reveal. From overt mannerisms (i.e. "tells") a skilled observer could pick up on the secrets another unintentionally disclosed. With respect to jeopardizing an acquaintanceship, however, Simmel considered taking advantage of such inferences no different than eavesdropping outside a door or reading a discarded letter.

At the same time, Simmel recognized that even when the parties to a relationship require no intimate knowledge of each other, there is frequently some need to see beyond that which is external and superficial. If business people are establishing a long-term relationship, for example, each may feel entitled to know something about the other's past, temperament, moral standards, etc. It may be considered indiscrete, and it may yield guilty knowledge, but,

> "all of human intercourse rests on the fact that everybody knows somewhat more about the other than the other voluntarily reveals . . . and those things . . . are frequently matters whose knowledge the other person . . . would find undesirable."[20]

The exemplars of relationships involving detailed reciprocal knowledge of each other's total personalities are friendship and love. They are a distinct type because these relationships are based, in principle, on the total involvement of participants. Particularly during the first stages of such relationships, Simmel observed, people are tempted to let themselves "be completely absorbed by the other" and lose themselves to the other "without reservation."[21] They fear not giving enough of themselves to the relationship, and it induces them to give more than they should. To succumb to this temptation can seriously threaten the future of the relationship because most people's inner lives are not unlimited. Every disclosure therefore leaves them with less of themselves to reveal in the future. In short, they become boring because the other knows all there is to know about them. There are no more surprises because they retain no more little delights to disclose about themselves. It is exceptional people whose psychic treasures continue to grow and provide them with an inexhaustible reservoir of psychological capital. It keeps them interesting because they are always a little unpredictable.

With respect to marriage, in particular, Simmel stressed the importance of discretion: guarding against revealing too much *and* against trying to get the other to reveal too much. If they go too far, the marriage can be the casualty. Husband and wife "lapse into a trivial habituation without charm, into a matter-of-factness which has no longer any room for surprises."[22] What is required, he concluded, is self-discipline that keeps each from probing too far into the other's "inner private property," respecting the other's right to intentionally withhold some potential self-revelations.

Maintaining a degree of secrecy can contribute directly to maintaining a marriage or close friendship in still another way. Suppose, Simmel wrote, one party has committed an act the other would consider a betrayal, and feel offended. Keeping the act secret may be the only way to prevent the termination of the relationship. Further, if the transgression is kept secret, a troubled conscience can induce the guilty party to be more accommodating and considerate, making the relationship more attractive to the other party.

The Secret Society

When a person has a secret, Simmel wrote, it tends to have an isolating effect, separating the person with something to hide from others. Too much intimacy could lead to inadvertent disclosure. However, when secrecy characterizes the group in totality, it has the opposite effect. It ties together members of a group who work to maintain and protect each other's invisibility. Simmel was thinking of such "secret societies" as a gang of swindlers, an association formed for engaging in sexual orgies, underground religious cults, etc.[23] The members of secret societies can openly interact with each other if they happen to belong to the same social circle, have business dealings or the like. However, they cannot openly interact with each other as members of the secret society. Their shared secret is the portal to a hidden world that exists alongside of the manifest social world.

In further contrasting the secret of an individual with a secret society, Simmel noted that an individual can hide a secret, but not an existence. A person can ordinarily hide (become invisible) for only brief periods. By contrast, when the social unit itself is the secret, its identity might be permanently concealed. Helping to maintain secret societies, but not the secrets of individuals, are rituals: handshakes, codes and the like that only group members share. What was most striking to Simmel was not only the careful way members observed the ritual, but the lengths to which they went to keep it from being publicly known. "Its disclosure appears to be as detrimental," he wrote, "as that . . . of the very existence of the society.[24]

The study summarized in Research Box 9-3 examines single women who were in secret, forbidden relationships with married men. The investigation tries, following Simmel, to clarify the effects of the secrecy upon their relationships. Note how, as Simmel anticipated, ritual was found to play an extremely important part in maintaining the secret relationship.

RESEARCH BOX 9-3
Women in Secret, Sexual Relationships

The Publication

Laurel Richardson, "Secrecy and Status: The Social Construction of Forbidden Relationships." *American Sociological Review*, 53, 1988.

The Research Question

Simmel contended that a degree of secrecy was characteristic of most relationships and that it strongly influenced the form of the relationship. This study examines the consequences of the most extreme secrecy: where the very existence of the relationship, itself, must be hidden. Specifically, Richardson focused upon a sample of single women who were sexually intimate with a married man over a period of time, and she questioned how the couple's need for secrecy shaped the entire relationship.

The Data

The investigator frequently gave public talks, at which she regularly mentioned this research project and asked for volunteers (with an appropriate experience) who were willing to be interviewed. Over time she obtained a sample of 65 single women who were, or had been, in long-term affairs with married men. The women's average age was 28 years, and over three-quarters of them were younger and less established than the man with whom they were intimate. (Richardson wondered whether these status differences influenced the type of relationship that typically developed, but could not really answer this question. Note also that all of the interviews were conducted with the women, so it is their view that is presented.)

The Findings

The early part of most of these relationships involved a process described by the investigator as, "becoming confidantes." It entailed laying aside the norms and roles of the outside world, and constructing a cocoon-like relationship. Each party was vulnerable: he was trying to conceal the affair from his wife and she was trying to protect her reputation. Each had to trust the other, which drew them closer to each other and encouraged varied types of self-disclosures that each would have been very reluctant to share with anyone else. These revelations about one's self further increased the couple's shared sense of intimacy.

　　After a while it was common for the woman in the secret relationship to begin to feel lost and uncomfortable because no one outside of the relationship socially defined it as real. If one becomes a member of a church, editor of a newspaper or gets married, the new role the person assumes is responded to by others. Their responses "validate" the role, that is, make it feel real to the incumbent. Lacking such validation in the secret role and relationship, every woman reported focusing upon a ritual or object which proved to her the relationship existed, even when she was alone. For example, many of the women saved mementoes, such as: matchbooks, Valentine cards, photos, even movie ticket stubs. These symbolic objects represented the relationship, made it feel real, and the women typically treated the items with an almost religious-like reverence. When the secret relationship ended, the women destroyed the symbolic objects in a very deliberate manner, such as burning them or throwing them in the trash; sometimes saying "good-by" aloud as each item was destroyed.

MONEY

During the 1890's, Simmel wrote a number of essays examining money from historical, philosophical and psychological perspectives. His most complete and systematic treatment appeared in 1900 in his book, *The Philosophy of Money* (hereafter, *Money*). It was immediately praised in reviews in German journals as well as by Durkheim, in *L'Année Sociologique*, in the *American Journal of Sociology*, and elsewhere. Reviewers called attention to the book's strong connection to other major works in social theory, and in particular, to Marx's *Capital*.[25]

In the preface to *Money*, Simmel made it clear that one of his intents was to modify Marx's historical materialism. Specifically, he believed it was not adequate to view ideas and values (Marx's superstructure) as resulting from economic structures (Marx's base). Simmel believed they were connected, as Marx had proposed; but Simmel contended, if one looked beneath the economic base, one would find ideas and values. Dig further, and one would find the economic base. Thus, each continuously led to the other. This reformulation of base and superstructure was consistent with Simmel's general assumption that all aspects of the social world were inter-connected.

The first part of *Money* focused upon the process of *exchange*. It is the core of any economic system, Simmel wrote, regardless of its complexity or specialization. It is central because objects have no intrinsic worth; their value is determined by exchange. Further, Simmel insisted, exchange is one of the most important processes underlying society because for a society to exist, there must be interaction among people. Otherwise, they are just, "a mere collection of individuals."[26] And the purest, most complete form of interaction involves exchange in a money economy.

What makes money of sociological significance, Simmel continued, is the fact that it is the embodiment of exchange. To be specific, it is only in a money economy that people can be divorced from their products so that true exchanges, with equal reciprocity, can occur. With barter, by contrast, negotiations are impeded because it is difficult to assign (non-monetary) objective values to people's subjective desires. While permitting true exchange, money simultaneously enables the value of objects to be precisely determined.

To be more specific, Simmel wrote, money sets value by arranging objects further or closer to people. When objects are exorbitantly expensive they are too far removed to seem attainable, leading people to value them less, even though there may be an element of "sour grapes" involved in their feelings. When objects are too close, the fact that they are so easy to obtain also makes them less desirable. It is when objects are distant, and yet almost within one's reach, that they attain the greatest value. (Note that Simmel regarded value much like the stranger: possessing a combination of closeness and distance.)

In addition, money contributes to a calculating and weighing tendency that is pervasive in modern societies. In an analysis that closely paralleled the examination of rationality by his colleague and friend, Max Weber, Simmel contended that money's mathematical quality reinforced the importance of precise counting and exactness in all aspects of social life. It introduced precision and ended ambiguity, he wrote, in the same manner as the pocket watch.

Prior to a money economy, each person was dependent upon a small number of other people, and they were all personally tied to each other. With the advent of a money economy, people became dependent upon more people, but less dependent upon any one of them. In addition, transactions within this broader network became impersonal. Money is the only thing of ours, Simmel wrote, that we are willing to give to anyone. People entered into relationships to buy and sell goods, purchase raw materials, obtain credit or the like. Who the people were outside of these economic relationships was irrelevant to the people who entered into an economic exchange with them. This form of interaction only requires money,

> "and leaves the rest of the personality untouched. It is an organization which unites people by combining what is impersonal in them, while leaving out everything that is personal and specifically individual."[27]

Thus, economic exchange meant impersonal relations and no overwhelming dependence upon any particular person. The result was a liberating sense of freedom. There was also a down side, however, because the growth of impersonal transactions also raised the specter of wide-spread alienation as people became so unattached to each other. And Simmel anticipated that the growth of the modern economy, with all of its products and money with which to buy them, meant that people would become more dependent upon objects and upon more different objects, and this dependence would ultimately provide another source of alienation.

Endnotes

1. A number of essays on Simmel's place in, and contributions to, contemporary sociology are included in Michael Kaern, Bernard S. Phillips, and Robert S. Cohen (Eds.), *George Simmel and Contemporary Sociology*. Dordrecht, Netherlands: Kluwer Academic Publishers, 1990.
2. Ralph M. Leck, *Georg Simmel and Avant-Garde Sociology*. Amherst, NY: Humanity Books, 2000.
3. Ibid., p 273.
4. Noted in, David Frisby, *Georg Simmel*. New York: Routledge: 2002. For thorough discussion and analysis of the book, see Gianfranco Poggi, *Money and the Modern Mind*. Berkeley: University of California Press, 1993.
5. Frisby.
6. See Leck, p 46.
7. Ibid., back cover.
8. Ibid.
9. Georg Simmel, "Sociability: An Example of Pure, or Formal, Sociology." In Kurt H. Wolff (Ed.), *The Sociology of Georg Simmel*. Glencoe, IL: The Free Press, 1950, 1964.
10. Georg Simmel, "The Isolated Individual and the Dyad." In Wolff, ibid., p 135.
11. Ibid.
12. Georg Simmel, "On the Significance of Numbers for Social Life." In Wolff, ibid., p 90.
13. Georg Simmel, "The Stranger." In Wolff, ibid., p 408.
14. Georg Simmel, *Conflict and the Web of Group-Affiliations*. New York: Free Press, 1955, p 146.
15. Lewis A. Coser, *Greedy Institutions*. New York: Free Press, 1974.
16. *Web*, p 158.
17. Simmel's essay, commonly translated as the web of group affiliations would be more literally translated as, "Intersection of Social Circles." See the comments by Reinhardt Bendix, the translator. Ibid., p 124.
18. Bernice A. Pescosolido and Beth Rubin, "The Web of Group Affiliations Revisited." *American Sociological Review*, 65, 2000.
19. Georg Simmel, "Types of Social Relationships." In ibid., p 317.
20. Ibid., p 323.
21. Ibid., p 328.
22. Ibid., p 329.
23. Georg Simmel, "The Secret Society." In ibid.
24. George Simmel, "Secrecy." In Wolff, p 359.
25. Discussion of the book's reception is in, David Frisby.
26. The most current edition is, George Simmel, *The Philosophy of Money*. New York: Routledge, 2004, p 175.
27. Ibid., p 386.

INDEX